Transnational Hallyu

Asian Cultural Studies: Transnational and Dialogic Approaches

The series advances transnational intellectual dialogue over diverse issues that are shared in various Asian countries and cities.

Series Editor:

Koichi Iwabuchi, Professor of Media and Cultural Studies and Director of Monash Asia Institute, Monash University, Australia

Editorial Collective

Ien Ang (University of Western Sydney)

Chris Berry (King's College London)

John Erni (Hong Kong Baptist University)

Daniel Goh (National University of Singapore)

Ariel Heryanto (Australian National University)

Kim Hyun Mee (Yonsei University)

Titles in the Series

Transnational Hallyu

The Globalization of Korean Digital and Popular Culture

Dal Yong Jin, Kyong Yoon
and Wonjung Min

ROWMAN & LITTLEFIELD
London • New York

Published by Rowman & Littlefield
4501 Forbes Boulevard, Suite 200, Lanham, Maryland 20706, USA
With additional offices in Boulder, New York, Toronto (Canada), and Plymouth (UK)
www.rowman.com

British Library Cataloguing in Publication Data
A catalogue record for this book is available from the British Library

Library of Congress Cataloging-in-Publication Data
Names: Jin, Dal Yong, 1964–. | Yoon, Kyong, 1974–. | Min, Wonjung, 1967–.
Title: Transnational hallyu : the globalization of Korean digital and popular culture /
    Dal Yong Jin, Kyong Yoon and Wonjung Min.
Description: London ; New York : Rowman & Littlefield, [2021] | Series: Asian cultural
    studies : transnational and dialogic approaches | Includes bibliographical references
    and index.
Identifiers: LCCN 2021003824 (print) | LCCN 2021003825 (ebook) |
    ISBN 9781538146965 (cloth) | ISBN 9781538146972 (epub)
    ISBN 9781538146989 (pbk)
Subjects: LCSH: Popular culture—Korea (South) | Mass media and culture—Korea
    (South) | Popular culture and globalization. | Civilization—Korean influences.
Classification: LCC DS923.23 .T73 2021 (print) | LCC DS923.23 (ebook) |
    DDC 306.095195—dc23
LC record available at https://lccn.loc.gov/2021003824
LC ebook record available at https://lccn.loc.gov/2021003825

Contents

Preface

The globally acclaimed Korean film *Parasite* (2019) and BTS' recent album *Map of the Soul: 7* (2020) exemplify the dynamic cultural flows of Korean digital and popular culture. Korean movie director Bong Joon-ho's black comedy-thriller *Parasite* made history in 2020 when it became the first non-English-language film to win the Best Picture Award at the Oscars. BTS—a seven-member Korean boy band—continued to amaze global music fans with their new album, which became their fourth No. 1 album on the Billboard 200 chart. These two historical moments not only show the continuously growing transnational cultural flows but also call for a new framework for multidirectional processes of cultural globalization.

In the early 2020s, Korean digital and popular cultures have continued their global rise. Despite some ebbs and flows, this cultural trend, which is widely known as the Korean Wave or Hallyu, appears to be irreversibly growing. Until the end of the 2010s, Hallyu might not have been globally pervasive but had rather been considered as a niche cultural trend. However, *Parasite* and BTS, alongside other cultural content and artists, have greatly expanded global audience bases for Korean popular culture. These recent developments demonstrate how Hallyu is no longer for the niche market but is instead increasingly exposed to global mainstream media and audiences. Moviegoers in Europe, North America, and Latin America, many of whom have never been interested in Korean films, have gone to the cinema to watch *Parasite* and looked for other Korean films. Music listeners in their forties and even fifties have increasingly been interested in BTS and other K-pop musicians. The circulation of Korean cultural content in the global markets and the expansion of its fan base, increasingly including various age groups, already started a decade ago. However, the current circumstances in the early

2020s seem to provide a new impetus in which Hallyu is incorporated into global audiences' everyday lives.

We started our book project with this trend in mind. We originally began to develop a book project on the popularity of Hallyu in the Global North, including North America, as two researchers of the book—Dal Yong Jin and Kyong Yoon—had worked together for several years to advance coresearch on Hallyu in the North American context. Later, Wonjung Min whose expertise lies in Latin America joined, and we further decided to expand the scope to include both the Global North and the Global South, aiming to analyze the transnationality of Hallyu in the truly global scene. Consequently, this book has been a long time in the making; however, it has been blessing for us to witness several historical moments that might redirect the contours of the Korean Wave phenomenon in the future. Due to our different academic backgrounds and regional foci, we also believed that this book would be a significant contribution to the literature, as we combined our academic strengths in different fields, including political economy, cultural studies, and area studies.

In this book, we aimed to historically document the growth of transnational Hallyu by examining its recent breakthroughs as well as the pre-Hallyu era. We also wanted to understand overseas audiences' engagement with the Korean Wave phenomenon. In so doing, we explored how cultural globalization might be redirected and renegotiated through transnational cultural practices. Through wide-ranging interviews with fans in North America, Latin America, and Western Europe, we illustrated how Hallyu has become part of global fans' everyday contexts.

Most of all, we do not simply define Hallyu as a popular cultural flow but rather expand this cultural trend as a process of the convergence of digital media and popular culture. As BTS's social media-driven world that comprises idols, fans, content, technology, and live performance vividly shows, Hallyu in the recent phase has benefited from evolving media convergence, through which cultural content and digital media are synergistically articulated and thus facilitate transnational and transmedia storytelling. Hallyu diversifies the way its stories are narrated and disseminated through transmedia convergence and transnational flows. By effectively combining interview-based audience studies with the political economy analysis of industries and cultural policies, we examined both the structure and lived experiences of Hallyu on a global scale. The book, thus, provides a comprehensive and comparative analysis of what Hallyu is and how it evolves at macro and microlevels. We hope that the book's critical discussions of the structural complexity and audience engagement in Hallyu will contribute to advancing transnational media studies.

We would like to acknowledge that while extensively updated and expanded, some parts of this book were originally published in scholarly journals. A portion of chapter 4 was published as "The Social Mediascape of Transnational Korean Pop Culture: Hallyu 2.0 as Spreadable Media Practice" in *New Media and Society* 18 (7): 1277–92. An earlier version of chapter 7 was published in the *Journal of Intercultural Studies* 41 (2): 132–47.

Chapter 1

Emerging New Wave: Transnational Hallyu

INTRODUCTION

In the early twenty-first century, South Korean (Korean, hereafter) cultural content, such as pop music (K-pop), films, animation, TV programs, webtoons, and digital games, has become increasingly integrated into the global mediascape. Korea has emerged as one of the most recognizable non-Western cultural hubs for the production of vibrant transnational popular culture and digital technologies. The rapid growth of local cultural industries and spread of Korean popular culture, first in East Asia and then in a wider range of overseas countries, which has been referred to as the Korean Wave, or *Hallyu* in Korean, has attracted scholarly and media attention because of its implications for diversified modes of global media and cultural flows. The term "Hallyu" reportedly emerged in the Asian news media in 1997, and thus, 2017 marks its twentieth anniversary (e.g., Yoon and Jin 2017). However, what is more important than the history of the term is the fact that Hallyu was not simply born in 1997 from scratch but gradually evolved over decades. By and large, Hallyu can be seen as a trend that comprises two different phases: the first between the late 1990s and the 2000s and the second since the late 2000s or early 2010s; in comparison with the first wave, the recent wave is often referred to as "Hallyu 2.0" (Lee and Nornes 2015) or the "New Korean Wave" (Jin 2016).

In the phase of Hallyu 2.0 or the New Korean Wave, Hallyu has become a global cultural phenomenon that extends far beyond Asia. While Asia, including Japan, China, Taiwan, Singapore, and Vietnam, has been the largest market for Korean popular culture, Korean cultural content has increasingly been circulated in other regions, such as North America, Latin America, Europe, the Middle East, and Africa. Korea has indeed expanded its export of

5

cultural products, from $188.9 million in 1998 to $6,240 million in 2018—a thirty-three times increase (Korea Creative Content Agency 2018b, 2019; Ministry of Culture, Sports, and Tourism 2017).[1] This phenomenal growth of the Korean cultural economy in terms of foreign exports could not have been achieved without its new audience bases far beyond Asia.

K-pop's popularity has been observed in various overseas locations, as evidenced, for example, by BTS's ongoing global stardom since the late 2010s. In Europe and Latin America, several K-pop bands, including BTS, EXO, Blackpink, and TWICE, have embarked on successful world tours. Several TV dramas and reality shows have also expanded their overseas viewership in Asia and, more recently, in other regions. *Descendants of the Sun* (*Taeyangui Huye*), a sixteen-episode KBS 2 (Korean Broadcasting System) TV drama, recorded 440 million cumulative online views in China while achieving successful ratings in other countries, including Singapore, Malaysia, Vietnam, and the United States, primarily via online platforms, such as iQiyi, Viu, and Viki (E.J. Jung 2016).

Several popular Korean dramas (hereafter K-dramas) have been remade and have achieved high viewer ratings in the United States. For example, ABC's medical drama *The Good Doctor* (2017–present), a remake of a KBS drama of the same title, recorded as a highly popular show among a wide range of audience groups in the United States. Furthermore, the format of TV content has recently emerged in several countries as a new Hallyu export item: for example, Fox's *The Masked Singer* (2019–present) is a U.S. version of the Korean music show *The King of Mask Singer* (2015–present).[2]

The Korean Wave includes newer media content and genres—in particular digital (online and mobile) games and digital cultural activities, such as electronic sports (esports)—which have attracted numerous overseas players. Although Korea is not the only country witnessing the growth of esports, the country developed several esports leagues in the early 2000s, thus leading the new cultural trend of esports (Jin 2010). Hallyu is also represented by several Korean animations and characters, such as *Pororo* and *Pucca*, which were sold to more than 150 countries in the early 2010s (Ministry of Culture, Sports, and Tourism 2012).

There are ongoing debates about whether Hallyu is a global and, furthermore, a globally hegemonic cultural trend, and Korea has achieved superpower status in the global cultural market. Epstein (2017) claims that Hallyu may constitute transnational niche markets among a limited number of overseas fans. However, the global rise of Hallyu is more than what is captured by conventional market share criteria—such as sales of media content in official markets and the size of consumer demographics. Hallyu cannot necessarily be measured and determined by conventional market evaluation mechanisms (such as sales and the exportation of ready-made content and merchandise);

rather, it signals a new means of transnational production, distribution, and consumption of popular culture.[3]

In particular, as Hallyu is deeply integrated into the social and digital media environment, which has been referred to as the "social mediascape" by Jin and Yoon (2016a), its scope and speed of circulation often far exceed that of the official cultural market. Accelerated by the increasing role of social media both in and outside Asia, the recent phase of Hallyu—that is, since the late 2000s—is comparable to its earlier phase, which was based on the exportation of cultural products (Jin 2016). In this book, we propose that the transnationalization of Hallyu since the late 2000s distinguishes itself from both its earlier wave and other transnational cultural flows—especially in its integration into new digital media and its multidirectional and extensive flows. The transnational Hallyu phenomenon offers a fascinating example that signals the multiple routes in cultural globalization and participatory audience engagement through digital technology (K. Yoon 2019; Y. Kim 2013).

THE DIMENSIONS OF HALLYU

In what ways can Hallyu be compared with other transnational cultural flows? Hallyu—especially its recent phase since the late 2000s—is an intriguing cultural phenomenon that embodies the convergence of culture and technology on the one hand and the global–local cultural conjunction on the other. In other words, the new Korean Wave differs from other cultural flows because of its extensive digital technology integration (a "digital wave") and transnational circulation (a "transnational wave").

Hallyu as a Digital Wave

A distinctive characteristic of the recent Hallyu trend is its nearly seamless integration into digital media environments—including social media/platform technologies—which exponentially enhances the transnational flow of cultural content. As demonstrated by the recent rise of K-pop and its fandom overseas, which will be further discussed throughout the remainder of this book, Hallyu's increasing integration into the social mediascape has shifted the methods, directions, and meanings of cultural flows. Social media platforms like YouTube, Facebook, and Twitter have been particularly important tools in the recent rise of BTS and its global fan community, the Adorable Representative M.C. for Youth, otherwise known as the ARMY (Chang and Park 2019). In addition, the global digital platform Netflix has been extensively utilized in the recent Hallyu phenomenon, as evidenced by the Korean film and TV industry's integration into the service. Acknowledging the global market potential of Korean cinema, Netflix invested in the local production industry and created several local content, including *Okja* (2017). This ungainly mix of a benign monster movie, action comedy, and coming-of-age fable, directed by Korean film auteur Bong Joon-ho and his production team, stars a global cast that includes Hollywood A-list actors Jake Gyllenhaal and Tilda Swinton. *Okja*, which was fully funded by and globally released through Netflix in May 2017, illustrates the increasing collaboration between Western and non-Western cultural industries in the era of digital platforms (H.W. Lee 2017).[4] Netflix has also invested in *Kingdom* (2019)—the company's first original Korean drama—and its second season, *Kingdom 2* (2020).

The increasing transnational flows of K-pop, K-films, and K-dramas demonstrate that Korean cultural content and industry have increasingly been integrated into social media and digital platforms (e.g., Netflix) and, in so doing, have generated networked audiences and markets while often bypassing the conventional national gatekeeping institutions. Due to the ubiquitousness of social media technologies, mobile and networked modes of media consumption have become the default with regard to the transnational circulation of Hallyu. Moreover, in terms of the Hallyu phenomenon, digital technology is not only the vehicle by which local content is delivered globally but is also important content itself, as exemplified by the global penetration of Korean-made smartphone technology and its applications (apps), such as KaKaoTalk and LINE—two free instant mobile messengers.

Compared to other transnational cultural flows—and even its own earlier wave, or "Hallyu 1.0"—the recent Hallyu phenomenon seems more deeply immersed in the process of media convergence: "the flow of content across multiple media platforms" (Jenkins 2006a, 2). As further discussed in chapter 2, Hallyu benefits from media convergence and media convergence benefits from Hallyu. In the following chapters, we will examine the convergence of digital technologies (e.g., smartphones, apps, and social media) and content (e.g., K-pop, TV dramas, and webtoons), which entails a transformation that maximizes the benefits to both users and industries. Hallyu and its digital media convergence show that popular culture is seamlessly integrated into technology and other areas of everyday media use.

Hallyu as a Transnational Wave

Hallyu's extensive transnational circulation illustrates that Korea has become the first non-Western country to strategically export a wide range of cultural genres and forms, such as television programs, films, pop music, animation, online gaming, and smartphones, to both Western and non-Western countries (Jin 2016, 5). While several countries' cultural products have penetrated the global markets, they primarily export one or a few specialized cultural genres, rather than an extensive range of cultural genres (Jin 2016; Lukács 2010). For example, Mexico and Brazil have exported television programs, known as *telenovelas*, to Latin American media markets, while Hong Kong and India have exported films—kung fu movies and the Bollywood cinema, respectively—to both regional and global markets. However, these countries' exported cultural content tends to be limited to one particular cultural form—either television drama or film.

Japanese popular culture, which has had a substantial impact in many parts of the world, including Asia, North America, and Western Europe (Iwabuchi 2002), may offer a case that is comparable to the recent Hallyu phenomenon. The Japanese cultural industry enjoyed its heydays in global markets throughout the 1990s. Japan's exportation of popular culture products tripled between 1992 and 2002, with the *Pokémon* cartoon, the *Sailor Moon* TV animation series, and the cat-like character Hello Kitty being among the most popular (Iwabuchi 2002). However, other than animations and video games, Japanese popular cultural forms—for example, the trendy drama (known as *J-dorama*) in the 1980s and 1990s—have not achieved a continuous presence in global markets, despite their selective and rather unintended success in East Asian markets (Lukács 2010). While Asia has enjoyed a rich diet of contemporary Japanese popular culture (e.g., fashion, music, TV shows, and film dramas, as well as anime and manga), North American and European audiences' interest in Japanese cultural content is almost exclusively focused on cartoon creations (Cooper-Chen 2012). Moreover, although Japanese pop music (e.g., Sakamoto Kyu) entered the overseas market as early as the 1960s, its global success has been intermittent and is applicable to only a few exceptional individual musicians (BBC 2014; Jin 2020a; Stevens 2008).[5]

The recent phase of Hallyu seems to be more expansive in terms of scope and degree of transnational flows and to comprise various cultural forms and reaches global audiences. While cultural industries of other non-Western countries—such as Japan, Mexico, Brazil, and India—have attempted to infiltrate the global cultural markets, the emerging global presence of Korean cultural forms through digital media platforms appears to signal an unprecedentedly extensive flow of culture from a non-Western country to different cultural markets.[6] The Hallyu phenomenon also reveals how a cultural form is integrated into different geocultural contexts through, with, and without reference to the center. It illustrates diversified directions of cultural globalization.

Hallyu does not simply refer to the exportation or dissemination of Korean cultural products to an increasing number of countries; rather, the wave has been shaped by the dialectics of global–local forces. As discussed further in chapters 2 and 3, Korea's cultural and digital industries have developed in relation to national policies on the one hand and the global economy on the other. The global division of labor and the consideration of transnational markets have become a default setting for major K-pop corporations (I. Oh 2013), while local ethos, such as the "collective moralism" of respecting elders and emphasizing family-oriented values, may be incorporated into the global K-pop package (Kim and Kim 2015). Meanwhile, the reception of Hallyu becomes a practice that is simultaneously global and local. Hallyu audiences are continuously networked with other audience groups both locally and globally through digital technologies. For example, Korean fans (in Korea), diasporic Korean and Asian fans, and international fans are able to collaborate, support, explore, and spread K-pop locally and globally, albeit with occasional conflicts (K. Yoon 2018).

UNDERSTANDING THE TRANSNATIONAL
CULTURAL FLOWS OF HALLYU

How can the Hallyu phenomenon, and especially its recent phase, be theoretically explained and understood? For an in-depth understanding, the context and process of how Hallyu emerged and has evolved can be examined using historical, ethnographic, and theoretical approaches. In this regard, before presenting a historical analysis of Hallyu and a close-up, ethnographic observation of its overseas audiences in the following chapters, we will first discuss the theoretical frameworks that are relevant to understanding Hallyu as a trend of transnational media and cultural flows.

As previously discussed, even prior to the emergence of Hallyu, several popular cultural exports originating in non-Western countries—such as *telenovelas*, Japanese anime, and Bollywood and Hong Kong cinema—attracted significant overseas audiences. In the 2010s, television dramas from Turkey have also been noticeable around the globe.[7] These precedent and ongoing examples have called for critical revisions of the previously dominant view on media flows—such as cultural imperialism—that drew on the binarism between the center and the periphery of global media industries. In particular, the recent phase of Hallyu vividly illustrates not only "the alternative circuits of media flows that operate outside the West" (Ginsburg et al. 2002, 14) but also the contraflows of non-Western cultural forms into the West (Thussu 2006). Media and cultural studies have examined transnational cultural flows based on different perspectives of the size, direction, and meanings of transnational culture. In particular, the early cultural imperialism thesis has been questioned and responded through several different theoretical discussions, such as the cultural globalization thesis (Featherstone 1990; King 1997), the cultural proximity thesis (Straubhaar 1991), and cultural hybridity thesis (Kraidy 2005).

The Cultural Imperialism Thesis

While earlier discussions of transnational media focused on the dominant influence of American pop culture and media industries, recent studies have increasingly addressed the diversification of media flows. In the early period of media globalization—especially before the 1990s, which was character-ized by American pop culture's significant global influence—critical media researchers were concerned about the penetration of American and Western media and pop culture in the developing world. From a critical political econ-omy perspective, a group of scholars proposed the cultural imperialism thesis, in which the globalization of the media is primarily considered as the dis-semination of U.S.-driven cultural hegemony around the globe as a one-way flow of culture from the West to the non-West (Boyd-Barrett 1977; Dorfman and Mattelart 1975; Guback 1984; Schiller 1976). This theoretical position was especially appealing in the 1970s and 1980s, during which American movies, TV programs, and pop music dominated the global cultural markets. This thesis also resonated with UNESCO's (1980) claim that the global com-munication system was characterized by imbalances and inequalities between a few rich countries and the majority of the developing "Third World" ones and that these imbalances were deepening the already-existing economic gaps between the two camps (Tomlinson 1991).

However, since the early 1990s, the cultural imperialism thesis has come under severe criticism because of increasing counterevidence, calling for further theoretical articulation. Several non-Western countries have advanced their cultural industries and penetrated other countries' markets, starting pri-marily in the early 1990s. In particular, again, Japanese pop cultural products, including animation, manga, and games, have been exported to overseas mar-kets in East and Southeast Asia (Iwabuchi 2002; Otmazgin 2013). Japanese animation and character products, such as *Doraemon*, *Pokémon*, *Sailor Moon*, and *Hello Kitty*, have attracted global fandom (Allison 2003; Yano 2013), while Sony and Nintendo have continued to be the global leaders in the field of digital games (Consalvo 2017). The cultural imperialism thesis has also been criticized due to its lack of discourse on the diversity and dynamics of global cultural flows (Crane 2014). As van Elteren (2014) noted succinctly, the thesis assumes a totalizing view in which the complexity of culture is not fully considered; it also arguably denies the possibly liberating effects of American culture or any hybrid cultural forms.

The Cultural Globalization Thesis

In contrast with the cultural imperialism thesis, in which cultural flows are considered primarily as unidirectional (from West to non-West), numerous recent studies have aimed to move beyond the rigid center—periphery (or West–Rest) binarism on which cultural imperialism is predicated. In this recent theoretical tendency—the "cultural globalization thesis"—especially since the 1990s (Kraidy 2005), the diversification of cultural flows has been explored in several different ways by cultural studies-inspired media researchers and media anthropologists (e.g., Appadurai 1996; Ginsburg et al. 2002).

Most notably, Appadurai's (1996) study elaborates on the plurality of cultural centers, suggesting that the existing global forces of homogenization are "repatriated as heterogeneous dialogues" (42) between different stakeholders and are, thus, localized. Thus, for Appadurai (1996), American or Western dominance is not universally hegemonic; rather, global power dynamics are locally redefined and operate in the "fundamental disjuncture between economy, culture, and politics" (33).[8] He proposed a diversified understanding of global cultural power, which implied that American dominance could no longer remain sustainable as several national forces emerged. However, while Appadurai (1996) analyzed media as one of the key areas of cultural globalization, he did not address in detail the nature and feature of transnational media.

In comparison, a growing number of media researchers have empirically analyzed the role of media in cultural globalization. They have provided empirical evidence of complex and diverse media flows and, thus, challenged the cultural imperialism predication on Western-oriented cultural flows (Iwabuchi 2002; Straubhaar 1991; Y. Cho 2011). Straubhaar (1991, 2007), in particular, analyzed telenovelas among Latin American and/or Latino audiences, emphasizing the importance of geocultural proximity in international media consumption. In Straubhaar's (1991) study, geocultural similarity is identified as a key motivational factor that facilitates the flows of media texts in particular regions; that is, audiences tend to prefer their own local or national media content and otherwise that of similar cultures and languages (Straubhaar 1991, 2007).

More recently, intra-Asian cultural flows have been analyzed as media consumption that is driven by the desire for and feeling of cultural proximity among regional audiences (Iwabuchi 2002; K. S. Lee 2008; Otmazgin 2013; Y. Cho 2011). In particular, in the 1980s and 1990s, Japanese pop culture, such as animation, TV dramas, and pop music, appealed to East Asian audiences in the official markets and via piracy. Of course, intra-Asian cultural flows have recently been led by the Korean Wave; thus, Otmazgin (2013) characterizes ongoing intra-Asian cultural flows as cultural regionalization—that is, "an undirected process that increases proximity among markets and communities in three or more geographically proximate economies" (23).

However, these studies that emphasize the role of geocultural proximity in transnational cultural flows—which can be categorized as the "cultural proximity thesis"—do not simply assume the homogeneity of geocultur- ally proximal texts and audiences. As Iwabuchi (2002) pointed out, cultural proximity "is not something 'out there'" and, thus, "should not be regarded as a predetermined attribute" (124). A few recent studies have critically engaged with and articulated the cultural proximity thesis by focusing more on the ongoing and flexible affinities between the text and the audience than on the inherited aspects of cultural proximity, which include factors such as geography, language, and race/ethnicity (B. Han 2017; Larkin 2008). Larkin (2008) illustrated that northern Nigerian audiences perceive Indian culture as being similar to their own and popularly consume Indian films. Larkin (2008) thus claimed that, despite geographic and linguistic differences, Indian films appeal to Nigerian viewers as "a way of imaginatively engaging with forms of tradition different from their own at the same time as conceiving of a modernity that comes without the political and ideological significance of that of the West" (199). Larkin's (2008) study effectively showed how non- Western media attract audiences beyond their geocultural boundaries. Simi- larly, several recent studies of media fans have illustrated that media texts offer cultural and emotional resources even to audiences who are far away from the geocultural contexts in which the texts are produced (Annett 2011; B. Han 2017; Chin and Morimoto 2013).

A growing number of studies do not focus only on regional flows but also address the diversified cultural flows that occur outside Western contexts. In particular, the body of research that is often referred to as the contraflow the- sis (Thussu 2006) has addressed how non-Western cultural texts penetrate or are integrated into the Western mediascape. With particular reference to the rise of several non-Western media texts, a few scholars have redefined global media flows that reverse or at least question the previously dominant model of West to non-West cultural flows. Thussu (2006) emphasized the potential of the global circulation of media products emanating from non-Western countries, referring to them as contraflows or subaltern flows "originating from the erstwhile peripheries of global media industries" (10). As Thussu (2006) suggested, the contraflows should not be simply celebrated as the rise of a counter-hegemonic or alternative culture; rather, there are disparities and complexities in contraflows, and more significantly, the dominant cultural flows, including the Hollywood film industry, continue to be influential in many regions worldwide.

The Cultural Hybridity Thesis and Hallyu

The aforementioned studies arguing for the diversification of cultural flows have challenged the assumed unidirectional flows of cultural content and media, moving from the rigid framework of cultural imperialism to that of cultural globalization (Kraidy 2005). In addition to these recent theoretical frameworks of transnational cultural flows as multidirectional processes, a newer approach—one that emphasizes the hybrid nature of transnational culture—is worth reviewing. The concepts of hybridity and hybridization have increasingly been utilized to analyze global cultural flows as a syner- getic process through which new cultural forms and meanings are generated. Hybridity is more than a cultural mixture; echoing and appropriating postco- lonial studies, it is considered "a sign of empowerment" or "a symptom of dominance" in critical media studies (Kraidy 2005, 5). The hybridity thesis explores the complex interactions between global and local cultural pow- ers. The cultural hybridity framework has increasingly been appropriated in transnational media studies, including research on Hallyu. With reference to the Korean Wave in the 2000s, Ryoo (2009) argued that "cultural hybridiza- tion has occurred as local cultural agents and actors negotiate with global forms, using them as resources through which Asian people construct their own cultural spaces, as exemplified in the case of the Korean wave" (147). In particular, contemporary Korea's postcolonial context and rapid integration into globalization inevitably entail the hybridization of the local culture. In this regard, Hallyu is an example that vividly reveals the tendency of global- ization or transnationalization to reify the logic of hybridization (Ryoo 2009). Researchers have also analyzed empirically how particular Hallyu-related cultural texts engage with hybridity, as well as the cultural meanings that emerge from such hybridity (e.g., Ono and Kwon 2013; Jin and Ryoo 2014).

Despite the increasing importance of hybridity as a theoretical tool for analyzing transnational cultural flows, Kraidy (2005) lamented that media studies has often focused on the hybridity of media texts without sufficiently addressing the structural issues involved in textual hybridity. Thus, hybrid media texts have been reduced to "symptoms of cultural pluralism, not indi- cators of dominance" (Kraidy 2005, 5). Moreover, the notion of hybridity and hybridization has been misunderstood and romanticized, as it is often reduced to the celebration of cultural mixture. The romanticized version of the cul- tural hybridity thesis does not sufficiently examine the existing global power geometry (Kraidy 2005). In reality, while some countries have developed hybrid cultures based on their initiatives, many locally driven hybrid cultures have not developed unique cultures representing their own identities due to the strong influence of Western forces (Jin 2016).

Meanwhile, some non-Western cultural industries have intentionally hybridized their local cultures, influenced by Western cultures, without exploring the possibility of hybridity as a "third space" (Bhabha 1994). Thus, Kraidy (2005) proposed a critical version of the cultural hybridity thesis, referring to as "critical transculturalism." The critical transculturalism frame- work redefines cultural hybridity as a social issue through which structural power relations and agency are articulated with each other; thus, the framework pays due attention to "hybridity's ability and inability to empower social groups to have influence over the course of their lives" (Kraidy 2005, 151).

Considering Audience Engagement

The theoretical discussions about transnational media flows mentioned above have focused on macrolevel transactions of media content and cultural products. Consequently, the lived experiences of transnational audiences are not sufficiently considered. Thus, it is worth noting that several studies have shed light on audience engagement in transnational media flows from the perspective of transnationalism. They examine how audience engagement has been transnationalized through new digital technologies both within and outside conventional media markets and institutions. This process of media engagement has enhanced a particular form of transnationalism in which local audiences tend to bypass the official media market and export/import routes while engaging with "alternative (bottom-up) practices of media circulation" (Lukács 2010, 179; see also Georgiou 2006; Larkin 2008).

For example, media fans' digital reproduction (sometimes in the form of piracy) and consumption have exposed the emerging non-Western cultural content to a wide range of Internet-networked audiences. Digital technologies—social media in particular—have contributed to the viral circulation of Hallyu and its participatory culture. Regarding the rise of Hallyu, the cultural industries, as well as cultural policies, have rigorously exploited digital technologies and have, thus, developed a new revenue model of pop culture that is key to the emerging cultural and creative economy. Equally importantly, global fan audiences have appropriated digital technologies in their process of translating, sharing, and interpreting Hallyu. Indeed, Hallyu has spread beyond the gatekeepers and conventional cultural regulations (such as copyright law) and enhanced the tendency of bottom-up transnationalism. Technologies in the Hallyu mediascape not only enhance virality but can also transform the existing cultural norms and conventional methods of cultural consumption (Nahon and Hemsley 2013).

The viral circulation of Psy's *Gangnam Style* video, for example, generated numerous different ways of interpreting and participating in the original text—that is, by clicking, sharing, commenting, and making user content, such as reaction videos and user-generated parody videos. The K-pop industry's strategic exploitation of the YouTube platform may contribute to the virality of *Gangnam Style* and, more recently, BTS's music videos; however, perhaps more importantly, audiences' bottom-up experiences of transnationalism accelerated the virality of Hallyu. Transnational media can enable local audiences to "critically reflect on the legitimacy of their own social system and imagine new possibilities within the multiple constraints of their social context" (Y. Kim 2013, 79). By engaging with Hallyu's digital mediascape, audiences who would not have otherwise been intensively exposed and attracted to such non-Western media are integrated into transnational cultural flows and, thus, reimagine their possible lives.

While the existing discussions of transnational media flows offer theoretical tools for understanding the recent Hallyu phenomenon, they seem to inadequately address the shifting media ecology surrounding the rise and integration of local cultural forces into the transnational mediascape. A new theoretical framework that effectively addresses the structural (governments, industries, and technologies) and agentic (audiences) forces behind Hallyu is required. In so doing, the meanings, directions, and effects of Hallyu as a form of transnational cultural flow can be effectively analyzed.

METHODOLOGICAL FRAMEWORK

To comprehensively and critically analyze Hallyu as an emerging transnational cultural flow, this book proposes the integration of a political economy approach (a macrolevel structural analysis) with ethnographic reception research (an in-depth microlevel analysis). The political economic approach examines Hallyu's economic and industrial aspects and explores questions related to the interaction of politics and economy. It involves a structural understanding of the production and circulation of Hallyu as a process that articulates the relationships between cultural industries, global markets, and governments. In addition, the political economy approach critically examines the role of technology, which is imperative to all stages of the marketing culture and especially to the recent Hallyu phenomenon. Chapters 2 and 3 will trace different forms of discourses and data to historicize the evolution of Hallyu on both the local and global scales.

In comparison, as will be discussed in chapters 4, 5, 6, and 7, this book engages with ethnographic audience research to examine how overseas fan audiences interpret and consume Hallyu. With this, the book's political economy approach is articulated with a cultural studies approach. For this project, we conducted 152 individual interviews with Hallyu fans in countries in Europe and the Americas—that is, the United States, Canada, Chile, Germany, and Spain—between 2014 and 2018. Of course, despite the extensive nature of the interviews, these five countries and the interviewees may not fully represent Hallyu as an entity. Nonetheless, they reveal the vibrant moments and momentums of transnational flows of Hallyu, especially as these countries are rapidly emerging overseas reception points. According to the music-streaming site Spotify's 2019 estimate, these five countries were among the top ten largest consumers of K-pop outside Asia: the United States (first), Germany (fifth), Canada (seventh), Spain (eighth), and Chile (ninth) (Llanos Martínez 2019).

Although we attempted to inclusively recruit various types of fans of Korean popular culture in the aforementioned regions, most participants turned out to be under the age of thirty, and women far outnumbered men in all five locations. According to the interviewees, for whom pseudonyms were used for confidentiality reasons, K-pop was the most popular Hallyu content, although other Hallyu genres, such as dramas, variety shows, films, animation, and video games, were also enjoyed. This demographic of dedicated Hallyu fans resonates with the findings of recent empirical studies, in which young women were observed to be the core fan group of K-pop as a leading genre of the recent phase of Hallyu (e.g., Capistrano 2019).

In this regard, it was unsurprising that most of the participants in our field studies were more enthusiastic about K-pop than any other Hallyu content. K-pop was intensively appealing to the young overseas fans who were interviewed for this study. Various other Hallyu content, such as K-dramas, variety shows, films, animations, and online games, were consumed primarily because of their relationship to K-pop. For example, many participants watched Korean variety shows because they often starred K-pop idols. Watching Korean TV was an activity that synergistically enhanced the fans' understanding of and interest in K-pop and its idols. The overrepresentation of K-pop and its fans in the chapters of the book that address audience studies might be related to the recruiting strategies used in the field studies. All participants were recruited via online advertisements or snowballing, and thus, more young K-pop fans, who are known to be relatively active on social media compared to K-drama fans or any other types of Hallyu fans, might have responded to the interview requests.

While more systematic and representative sampling could have been conducted, the aim of this study is not to identify a representative sample and generalize Hallyu as a cultural trend. Instead, the aim of the book's audience studies section is to explore the in-depth meanings of Hallyu fan activities, and thus, voluntary response sampling allowed those who were willing to tell their stories about being Hallyu fans and consuming its content to participate in this project.

The interview participants comprised the following groups. In North America, sixty American and Canadian fans (thirty-five in 2014 and twenty-five in 2016) participated in individual interviews either face to face or online. In Chile, thirty-six individual face-to-face interviews were conducted in 2017. With the exception of one individual who identified herself as upper-middle class, all the participants were from lower-middle or working-class families. In Germany, forty individual interviews were conducted in 2017 and 2018.

The participants, who lived in Berlin, Frankfurt, or Tübingen, were far more ethnically diverse than their counterparts in the United States, Canada, and Chile; nearly half (eighteen out of forty participants) were ethnic minorities.[9] In Spain, sixteen individual interviews were conducted face to face (n = 12) or online (= 4) in the second half of 2018. Interestingly, interview participants in Spain included a total of four interviewees in their thirties and forties, which constitute an older group among all participants we interviewed for this book.

The interview data collected from different sites in Europe and the Americas are presented in chronological order of the field studies and offer comparative points in terms of their chronological order and geographical differences. Due in part to the emerging social media ecology, which allows for flexible and fragmented yet networked media consumption, the Hallyu fans interviewed for this book neither devoted to one cultural genre or object nor clearly distinguished from ordinary audiences. Many of the interviewees whom we met were also "cultural omnivores" (Peterson 1992) who engage with a wide range of cultural genres across nationalities, social classes, and ethnicities.

While our field research labor and time were divided to interview and observe more Hallyu fans, we continuously collaborated with each other while undertaking a comparative analysis of transnational Hallyu. We participated in a few scenes of Hallyu cultures, such as K-pop events, as (semi-)fans at one point and observed the context of fandom at another. In other words, we attempted to be participants (aca-fans) and/or observers (academics). This dual positioning of the participant and the observer seems necessary for exploring Hallyu as a complex cultural practice that involves diverse meanings and powers—that is, a bottom-up flow of transnationalism and a new wave of the global–local cultural economy.

By investigating the structural complexity of Hallyu and audiences' reception of it, this book contributes to advancing transnational media scholarship. This examination of the global growth of a popular culture phenomenon that originated in a non-Western location vividly illustrates how transnational cultural flows are configured and reconfigured in relation to digital media environments and participatory audience cultures. The Hallyu phenomenon is not simply an example of reverse cultural imperialism nor a counter-hegemonic cultural phenomenon; rather, it is an ongoing process of transnationalization. This book analyzes the transnationalism of popular culture not only through the exportation of domestic popular culture to other countries but also through its increasing appropriation, hybridization, and digital mediation. Through the articulation of political economic and cultural analyses of Hallyu as a unique global cultural phenomenon, we enrich the ongoing media globalization debate.

The evolution of Hallyu provides new theoretical and methodological tools for understanding the transforming media environments and practices. Despite an increase in Hallyu studies and conferences, the theoretical configuration of Hallyu is still emerging. The existing literature attempts to situate Hallyu in the context of the dominant global media theories (e.g., Ryoo 2009; Y. Kim 2013) or to identify major themes in the Hallyu discourse (e.g., Hong et al. 2019; J. Choi 2015; Kim and Kim 2015; Yoon and Kang 2017) rather than sufficiently developing its own theoretical perspective. Drawing on extensive field studies in five different countries and the political economic study of industries and cultural, this book provides a macro- and microlevel analysis of transnational Hallyu, while exploring the probable new theoretical frameworks to arrive at a critical understanding of Hallyu as transnational media and cultural practices.

THE ORGANIZATION OF THE BOOK

The book is organized as follows. Chapter 1 provides the fundamentals, addressing the question of why Hallyu matters. While defining Hallyu as a digital and transnational cultural wave, it engages with the research questions, context, methodologies, and major approaches. It also provides a summary of the ensuing chapters.

Chapter 2 investigates the shifting role of the Korean cultural industries in the context of the broader social structure of society. It historically analyzes the development of Hallyu by discussing its three major phases: the mid-1990s, late 1990s, and late 2000s. The continuity and changes in Hallyu practice and discourse are examined.

Chapter 3 addresses the emergence of digital technology-driven cultural flows as a major part of transnational Hallyu in the 2010s. The digital wave of Hallyu includes not only the exportation of Korean-created digital technologies to global markets but also the convergence of digital technologies and cultural content, whereby cultural genres are transnationally circulated and hybridized. It suggests that the digital Korean Wave has changed the map of Hallyu and influenced the global youth culture.

Chapter 4 examines the reception of Hallyu in the United States and Canada. Drawing on interviews with American and Canadian fans, it explores the interplay between Hallyu's texts, technology, fan sociality, and political economy. Hallyu in North America illustrates how social media is becoming the default media for transnational cultural flows and how Hallyu reaches global audiences via social media platforms. It shows the bottom-up fan experiences of transnationalism as well as the top-down forces of transnational media convergence led by corporations.

Chapter 5 examines how Hallyu is integrated into the everyday lives of young people in Chile. Drawing on field studies conducted in Santiago, a vibrant Hallyu fan site, it analyzes the process of fans' participation in and translation of Hallyu. It reveals that the Chilean fans engaged with Hallyu as an alternative cultural resource through which they negotiated the realities. Hallyu in Chile was, to some extent, reliant on English translation and, thus, involved in what we call "secondhand translation," which included not only time lags and misunderstandings but also left room for local participation and appropriation.

Chapter 6 focuses on young Hallyu fans in Germany. By focusing on their consumption of Korean popular culture, it reveals that young Germans engaged with Hallyu by negotiating structural forces, such as pervasive stereotyping and technological regulation. The German fans, who appeared to be highly individualized rather than organized or collective, considered Hallyu as a *Gesamtkunstwerk* (a total work of art) that was distinguished from mainstream American or German culture, and they, thus, found within it diverse dimensions that could be related to their everyday lives.

Chapter 7 examines Hallyu's recent arrival in Spain. The chapter illustrates how Korean popular cultural forms are consumed as a new trend in relation to the existing Asian cultural repertoire. This chapter provides an intriguing comparison with the Chilean context (chapter 5), revealing how, on the one hand, Korean popular cultural forms are consumed similarly or differently in the same linguistic zone (Spanish) and offering a comparison with the German context (chapter 6), thereby illustrating how the European reception of Hallyu may be heterogeneous, on the other.

Chapter 8 summarizes the major characteristics of the new phase of Hallyu in the era of digital technology and the networked fan culture. By revisiting the two interwoven aspects of the new Korean Wave—digital and transnational—this concluding chapter proposes how transnational cultural flows can be theorized and how the Hallyu phenomenon contributes to this theorization.

NOTES

1. These data include only the major cultural forms, such as broadcasting, movies, animation, music, games, characters, and manga; however, when other cultural forms, such as webtoons and digital technologies, are included, the magnitude becomes much greater than this figure indicates (see table 2.1).

2. The exportation of TV show formats has increased, as illustrated by several examples, including NBC's highly rated reality show *Better Late Than Never* (2016–2018), which is a U.S. remake of the Korean show *Grandpas over Flowers* (2013–2018), and the Chinese reality TV show *The Great Challenge* (2015–2016), which is a remake of the long-running Korean reality TV show *Infinite Challenge* (2005–2018). Format sales as a trend of global Hallyu are not limited to the TV drama genre. Due to the high-quality and unique storytelling of Korean films, Hollywood

has continued to remake Korean films, including the romantic comedy *My Sassy Girl* (2008), which is a remake of *My Sassy Girl* (*Yeopgijeogin geunyeo*, 2001); the neo-noir *Oldboy* (2013), which is a remake of Korean author Park Chan-wook's film of the same title; and the horror movie *The Uninvited* (2009), which is a remake of *A Tale of Two Sisters* (*Janghwa, hongryeon*, 2003). The Korean reality television format has also been especially popular in Asia. The increasing popularity of the Korean TV show format is demonstrated by the numerous Asian TV shows that have allegedly copied the format of Korean TV shows without acquiring a proper license. A recent report presented in the Korean National Assembly accuses at least twenty-nine Chinese TV shows of engaging in the unlicensed reproduction of the Korean TV format (J. Han 2017). Chinese knockoffs of Korean television content and pop culture may resemble the Korean culture industry's occasional plagiarism of American or Japanese pop culture content prior to the rise of Hallyu.

3. Of course, the culture and media industries have been keen to reinvent their measurement systems. For example, as the Internet-mediated consumption of conventional media forms (e.g., television, radio, and magazines) has become increasingly common, user rating systems have been updated to more accurately reflect users' increasingly mobile and individualized nature. Sedentary and sample-based user measurements have gradually been supplemented or even replaced by newer data mining-type systems that aim to capture media users' personalized experiences (Buzzard 2012). In 2013, the famous Billboard music charts began to include YouTube views as an important criterion for its Hot 100 chart, which has increased the visibility of several musicians who are not necessarily reliant on the U.S. network media, including K-pop idol groups. However, in 2017, Billboard announced that paid, subscription-based streaming services data will be more weighted than the data of ad-supported streaming services—YouTube in particular. This change in Billboard's measurement system is intriguing, as it illustrates how conventional measurement systems have evolved by encompassing Internet usage. However, as exemplified in its recent change geared toward reducing the weight of YouTube data, the mainstream media environment still values "paid" rather than "free" use. In this evolved yet mainstream measurement system, the impact of Hallyu, which is still largely reliant on underground, unofficial, digitally driven media consumption, on its global audiences might not yet be fully measured.

4. Moreover, several Korean television series were funded and/or distributed by Netflix and were, thus, released to global audiences. The most recent and prominent example is *Mister Sunshine* (2018), a twenty-four-episode historical melodrama set in colonial Korea (discussed in detail in chapter 2).

5. Another important point for comparison between Japanese and Korean pop culture is the role of the government and the local industries' strategies for targeting overseas markets. Japanese trendy dramas' popularity among intra-Asian audiences in the 1980s and 1990s was an unexpected consequence that was largely reliant on underground and pirate consumption. The Japanese pop culture industry was not keen to export its products widely to overseas markets because the expected profits from the sale of Japanese products, such as TV dramas, were rather minimal (Iwabuchi 2002; Lukács 2010). However, as discussed later in this book, the global rise of Hallyu is considered to have benefited from successive Korean governments' investments in information and technology (IT) and cultural industries, as well as the entertainment

industry's rigorous expansion into overseas markets (K. S. Lee, 2015). As evident in the global circulation of K-pop via social media channels, the industry has effectively explored a new, Internet-driven revenue model partly in response to decreasing domestic/offline music sales and partly in its effective deployment of new technologies, such as social media. The industrial strategies have often been synergized with the Korean government's or public organizations' outreach programs geared toward overseas audiences. For example, the Korean Cultural Centre, a nonprofit organization aligned with the Korean government, has offered free K-pop education programs, known as the K-pop Academy, in many overseas locations for K-pop fans (Um 2014).

6. When we use the term "West" in this book, it refers to the region inherited from the legacy of Western modernity. The meaning of the term West has been virtually identical to that of the word "modern" (Hall 1996) and in this regard several countries located outside the Western Europe and North America have taken ambivalent positions. For example, Japan is situated in a very complex situation (Jin 2009, 267–68); despite its non-Western location, Japan has been "a name always associating itself with those regions, communities, and peoples that appear politically or economically superior to other regions, communities and peoples"—that is, the West (Sakai 1988, 95). Japan can be considered as the West in that it has sought and achieved a type of Western modernity; however, it may not be sufficiently West, because it has been racialized in the hegemonic racial discourse of Orientalism. Thus, throughout this book, we critically use the concept/category of the West as a hegemonic discursive construct, wherein the Orient is racialized, marginalized, and othered (Said 1978).

7. According to the BBC (2016), Turkish TV shows have been popular in many countries since the mid-2000s. In 2015 alone, Turkey earned $250 million from overseas sales of TV shows, up from only $10,000 in 2004. Turkish TV dramas are now watched in more than 140 countries. In particular, many people in South America enjoy Turkish television programs because they explore societal changes that resonate in South America, such as migration from rural villages to cities.

8. While questioning the myth of American cultural dominance in the context of globalization, Appadurai (1996) discussed examples of regional domination, such as Japanization for Koreans, Indianization for Sri Lankans, and Vietnamization for Cambodians, which could be greater "fears" than American domination for the local people. He claimed that some Asian countries have been concerned about the new trends of the emerging regional dominance of neighboring countries, as well as continuing American dominance. Appadurai's (1996) discussion on the fear of regional domination seems open to further revision, especially given the increasingly complex nature of cultural flows. For example, the Korean government banned the exportation of Japanese cultural content until the 1990s for primarily traumatic history of Japan's colonization of Korea in the early twentieth century. However, in the twenty-first century Korea's cultural content has seemed to cause fear in Japan, as shown in the Japanese government and media's expression of concern about a Korean cultural boom in Japan.

9. The interviews with the German participants were conducted in English, which is not the native language of the researcher or of the interviewees. However, the participants, most of whom were undergraduate students, had a high level of English-language proficiency and, thus, seemed to express their feelings without encountering language barriers. To triangulate the interview data, the field researcher observed Hallyu fan clubs and dance events, while communicating casually with local Hallyu fans.

Chapter 2

Evolution of the Korean Cultural Industries

INTRODUCTION

Hallyu has become a global phenomenon in the early twenty-first century. People from many parts of the world have enjoyed Korean cultural content, which is not precedent. Due to the soaring popularity of local popular culture beyond a national boundary, the Korean Wave has become an intriguing topic in transnational studies, as it has increasingly been considered as evidence of a new form of transnationalization (Fuhr 2016). Korean popular culture has been cited as the most vibrant transnational form in several recent media studies textbooks (e.g., de Beukelaer and Spence 2019; Takacs 2014). Prior to the early 1990s, the idea of exporting cultural products would have struck most Koreans as bizarre, therefore, this is a surprising development (Lie 2012). This development indeed has been rapid. Globalization has been identified as the primary feature of Korean cultural industries and has constituted the central trend of Hallyu. Since the mid-1990s, Korea has emerged as one of the global cultural hubs that produces several forms of popular culture and digital technologies.

Hallyu has had ebbs and flows. Due to the wave's relatively small size and influence, scholars in several academic disciplines, policy makers, and cultural producers once considered it a fad in the 2000s (Hanaki et al. 2007). In the early 2000s, several Asian countries especially witnessed anti-Hallyu movements in response to the rise of Korean television dramas and films; thus, Hallyu appeared to dissipate for a while (Chen 2017; Kwon 2016; H. Lee 2017). However, since the late 2000s, Korean cultural industries have created several new driving forces to expedite the wave through the social media-driven dissemination of K-pop and other cultural products, including digital games, far beyond Asia.

The history of the Korean media and cultural industries suggests that Hallyu as a cultural trend has experienced several significant shifts over more than two decades. To contextualize Hallyu, we investigate the shifting role of the Korean cultural industries in relation to the broader social structure of society. By comprehensively documenting the context and process behind the growth of Korean cultural industries and policies, as well as technological development, we explore how Hallyu has become a popular cultural trend in the global markets. We examine how the term Hallyu was coined and introduced. The etymological review will be followed by a structural and historical analysis of the three significant Hallyu periods. In other words, we trace the development of Hallyu since the 1990s by addressing its structural shifts. Here the evolution of Hallyu is divided into three major periods based on several characteristics, such as its global reception, cultural policies, and technological advancements. The first period is the wave's seed phase in the mid-1990s, the second is its rise in Asia starting in the late 1990s, the so-called intra-Asian phase, and the third is its digital media-driven global penetration since around 2008. In examining characteristics of these periods, we historicize the Korean Wave as a series of waves beginning in the 1990s. It, therefore, provides structural and historical frameworks for a comprehensive understanding of the development and transnational flows of Hallyu.

ETYMOLOGY OF HALLYU

Hallyu has benefited from the rapid growth of the Korean media and cultural industries over the past two to three decades. Prior to the 1990s, Korea's media and cultural industries were not particularly significant in size or diversity, even compared to other countries with a similar economic capacity. In 1980, the number of movie theaters in Korea stood at 447, while Mexico and Argentina had 2,831 and 1,136 cinemas, respectively (Jin 2011; United Nations Educational, Scientific, and Cultural Organization 1999). Korea's broadcast media industry was also nascent until the early 1980s, during which only three television channels were available. This is, however, no longer the case in the Korean media and cultural industries, as media and cultural corporations have greatly increased, which has been the stepping-stone for the growth of the Korean Wave (Jin and Kwak, 2018).

In fact, Korea has become one of the largest media and/or cultural markets worldwide. As figure 2.1 shows, Korea earned US$57.1 billion and ranked eighth, surpassing Canada and Italy, in the global media markets in 2018 (PricewaterHouseCoopers 2018). The number of media and cultural firms rapidly increased. Korea has embraced the multichannel television era. Thirty-two terrestrial broadcasting channels and 199 cable channels have

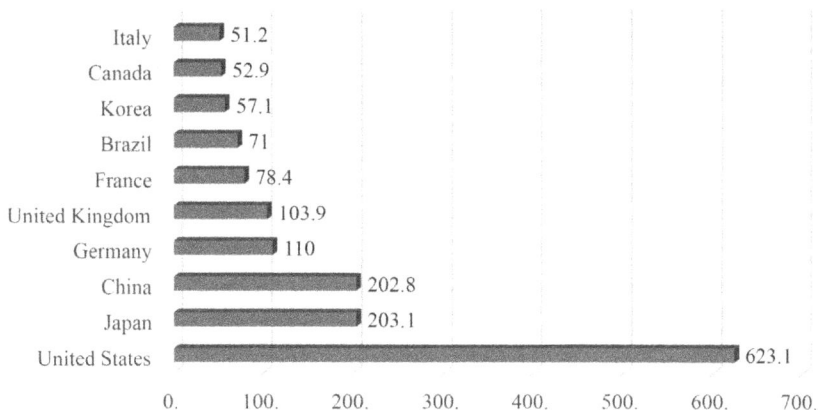

Italy — 51.2
Canada — 52.9
Korea — 57.1
Brazil — 71
France — 78.4
United Kingdom — 103.9
Germany — 110
China — 202.8
Japan — 203.1
United States — 623.1

0.   100.   200.   300.   400.   500.   600.   700.

Figure 2.1.   Largest Media Markets Worldwide by Revenue in 2017 (Unit: Billion USD ($)).
Source: **PricewaterHouseCoopers (2018).**

been established since the mid-1990s, and as of December 2013, there are 425 functioning broadcasting companies (Korea Press Foundation 2004, 2014). Since the late 1990s, Korea's film industry has also grown exponentially in areas such as production and distribution, and box-office revenue has soared. When this figure reached U$510 million in 2001, Korea ranked twelfth, lagging behind several countries, including the United States, Japan, the United Kingdom, France, India, Germany, Australia, Spain, and Canada. However, in 2017, Korea ranked sixth, with a record high of $1.6 billion, lagging behind only the United States, China, Japan, the United Kingdom, and India (Motion Picture Association of America 2017; PricewaterHouseCoopers 2006). As such, the Korean cultural industries have rapidly grown to become one of the major cultural hubs in the global scape, which means that local cultural industries have played a primary role in the formation and growth of the Korean Wave in the early twenty-first century.

Against this backdrop, it is important to examine how the term Hallyu emerged and was popularized as a cultural trend and discourse, because it enables a comprehensive understanding of transnational Hallyu and its origins. The term Hallyu (韓流) was coined in 1999 by Chinese newspapers, which used the expression to represent the success of Korean singers in China (Hong et al. 2017; Yoon and Kang 2017). In 1999, the Ministry of Culture and Tourism produced and distributed a music CD to publicize K-pop in East Asia. The title in English was *Korean Pop Music*, while its Chinese version was called *Hallyu—Songs from Korea*.

However, it is allegedly a Taiwanese newspaper that used the term Hallyu for the first time. On December 17, 1997, a Taiwanese newspaper (中國時報) stated that the Korean Wave had invaded Taiwan (You 1998), and other

Taiwanese newspapers began to use the term Hallyu to warn of the increasing competition power of Korean dramas in the mid-1990s (C. Hong 2012). While being produced as Hallyu, the meaning of the term was not the Korean Wave at that time; in Chinese characters, it initially meant "the coldest wind" (寒流).

The context surrounding this etymology and its interpretation is more important than the origin of the term Hallyu itself. The birth of a new term does not occur in a vacuum; rather, there are precedents and continuous trends before its formation. Thus, as will be illustrated later, a historical analysis of the pre-1997 period is required. In response to the increasing intra-Asian flows of Korean media, researchers have attempted to define this cultural phenomenon. An emerging group of studies, sometimes referred to as "Hallyu studies" (Yoon and Jin 2017), has defined the phenomenon as media and cultural flows while often describing it as a "rise" or "growth." For example, several media scholars, such as Shim (2006b), Y. Kim (2013), and Jeong et al. (2017), have defined Hallyu as media flows, while Hanaki et al. (2007) included a wider range of products, such as clothes, hairstyles, and cosmetics. These studies focused on the "rise," "spread," and "sudden growth" of Korean popular culture in the Asian and overseas markets.

After its seemingly sudden growth, Hallyu has rapidly moved beyond Asia and has, thus, been one of the few successful examples of cultural trends originating in non-Western countries (Marinescu 2014). In comparison with other transnational cultural flows, Hallyu can be characterized by its rapid market expansion around the globe; diversity in content, including both pop cultural content and digital technologies (e.g., smartphones and games); and social media-saturated consumption. Contemporary Hallyu has been popularly received in both Asian and Western markets due to the increasing role of social media while extending its scope to include digital technologies, such as Korean digital games, online and mobile games, smartphones, and free instant mobile messengers (Kakao Talk and LINE) (Jin 2016). The technological landscape of the smartphone has proven to be an interesting trend as locally produced media and telecommunications technologies have become popular worldwide (Goldsmith et al. 2011, 70).

Thus, contemporary Hallyu can be identified as the global popularity of Korean popular culture and digital technologies through both global trade and social media platform-driven consumption, which are embedded in transnationality. Of course, some recent studies continue to use expressions such as "rise" and "sudden growth" to describe Hallyu and its surprising overseas circulation. However, given the Korean cultural industries' continuous integration into the global mediascape for more than twenty years, this emphasis on Hallyu as an entirely new breed of cultural trend should be reconsidered. As Hallyu has advanced its visibility in the global cultural markets over the past few decades, it is time to redefine the notion by emphasizing continuity.

Given the significance of social media platforms in the contemporary Hallyu phenomenon, it is necessary to understand Hallyu as a process of media convergence in which different (old and new) media forms are synergistically mixed and articulated. Hallyu should be defined as the evolution of the Korean cultural industries and their content production through digital technologies at home and around the globe.

THE SEED PHASE OF HALLYU: THE EARLY AND MID-1990S

It is undeniable that Hallyu has emerged as extensive transnational cultural flows since the 2010s; however, this trend has a longer history than its global audiences might assume. Hallyu has evolved for over two decades, during which its notion and practices have shifted. Some scholars consider 1997 to be the beginning of Hallyu (e.g., Yoon and Jin 2017) because the year marked the first appearance of the term in the Chinese language media. If this is accepted, then 2017 marked a historical point as the twentieth anniversary of this cultural trend. When Korean culture started to enter several Asian countries in the late 1990s, Asian audiences and media critics considered it a fad. This response was not surprising, as Korea had never developed popular culture that had been well received in other countries. However, since the 1990s, Korea has continued to develop several forms of popular culture, followed by digital technologies, which have been exported to other parts of the world.

To historicize the early stage of Hallyu, as is well elaborated (Jin 2016; Yoon and Jin 2017), the Korean Wave started with a few well-made television dramas that were popular in East Asia, and the local cultural industries have advanced several forms, including films and K-pop, which have gradually arrived on the global market. Several Korean dramas then gained unexpected popularity in China and Taiwan. While acknowledging the significance of the late 1990s (1997 and onward) as a major point in Hallyu, it is important to historically examine this cultural trend in continuity. It is not easy to pinpoint the starting point of Hallyu because of the complexity of this cultural trend, which comprises several different contributing factors and effects. Instead of emphasizing the exportation of Korean cultural products to several Asian countries, a more nuanced approach is required to consider the political, economic, cultural, and technological components of transnational cultural flows. To enable a comprehensive understanding of Hallyu, this section examines the pre-1997 period, which can be referred to as the "seed phase"—that is, the period during which the term Hallyu had not yet been coined but motivational forces of this cultural trend grew—with reference to international cultural trade, the expansion of national cultural industries, and the implementation of national cultural policies.

International Cultural Trade

As exemplified by the success of Korean TV dramas and several pop music stars in Asia, the integration of the Korean culture industry into international cultural trade can be traced back to the pre-Hallyu era.[1] As early as the 1970s, preceding Hallyu's global rise, Korean cultural products were already being exported to several other countries, albeit in a haphazard fashion. Several Korean films were sold to overseas markets in the late 1970s, while Korean pop singers, such as Cho Yong-phil, Kim Yonja, and Kye Eun-sook, performed in Asian markets, including Japan, in the 1970s and 1980s—much earlier than the formal Korean Wave era.

More importantly, television drama is an important media genre that initiated more extensive exportation of Korean popular culture and contributed to the emergence of the Korean Wave in its early form. The Korean broadcasting industry started to export television programs in 1993. The MBC-produced drama *Jealousy (Jiltu)*, which depicted young couples' love and urban lives, introduced a new subgenre—"trendy drama."[2] This drama's domestic viewer rate soared to over 40 percent, and its main cast members, Choi Jin-sil and Choi Soo-jong, achieved their own stardom. *Jealousy* became the first Korean production to be broadcast in China in the same year. Amid the sweeping popularity of Japanese television programs across several Asian broadcasting markets, *Jealousy* caught the eyes of Chinese audiences; Harbin TV imported and aired it in 1993, as well as the thirty-six-episode *Eyes of Dawn*, an epic drama aired on MBC in 1991 and one of the first exported Korean drama series (C. Park 2015; J. Sohn 2016). The exportation of Korean television dramas started in the mid-1990s, paving the way for Hallyu to emerge in the late 1990s and the early 2000s. What they tell us is that Hallyu did not fall from the sky. Scholars in many fields schematically stated that Hallyu came suddenly in the late 1990s; however, several cases of transnational flows of Korean cultural content in the pre-Hallyu era certainly played a role as the foundation of the Korean Wave phenomenon. Although people do not consider them as they were very limited and marginal, they were unofficially the harbingers of Hallyu.

Expansion of Cultural Industries

Korea's cultural industries have rapidly expanded and developed since the 1990s, as briefly discussed. Along with the increased export economy of Korean popular culture, the remarkable expansion of domestic cultural industries and market has contributed to the rise of Hallyu. Some previous works have emphasized the domestic expansion of cultural industries and the emergence of new popular cultural forms in the mid-1990s. Lie (2015) emphasized that K-pop, which has been one of the most significant cultural forms in the Korean Wave, started in the mid-1990s when Seo Taiji and Boys performed between 1992 and 1996. Seo Taiji and Boys burst forth onto Korean TV in 1992 as the group's rap song "Nan arayo" (I Know, 1992) became one of the first rap tracks to use the Korean language (Howard 2006; Morelli 2001). Seo Taiji and Boys became a timely icon of Korean youth, as their music touched on sociocultural issues, such as the notoriously exam-oriented education system, and grasped the atmosphere of political liberation and the emerging consumer culture (Fuhr 2016). With the arrival of American hip-hop culture and rap music via Seo Taiji and Boys and a few other musicians in the early and mid-1990s, Korean popular music became more youth-oriented (E.-Y. Jung 2009).

Seo Taiji and Boys is estimated to be a true pioneer, helping to pave the way for contemporary K-pop (Howard 2006; Lie 2015). The group popularized rap and hip-hop in Korea, challenging and ultimately transforming the conventions of Korean popular music. From the standpoint of K-pop, the most consequential effect of Seo Taiji and Boys was its invention of a creative form of idol groups while introducing several different music genres and dances into the Korean music industry (Lie 2015). The early K-pop led by Seo Taiji and Boys suggests that Hallyu did not suddenly emerge in the late 1990s but has continuously evolved over a long period. In particular, K-pop was already led by several teenage idol groups, including H.O.T, NRG, S.E.S, Baby VOX, and Shinhwa, starting in the mid-1990s. The success of Seo Taiji and Boys and other early idol groups motivated the K-pop industry to develop its idol system. Major K-pop entertainment houses—some of which were established by early idol stars, such as Seo Taiji and Boys's Yang Hyun-Seok—developed in-house production systems that effectively train, produce, and distribute K-pop idols.

As shown in the K-pop idol manufacturing system, the expansion and development of domestic cultural industries are probably best observed in the structuralization of the music industry. There is no doubt that Korean entertainment houses are the primary driving forces of the process, and the strategic marketization of K-pop stars had already begun in 1995, when Soo-man Lee founded SM Entertainment (Jin 2016). After studying in the United States, Lee returned to Korea and established SM Studio in 1989, after which he changed the name to SM Entertainment in February 1995. The agency developed an in-house production system and produced a string of successful artists, including the boy group H.O.T in 1996, the girl group S.E.S. in 1997, and Shinhwa in 1998 (SM Entertainment 2018). By adopting and appropriating the typical Japanese idol production system, in which music production companies focused on fostering television-friendly young talents—those who had not only singing ability (or the lack thereof) but also dancing and general all-round television entertainer capabilities (J. Lee 2009, 491–92)—SM Entertainment fully systemized the total procedure of young pop-star making, with breakthroughs by the boy band H.O.T and the girl group S.E.S. Of these, H.O.T. was particularly popular in Taiwan and China, where they were accessed via traditional media (e.g., television) and online spaces (e.g., music-download sites and online broadcasters) as they formed active virtual fan communities in the early years of the twenty-first century (E.-Y. Jung 2014).

The development of digital technology industries in Korea has also been significant, as shown the remarkable market expansion of online and mobile games and smartphones, to be test beds in the global markets. As of October 2018, Korea's gaming industry is estimated to be the fourth largest in the world, behind only China, the United States, and Japan, in terms of revenue (Lee and Kim 2018). As the Korean cultural industries that are equipped with both new media and popular culture are among the most vibrant in the global media systems, they produce diverse cultural products and services, which they export to other countries, including in Asia, North America, Europe, and Latin America.

Implementation of Cultural Policies

National cultural policies have played a significant role in the growth of the country's cultural industries, especially since the Kim Young-sam government (1993–1998), which was the first civilian regime after three decade-long military regimes. Unlike the previous military regimes, the Kim government initiated several different policy measures, ultimately nurturing the cultural industries. While the Kim government continued to advance neoliberal cultural policies, which opened the cultural markets to foreign forces and deregulated the local industries, it started to develop some supportive cultural policies. In the midst of neoliberal changes in the political, economic, and social environment, the Korean government's perception of the cultural industries also shifted. Most of all, the Kim government acknowledged the economic importance of culture not as an art but as a commodity (Jin 2011; Kwon and Kim 2014). The Kim government brought the concept of cultural industries to cultural policy, shifted the focus of cultural policy from the arts to commercial cultural industries, and consequently intensified the commodification of popular culture (Jin 2016).

More specifically, the Kim government organized the Presidential Advisory Board on Science and Technology and submitted a comprehensive report

to the president suggesting that the new government promote media production as the national strategic industry. Within the same report, the board
indicated that *Jurassic Park*, a Hollywood movie created in 1993, equated
the exportation value of 1.5 million Hyundai cars. The comparison of a film
to Hyundai cars was sufficiently apt to awaken the Korean government to the
idea of culture as an industry, which became one of Kim Young-sam's earliest
cultural agendas (J. H. Kim 2004; Shim 2006b).

Following the report, the Korean government set up the Cultural Industries
Directorate in 1994. Established within the Ministry of Culture, the directorate focused on "the industrialization of culture and the internationalization
of Korean culture" (H. K. Lee 2013, 189). The government also initiated the
growth of the film industry by enacting the Motion Picture Promotion Law
in 1995 (Shin 2005). The Kim government began to support the cultural
industries, which became a basis for the spread of Hallyu thereafter. The
Korean Wave cannot be seen solely as a transnational cultural phenomenon;
rather, Hallyu must be seen as a national institutional policy initiative with
clear ambitions (J. Choi 2015). Jin (2016, 20) argues that Korea has emerged
as one of the major centers for the production of transnational popular culture, meaning that Korean cultural industries have developed a number of
recognizable cultural products of their own, such as television programs and
films. Korea has also developed new cultural forms, especially online games,
animation, and K-pop, and has expanded its role as a meaningful exporter of
locally made popular culture in other parts of the world, including Europe
and North America.

The changed cultural policies, which now aimed to support the growth of
national cultural industries, were accompanied by the loosening of the censorship system. Until the mid-1990s, the Korean government had censored
popular culture to uphold morals and prevent political agitation under the
military regime. In terms of cultural content, the military regimes had strictly
controlled films and television programs. However, the government gradually
changed the censorship system between the mid-1990s and the early twenty-
first century in the name of freedom of speech in artistic fields. Prompted by
the loosening of the censorship system, young Korean pop singers, including
Seo Taiji and Boys, could develop their music, which would not have been
able to prosper under the military regime. The cultural policies of the Korean
government centered on the proliferation of creativity (Yim 2002). In the
middle of the 1990s, the civilian government certainly fostered the growth
of the cultural industries and, therefore, eventually increased the exportation
of cultural products. In other words, until the early 1990s, cultural content
was heavily censored by the government in the name of upholding morals
and preventing political agitation under the military regime (Yang 2003).
However, the loosening censorship under the civilian government, starting

in 1993, increased new forms of cultural content and production, which later become seeds for Hallyu.

THE INTRA-ASIAN PHASE: THE LATE 1990S

While Hallyu has its roots in the development of Korean cultural industries in the early and mid-1990s, this trend gained overseas visibility in the late 1990s through the intra-Asian circulation of Korean pop culture content. Thus, the late 1990s can be referred to as the intra-Asian Hallyu phase. As several researchers (e.g., Ainslie, 2016; Hong et al. 2017; Jin and Kim 2018; Yoon and Jin 2017) commonly point out, Hallyu started to grow substantially with the birth of a few Korean TV dramas, such as *What Is Love All About?* (produced in 1991 and aired in China in 1997), *Autumn in My Heart* (2000), *Winter Sonata* (2002), and *Dae Jang Geum* (2003), which were popular in several East Asian countries. Among these, *What Is Love All About?* was tele-vised by Chinese channel CCTV 1 in June 1997; its viewer rating, recorded at 4.2 percent, was one of the highest among foreign programs, and CCTV 2 rebroadcasted the series at prime time due to high demand (You 1998).[3] Hal-lyu was also facilitated by the success of Korean films, such as *Joint Security Area* (2000), although their presence in the West was marginal.

Hallyu was visible in the intra-Asian circulation of Korean idol pop music, which was later commonly referred as K-pop. A few Korean musicians, including HOT and Shinhwa, continued to grow in popularity in East Asia; however, K-pop was relatively unknown to the global music markets until early 2001, when SM Entertainment began to promote a female teenage singer named BoA, especially in Japan. BoA's debut Japanese album, *Listen to My Heart*, was released in March 2002; it became a million-album seller and was the first album by a Korean artist to debut atop the Oricon charts (Poole 2009). However, in regard to its exportation and international influ-ence, K-pop remained nascent until the mid-2000s.

Overall, starting in 1997, the intra-Asian stage of Hallyu relied heavily on two major cultural forms: television dramas and films. This is understandable, because the structural transformations in Korean cultural industries occurred primarily in the broadcasting and film industries during this period. With the adaptation of neoliberal globalization since the late 1980s, the Korean government started to liberalize the cultural market. Until the early 1990s, only three television channels—KBS 1, KBS 2, and MBC—existed, and the quality of production and number of programs were limited. However, the significant transformation began with the introduction of a new terrestrial commercial broadcasting company, the Seoul Broadcasting System (SBS), in 1991, followed by numerous cable channels starting in 1995. That same year, the Kim Young-sam government also enacted the Motion Picture Promotion Law, which included diverse incentives, such as tax breaks for film studios to encourage *chaebol*—that is, the largest conglomerates in Korea, such as Samsung, Hyundai, and Lotte—to participate in the film and media production industry. The Kim government also developed several financial support programs, in particular for the media production industry (Jin 2011).

It is noteworthy that Hallyu emerged around 1997, when the financial crisis decimated the Asian and, in particular, the Korean economy. In a way, the economic crisis motivated investment in the development of creative and cultural content (Shim 2008). In the face of the financial crisis, the worst recession in Korean history, broadcasters and filmmakers had to produce quality programs instead of purchasing foreign television programs and films. Indeed, according to the Ministry of Culture and Tourism (2000), the importation of television programs continued to increase until 1996—by 40 percent between 1994 and 1995 and 49 percent between 1995 and 1996. However, when the financial crisis hit, this trend changed dramatically. In 1997, Korea imported $57 million worth of television programs, representing a 10.4 percent decrease from the prior year, and in 1998, this figure fell to $27 million, indicating a 52.8 percent decrease. In contrast, the exportation of television programs increased 38.7 percent in 1997 ($8.3 million) and 20.4 percent in 1998 ($10 million) (Ministry of Culture and Tourism 2000). The film industry experienced a similar trend. In 1996, the importation of foreign films decreased significantly from 483, the highest figure recorded up to that time, to 431 in 1997 and 296 in 1998, while their exportation gradually increased during the same period, from 30 in 1996 to 102 in 2001 (Korean Film Council 2009).

During the mid- and late 1990s, several East Asian countries also experienced the rapid growth of their cultural markets, as cable and satellite channels were introduced; they therefore needed programs to fill the channels (T. Lim 2008). They discovered a new resource, as locally produced cultural products in Korea were relatively inexpensive compared to their American and Japanese counterparts. The rapid rise of Asian media markets in the late 1990s was fueled by the expansion of the urban middle class in the region (Chua 2012; Y. Kim 2013).

The intra-Asian Hallyu phase (the late 1990s) is clearly distinguished from the early 1990s, as the former engaged with media globalization and witnessed the rapid overseas dissemination of Korean pop cultural content. While the early 1990s was a period when Korean cultural industries prepared their infrastructure in light of globalization, the intra-Asian Hallyu phase engaged with the rapid globalization of Korean cultural industries and paved the way for Korean media's dissemination beyond Asia. With the emergence and growth of new media, including cable, satellite television, multiplex cinemas being established in numerous countries in the late 1990s, global citizens (especially Asian urban middle-class audiences) were ready to enjoy other countries' popular culture, and some found Korean popular culture unique and enjoyable.

The transition from the seed phase to the intra-Asian phase shows how transnational cultural flows were implemented through different moments and momentums. Overall, the emerging cultural trend of Hallyu benefited from the massive effect of globalization, which impacted Asian countries in the 1990s, during which the movement of capital, commodities, and labor power began to be expedited to enhance the neoliberal global economy.[4]

THE HALLYU 2.0 PHASE: THE 2010S ONWARD

The third most significant historical period in the development of Hallyu is its 2.0 phase (Lee and Nornes 2015), or new Korean Wave phase (Jin 2016), which started around 2008. This period is distinguished from previous transnational cultural flows, owing to its seamless integration into the digital mediascape and its global reach across different cultural forms (Jin 2016). The Korean Wave has changed significantly, and the global popularity of Korean popular culture and digital technologies has increased substantially. The exportation of Korean cultural products increased from $1,675 million in 2008 to $6,240 million in 2018 (Korea Creative Content Agency 2019; see table 2.1). During the same period, digital games, K-pop, and animation became significant, while television programs and films were major cultural forms leading global trade until the mid-2000s. Among these, K-pop has become one of the most significant cultural forms of the new Korean Wave. As previously discussed, K-pop gained popularity in some Asian countries; however, it was not well received in the global market. Since the late 1990s, K-pop has gradually become a new powerhouse of transnational Hallyu. Most of all, precipitated by Psy's *Gangnam Style*, which became a global sensation in 2012, K-pop has positioned itself as the most significant Korean popular culture genre. The exportation of Korean popular music has soared from only $16.4 million in 2008 to $510 million in 2018 (Korea Creative Content Agency 2018a, 2019; Ministry of Culture, Sports, and Tourism 2017. See table 2.1).

On the consumption side, the most noteworthy element of the new Korean Wave starting in 2008 has been the advance of social media and its integration into the process of cultural circulation. Recently, Hallyu has been immersed extensively in the social mediascape and has opened up a new paradigm of cultural production and consumption that cannot be properly identified using the conventional market measurement model. Until the early 2000s, the major indicator of Hallyu was its exportation overseas; however, in the 2010s,

Table 2.1. Exports of Major Cultural Products, 1998–2018 (Unit: Million USD)

	1998	1999	2000	2001	2002	2003	2004	2005	2006	2007
Broadcasting	10	12.7	13.1	18.9	28.8	42.1	70.3	122	134	151
Movies	3.1	5.9	7.1	11.2	15	31	58.3	76	24.5	24.4
Animation	85	81.6	85	121.3	89.2	75.7	61.8	78.4	66.8	72.7
Music	8.6	8.1	7.9	7.4	4.2	13.3	34.2	22.3	16.6	13.8
Games	82.2	107.6	101.5	130.4	140.7	182	388	585	672	781
Characters	0	65.7	69.2	76.9	86	116	117	164	189	203
Manga	0	2.9	3.7	6.8	8.2	4.1	1.9	3.3	3.9	3.9
Total	188.9	284.5	287.5	372.9	372.1	464	732	1051	1107	1250

	2008	2009	2010	2011	2012	2013	2014	2015	2016	2017	2018 (P)
Broadcasting	171	185	184.7	222.4	233.8	309.4	336	320	411.2	493.3	550
Movies	21	14.1	13.6	15.8	20.1	37	26	29.3	43.8	40.7	40
Animation	80.5	89.6	96.8	115.9	112.5	109.8	115	126.5	135.6	145.8	160
Music	16.4	31.2	81.3	196.1	235.1	277.3	335	381	442.5	456.3	510
Games	1094	1241	1606	2378	2638	2715	2973	3214	3277	3906	4230
Characters	228	237	276.3	392.3	416.4	446	489	551	612.8	648.8	710
Manga	4.1	4.2	8.2	17.2	17.1	20.9	25	29.3	32.4	37.6	40
Total	1675	1786	2266	3237	3673	3915	4299	4651	4824	5729	6240

Sources: Ministry of Culture, Sports, and Tourism (2012, 2016, 2017); Ministry of Culture and Tourism (2006); Korea Creative Content Agency (2019)

global audiences enjoy K-pop and Korean films on various forms of social media, often bypassing conventional platforms and gatekeepers. Many global fans of Korean television dramas also watch these programs on YouTube and Netflix. Without digital technologies and/or social media, the current form of Hallyu would not exist. Of course, the popularity of K-pop relevant to the use of social media eventually triggers the growth of K-pop exportation, as many concerts have been held in North America, Latin America, and Europe, as well as Asia. This implies that the new phase of Hallyu has been greatly supported by the growth of social media and that the convergence of old and new media has, therefore, been a crucial factor in the recent Korean Wave.

As sociocultural and political milieus surrounding the growth of the cultural industries constituted a significant factor in the rise of early Hallyu, sociocultural contexts are important for enabling a comprehensive understanding of social media-driven Hallyu in its recent form. As is well known, Facebook was created in 2004, YouTube followed in 2005, and the first commercially successful smartphone—Apple's iPhone—was invented in 2007. As these social media platforms gained massive interest a few years after their creation, the global popularity of Korean culture and the growth of social media platforms coincide perfectly with this development. In other words, the popularity of Korean culture in the global markets is contingent upon a high penetration of social media and digital technologies through which soft pop cultural content flows with ease (Jin 2016). As exemplified in the viral circulation of K-pop idol groups' music videos, social media have shifted the ways in which process cultural content is transnationally circulated; cultural flows have increasingly been diversified, decentralized, expedited, and networked.

The importance of social media and digital technologies is not the sole factor behind the rise of the new Korean Wave; national cultural policies continue to contribute to its recent phase. Since the late 2000s, government policy has shifted from a hands-off approach (i.e., indirect support for the global trade of cultural products) in the early years of Hallyu to a hands-on (i.e., direct support) one in the new Hallyu era. It is necessary to analyze the influences of key cultural policies in the development of Korean popular culture and its cultural industries. In the early stage of Hallyu, the Korean government initially developed its cultural policy to support indirect intervention and deregulation with a view to enabling the private sector to advance the Hallyu phenomenon.

However, the governments in the 2000s and 2010s—the Lee Myung-bak (2008–2013) and Park Geun-hae (2013–2017) administrations—subsequently shifted their cultural policy emphasis toward a creative content policy and have become actively involved in the cultural sector. The creative industry discourse seemed to enhance the view that particular cultural sectors are considered to be drivers of national economic growth, which Potts and Cunningham (2008) have referred to as the growth model of cultural policy. Indeed, the two governments since 2008 have focused on the notion of "creative industries" (compared to the previous term "cultural industries") as a significant component of the national economy, with one of the emphases being placed on intellectual property. Intellectual property rights have also become some of the most significant revenue resources for Korean cultural industries and performers and are increasingly more important than future exports of cultural goods in terms of revenue. The government has developed strategic policies regarding the protection and enhancement of intellectual properties and rights, while Korean media and entertainment corporations have made strategic choices toward expanding revenues in such areas as licensing, royalty, sponsorship contributions, and advertising (Jin 2016; Oh and Park 2012). This does not mean that government policies directly enhance the growth of Hallyu. The point being emphasized is that Korean cultural industries have been influenced by government policies—sometimes direct and at other times indirect policy mechanisms.

Under these circumstances, recent Hallyu has become a global sensation, which distinguishes itself not only from its earlier wave but also from other countries' popular cultural flows. The phase of Hallyu 2.0 has continued to advance the convergence of popular culture and digital technologies, thereby facilitating media consumers' participation in production processes and the continuous hybridization of local and global content. As empirical studies presented later in this book, extensive and ongoing hybridization, which is evident in several forms of Hallyu content, such as K-pop and films, may provide resources for challenges to the Western hegemony in cultural industries (Ono and Kwon 2013; Yoon and Jin 2017). The commodification and commercialization of local cultural industries have been evident, as many cultural creators and cultural industries firms have emphasized the commercial success of cultural content in the global cultural markets. By emphasizing hybridization, for example, they are able to attract global fans more than expected; however, during the process, they lose cultural uniqueness embedded in traditional Korean cultural scenes.

CONCLUSION

This chapter has historicized the evolution of Hallyu by discussing its three major phases. While Hallyu is known for its emergence in 1997, our exploration began with the early 1990s due to several sociocultural considerations. As Hallyu has continued its evolution over the past two decades, it is important to acknowledge its histories and continuity. As evidenced by the influence of

Seo Taiji and Boys, Hallyu did not suddenly emerge in 1997 but, rather, was rooted in significant cultural practices from the early and mid-1990s. In this regard, we have shed light on the pre-1997 era and two additional historical breakthrough periods—the late 1990s and late 2000s—as the most significant historical moments for the evolution of Hallyu.

We have attempted to argue that Hallyu cannot be identified solely as the rise of Korean popular culture in Asia and around the globe. Rather, the popularity of Korean culture in foreign countries should be understood as a process and not solely as a conclusion. It is crucial to comprehend the socio-cultural, political, and technological milieus surrounding the Korean Wave. It is critical to pay attention to the growth of Korea's cultural industries as the infrastructure of the emergence of the Korean Wave. Since the 1990s, the Korean cultural industries have undergone a major transformation, growing rapidly alongside the political, economic, and sociocultural changes taking place within Korea (Ryoo and Jin 2020). Unlike the vast majority of previous works emphasizing the late 1990s as the starting point of Hallyu, we argue that it actually started in the early to mid-1990s as liberalization and techno-logical breakthroughs continued to occur.

Of course, Hallyu has experienced a quantum leap starting in the late 1990s, as K-pop, films, and dramas became some of the most significant cul-tural products embraced in East and Southeast Asia. Starting in the late 2000s, Hallyu witnessed another breakthrough: Due primarily to social media, this cultural trend became prevalent in the global market. More recently, it has obtained global popularity through the increasing role of social media and global audiences who actively use social media; in this recent phase, conver-gence of different media forms across national borders has been accelerated more than ever before.

In this chapter, by emphasizing sociocultural aspects, as well as the tech-nological elements embedded in the Korean cultural industries, we have suggested that Hallyu is the outcome of complex processes, including cul-tural industries' expansion, technological developments (e.g., cable channels and social media), government cultural policies, and the increasing role of overseas audiences. For better understanding of Hallyu as a socioeconomic process, it is important to historicize the evolution of this cultural trend.

NOTES

1. There are ongoing debates about how to historicize Hallyu. Investigating its starting point, several scholars have examined its nascent form by tracing the period in which even the neologism *Hallyu* or the *Korean Wave* did not exist. C. Park (2014) argues that Hallyu started in 1987, when Korea exported a few animated television programs. His example includes *Wanderer Kkachi*, which was created by KBS in

1987, and exported to France and several other countries interested in knowing about Korea around 1988 Summer Olympics; other animations, such as *Dooly the Little Dinosaur* and *Meoteol Dosa*, followed *Wanderer Kkachi*. However, given the limited scope of international trades of this early Korea animation products, C. Park's (2014) claim of 1987 as the origin of Hallyu seems far-fetched.

2. The term "trendy drama" originally refers to a Japanese subtelevision genre that was popular in the 1980s and 1990s. In contrast with the traditional "home drama"—that is, drama drawing on the stories of family relationships and targeting family-oriented viewers—the trendy drama formula emphasizes characters' individuality and lifestyles, rather than tensions between individuals and society. Japan's trendy drama genre has emerged in the country's bubble economy and its transition to the era of flexible accumulation and postmodernity (Lukács 2010). In a similar vein, Korean trendy dramas, which are influenced by their earlier Japanese counterparts, describe the urban lifestyles of young generations and coincide with Korea's booming economy and political liberalization of the 1990s (Yang 2003).

3. Among several early, successfully exported Korean TV dramas, *What Is Love All About?* tends to be considered as an initiator of the Hallyu phenomenon, as it is partly responsible for the creation of the neologism Hallyu. This TV drama, which was originally aired in 1991 and 1992 in Korea, was sold to China in 1994, but its air dates were delayed considerably because of technical issues (e.g., dubbing) and bureaucratic processes. This postponement demonstrates that transnational cultural flows were largely restricted by national and institutional gatekeeping in the pre-Internet era. Despite the difficulties with reaching out to Chinese audiences, Korean media industries made continuous efforts throughout the 1990s. Given these efforts, the Korean drama boom in China in the late 1990s is not accidental (K. C. Kim 2000).

4. Throughout the 1990s, Koreans increasingly participated in transnational migration through permanent emigration, overseas study, and tourism. In this regard, the Korean diaspora has played a significant role in spreading a new wave of Korean pop culture since the 1990s. As shown in several recent examples, such as Bollywood cinema and, more recently, Hallyu, the global circulation of local culture often begins with its own ethnic community and its spillover (Jenkins et al. 2013). However, despite their importance as the major consumers in the early stage of Hallyu, diasporic audiences have been significantly underresearched. In particular, young diasporic Koreans have participated in the emerging Hallyu fan culture by offering fan translation and facilitating the streaming and sharing Hallyu content (K. Yoon 2020). While the earlier Korean diasporic populations were regular consumers of Korean TV content in their neighborhoods (such as Koreatowns around the globe), new diasporic populations tend to be more involved in sharing, recommending, and translating Hallyu beyond their local neighborhoods (Dwyer 2012).

Chapter 3

Digital Convergence of Hallyu

INTRODUCTION

On March 26, 2012, during his official visit to South Korea, former U.S. president Barack Obama gave a speech on international collaboration and future cooperation at Hankuk University of Foreign Studies located in Seoul. During this speech, he mentioned Hallyu to emphasize the role of digital technologies in transnational connections and innovations: "And you know that in our digital age, we can connect and innovate across borders like never before—with your smart phones and Twitter and Me2Day and KakaoTalk (Laughter and applause). It's no wonder so many people around the world have caught the Korean Wave, Hallyu" (Obama 2012). This special moment clearly exemplifies that Hallyu has been well received in many parts of the world, and Korean digital technologies have been considered an important component and driver of the Korean Wave.

The discourse of Hallyu until the 2010s had not sufficiently addressed digital technologies as a key component of this cultural trend (e.g., Goldsmith et al. 2011). However, as illustrated in the following chapters on audience studies, transnational audiences that engage with Hallyu cannot be explained without considering the digital component of the flow. As Arora (2012) points out, the relationship between popular culture and networks, such as broadcasting media, has been crucial in the circulation of culture. The new Korean Wave has been greatly circulated through social media and digital platforms alongside traditional media, and therefore, we cannot imagine the dissemination of Korean popular culture without digital technologies, including social media. In addition, several digital culture forms, such as esports (electronic sports) and instant mobile messenger user culture on KakaoTalk and LINE, in addition to digital technologies like smartphones, have become globally popular and, thus, should be considered as integral parts of Hallyu. Despite the importance of the digital aspect of Hallyu, it has been insufficiently addressed in existing studies. The early studies tended to attribute the Hallyu phenomenon to solely the domain of popular culture (e.g., Chua and Iwabuchi 2008), whereas the recent studies have begun to partially address the importance of digital technologies in the phenomenon (e.g., Lee and Nornes 2015); exceptionally, some recent studies have increasingly paid due attention to the focal role of digital technologies in Hallyu (e.g., Holroyd 2019; Jin 2016, 2017a, 2017b; Jin and Yoon 2016; Song et al. 2014).

In this chapter, we suggest that the convergence of digital technologies and popular culture is a significant process through which contemporary Hallyu has emerged and flourished. We first explore the evolution of Korea's digital media industries that trigger the growth of the digital phase of Hallyu or Hallyu 2.0. By tracing several key moments of digital technology development in Korea, we document an early history of digital Hallyu. As discussed in chapter 1, it is important to historicize the emergence and evolution of the Korean Wave phenomenon. In a similar vein, we argue that it is important to examine the process of how digital infrastructure for Hallyu has developed since the early 1990s. In addition to the historicization of digital Hallyu, we investigate the role of digital media convergence in the rise of Hallyu, with particular reference to Korean webtoons, which provide a vivid example of transmedia convergence and transmedia storytelling. The recent global rise of Korean webtoons clearly shows how digital technology is not simply a vehicle of Hallyu but also the key content of Hallyu.

DEVELOPMENT OF DIGITAL INFRASTRUCTURE FOR HALLYU

Hallyu first earned its name through a few television dramas and films in Asia in the late 1990s, as already discussed in previous chapters. While the rise of the Wave was caused by engaging media content and its appeal to Asian audiences, the content cannot solely explain the rise of the Wave. What we propose is that we should also consider the digital infrastructure and capacity that have transformed Korean cultural industries and accelerated a new mode of media production. In particular, broadband services, mobile technologies, digital games, and social media have contributed to the rise and enhancement of Hallyu over the past two decades (Jin 2016). Since the early 2000s, Korea has rigorously advanced digital technologies and infrastructure as new growth engines for the national economy. Made-in-Korea digital technologies, including digital games, mobile instant messengers (e.g., KakaoTalk and LINE), and webtoons (web comics) have quickly penetrated the global and local markets. Both domestic and global users of smartphones enjoy K-pop and K-dramas on Samsung's Galaxy, while many gamers enjoy local-made mobile games on KakaoTalk (or simply KaTalk). Smartphone users in many countries have also increasingly been enjoying Korean webtoons (Jeong 2020). Broadband technology and social media provide a preliminary background to an appreciation of the scale of digital economy in Korea (Chung 2013). For a better understanding of the development of digital Hallyu infrastructure, we should consider the role of major stakeholders such as the government, users, and cultural industries.

IT Policies for Wiring the Country

It is fair to say that the global reputation of Korea's digital technologies started with the growth of broadband, which was first made available in the country in June 1998. Its national penetration rate rapidly increased to the highest in the world in 2000 (Kim et al. 2010); the country has been a leader in the number of households with broadband access since its early advancement. The rapid development of broadband technology in Korea benefited from state-led interventionism in the ICT sector since the early 1990s. The Kim Young Sam government (1993–1998) launched a project, titled the Korea Information Infrastructure (KII) in March 1995—the largest IT (information technology) project in the history of Korean government—aiming to transform the country toward a knowledge-based economy. While households had a maximum dialup service speed of 64 Kbps until the late 1990s, several telecommunications service providers introduced high-speed Internet services in 1998–1999, which contributed to transforming the country's digital landscape (Chon et al. 2013). The KII project acted as the primary policy mechanism to build a higher-level information technology-based economic model. The Korean government's emphasis on digital technologies for economic growth has continued during the following administrations, whether the two liberal governments—the Kim Dae-jung government (1998–2003) and the Roh Moo-hyun government (2003–2008)—or the two conservative governments—the Lee Myung-bak government (2008–2013) and the Park Geun-hye government (2013–2017). The Korean government has continued and even intensified its function to support the ICT sector (Jin 2017a). Based on the rapid growth of broadband, Korea has been able to advance several cutting-edge technologies and relevant cultures. As Holroyd (2019, 297) aptly puts it, Korea's large and rapid investment in ICT services and connectivity, "producing world-leading speeds and reliability, coupled with comparatively low costs," laid the foundation for Korea's emergence as an ICT power, which, in turn, "provided a technological foundation for the emergence of the digital content sector."

Vibrant User Culture

While several IT firms, including Samsung, LG, Naver, and Kakao, have greatly advanced new digital technologies, Korean consumers have also swiftly adapted to the new media environments, while demanding cutting-edge digital technologies faster than others have (Lau et al. 2005). For Koreans, the use of digital technologies, including digital games and KakaoTalk, as well as social media, implies digitally networking together, not individually, so that they work together, play together, and even organize social and political events together through these digital technologies.[1] Consumers previously consumed media infrastructure and content, but they now produce content themselves as major players (Jin 2017a, 2017b). The vibrant media user behaviors have, to some extent, accelerated the Korean IT industries' research and development. Several local corporations have been globally recognized by their cutting-edge technologies, such as smartphones, social media, and video games. The articulation of vibrant user culture and technology development explains why and how digital Hallyu is closely related to Korea's IT industries.

Early Social Media Experiences: Cyworld

Hallyu has effectively utilized different digital and social media platforms. Korean IT industries' endeavors to generate and test different platform technologies may have contributed to Hallyu industries' timely engagement with global media platforms. In this regard, the role of Korean-made social and digital media for paving the way to transnational Hallyu should not be underestimated.

First of all, prior to global social media, Korea already created and advanced its own local social media, Cyworld, earlier than U.S.-based social media. Cyworld was created as a personal information management system in 1999, although it technically became defunct in October 2015. This template-based, networked homepage service, called mini-hompy (J. H. Choi 2006), enjoyed phenomenal popularity among young Koreans, while pioneering as an online social networking tool.[2] Cyworld was intended to be a personal contact website, a way to connect to the user's immediate circle of acquaintances. Cyworld showed the nascent potential form of social media and media convergence, while functioning as a platform for various methods of media content consumption, such as background music and avatars, and as a virtual playground for young users in the digital age (Jin 2015). However, this Korean-made, early social media platform did not maintain its extensive and solid user base, as it failed to attract young people in the smartphone era in the 2010s (Jin and Yoon 2016).[3]

As Korean-made social media platforms, including Cyworld, have not extensively penetrated into other countries, the Hallyu industries have capitalized on global platforms such as YouTube and Twitter. However, we argue that, despite the trial and error, the early Korean social media Cyworld, as well as a few other digital media platforms that no longer exist, might have provided Korean cultural industries to explore the potential of transmedia platforms. Thus, the early endeavors might be incorporated into the development of transmedia storytelling strategies in recent digital Hallyu.

Hallyu industries have indeed extensively used social media platforms to reach a wider audience globally as fans of Korean popular culture rely on social media platforms to enjoy their favorite K-pop, dramas, and films. By entering the social media-driven space of Hallyu, global fans are networked, share their feelings, and translate the content to move beyond the linguistic and cultural barriers. For example, the Korean music entertainment houses have effectively integrated into the social media platforms on a global scale. Due to K-pop industry's vibrant music video production and distribution via social media, many K-pop idols have been highly recognized on YouTube, and their videos are virally circulated even without substantial mainstream media exposure in many countries. Korean films and TV shows have increasingly been available on major global social media or content platform services, such as YouTube and Netflix. In some cases, such as *Okja* (2017), global platforms have functioned as important outlets for digital Hallyu by funding and engaging with the process of production and global distribution of cultural content.

Evolution of the Gaming Industries and Culture

Online gaming and mobile gaming have swiftly grown and been integral areas of Hallyu, because the deployment of broadband and smartphones has provided a much necessary tool for these digital technologies. Online gaming has substantially increased in the Korean game market and moved beyond the national market. Online gaming had become the single largest cultural product in the Hallyu phenomenon until very recent years; however, with the rapid growth of smartphones, mobile gaming has become the largest segment in the export of digital games starting in 2016. In fact, in 2015, when Korea exported $3,214 million worth of digital games, online gaming was the largest, accounting for as much as 61.5 percent, followed by mobile gaming (37.9 percent); however, in 2016, Korea exported $3,277 million, and mobile gaming became the largest for the first time, consisting of 49.9 percent, followed by online gaming (49.4 percent). In the global game market, Korea also ranked fifth, only behind the United States, China, Japan, and the United Kingdom, accounting for 5.7 percent in 2016 (Korea Creative Content Agency 2016, 2017).

The recent growth of mobile games has been closely related to the rapid development and penetration of smartphone technologies in Korea during the

2010s. The smartphone revolution has been remarkable as Samsung and LG have become some of the largest handset makers. Domestically, Korea had 56 million mobile subscriptions at the end of 2017, and the number of smartphone users spiked to exceed 48 million during the same period, consisting of 86.7 percent of total mobile phone users (Ministry of Science and ICT 2017a). According to the global data, Korea stands out as the country with the highest smartphone penetration. As of 2018, Korea's smartphone penetration rate among adults was 95 percent, followed by Israel (88 percent), the Netherlands (87 percent), Sweden (86 percent), Australia (81 percent), and United States (81 percent) (Silver 2019). Based on this high use of smartphones, Korea's mobile game industry and market have rapidly grown, so much so that the mobile game market's size surpassed that of traditionally strong online games in 2017 (Korea Creative Content Agency 2018b). As discussed in this section, digital technologies created in Korea have significantly contributed to the rise of the new phase of Hallyu (Hallyu 2.0). In the following sections, we focus on two of the most significant digital technologies (smartphone applications and webtoons), which have generated unique user cultures and accordingly facilitated the Korean Wave.

Communication Apps as Driving Forces of Digital Hallyu

With the rapid growth of smartphone technologies, applications (apps) have become very important parts of people's daily activities. From commercial banks to platform corporations, such as Apple and Google, all kinds of companies have applications developed in order to meet people's needs while securing huge financial profits. In particular, due to its high smartphone penetration rate, advanced IT industries, and savvy user cultures, Korea has witnessed the rapid growth of the app economy—a range of economic activities encompassing the sale of apps, ad revenues, and digital goods on which apps are designed to operate (Jin 2017b)—in the 2010s. Among these, two major instant mobile messenger apps—KakaoTalk and LINE—have deeply integrated into Koreans' everyday lives. KakaoTalk has been the most popular messaging app in Korea while Line is highly pervasive in the Japanese market.

These instant mobile messengers have become some of the most important digital technologies as they are primary platforms for several applications. Released in 2010, KakaoTalk immediately became the most popular app in Korea. This app, operated by the Korean platform giant Kakao, offers free instant messaging, social media, and gaming services. KakaoTalk allows person-to-person and group chats by simply entering users' phone numbers without any limit on the number of participants and without registering or logging in (Jin and Yoon 2016). While the Kakao platform is predominantly used among Koreans and Korean diasporas, it has increasingly been adopted

and used by overseas Hallyu fans (B. Han 2017). Another instant mobile messenger app, LINE, which is operated by Korean search engine giant Naver,
has been favored by smartphone users in several Asian countries, including
Japan, Thailand, Taiwan, and Turkmenistan; it had nearly 600 million worldwide users as of August 2017 (S. T. Kang 2017).

These two instant mobile messengers—KakaoTalk and LINE—have
played a major role in spreading Hallyu as they facilitated Asian users and
Asian diasporas' information sharing and transmedia app activities such as
online gaming, watching K-pop idols' webcasts and postings, and networking
with other Hallyu fans. The two apps are increasingly introduced to global
users other than Asian diasporas, partly due to their convenient interface and
cutesy design and accessibility to other apps for Korean games and music. In
particular, K-pop fans are increasingly accessing these two Korean-developed
apps to get more intimate and immediate access to their favorite idols. Indeed,
being aware of the popularity of these Korean-based platforms, some K-pop
idols regularly use the Kakao platform and LINE, as well as other major
social media platforms, to keep their fans updated, and thus, overseas fans
access these platforms.

MEDIA CONVERGENCE AND HALLYU

The development of Korean IT industries significantly influenced the country's cultural industries in several different ways. Among others, digital
media's increasing convergence enabled different cultural content to be
merged with and translated into another form. Media convergence has been
one of the most important trends in the global cultural industries in the early
twenty-first century, and Hallyu industries adapted to this changing media
environment quickly. Different types of media and platforms have consequently merged together. For instance, smartphones are not just communication handsets; they are also computers, televisions, and gaming devices, all
rolled into one, which is a logical progression (Goodson 2012).

Cultural creators and corporations have increasingly developed convergence between diverse media technologies and cultural content (Jenkins
2006a; Jin 2015; Noll 2003). Hallyu may be one of the first transnational
cultural trends that has extensively appropriated the logic of media convergence. With the rapid growth of the Internet, followed by smartphones and
social media, including user-generated content platforms (e.g., YouTube),
cultural producers have clearly understood the significance of media convergence and actualized it. While media convergence in the realm of technology
primarily implies the mix of the old technology (e.g., TV and radio) and the
new technology (e.g., the Internet and smartphone) (Jenkins 2006a), media

convergence is also about the mix of digital technologies and cultural content (e.g., news, film, music, and television program) for achieving endless transformation to maximize the benefits to both customers (in a new way of convenience) and developers (in a new way of capital accumulation) in the digital technology era (Jin 2015).

As Jenkins (2004, 34) points out, media convergence does not only mean a technological shift but rather means certain impacts on "the way we consume media" by creating synergistic effects through the mixing of digital technologies and cultural content. For example, convergence can be made possible due to consumers' changing consumption habits. They previously watched television dramas on television sets at home; they now often enjoy television dramas on their notebook computers or smartphones anytime and anyplace. Fans of television dramas also participate and share their opinions with other fans as they summarize episodes, share their emotions, debate subtexts, create original fan fiction, record their own soundtracks, make their own movies, and distribute their content worldwide via the Internet. Networked and participatory audiences emerged through digital media convergence (Jenkins 2004).

As Jenkins (2006a, 2–3) aptly puts it, one of the major features of media convergence is "the flow of content across multiple media platforms," and the flow in the digital media era has been actualized through transmedia storytelling (see Jin 2020b), which is a process where integral elements of a fiction get dispersed systematically across multiple outlets for the purpose of creating a unified and coordinated entertainment experience (Jenkins 2011). Transmedia storytelling is considered an outcome of media convergence and enhanced horizontal (cross-media) media ownership (Freeman 2015, 215). However, whereas cross-media ownership constitutes one side of media convergence—what is referred to as "corporate convergence" by Jenkins (2006a)—the end users' bottom-up experiences ("grassroots convergence" in Jenkins' term) constitute the other side of convergence. The enhanced grassroots convergence in the new Hallyu era implies media corporations' top-down control of media circulation may no longer be in full effect (Jenkins et al. 2013).

Media convergence has played a key role in the growth of Hallyu in several ways. First, Hallyu content has been enjoyed by global fans through their smartphones and apps, some of which are made in Korea, and social media platforms, including Facebook and YouTube. Second, digital technologies have allowed different forms of Korean cultural content to synergistically engage with storytelling practices across media platforms. The rising popularity of Korean webtoons[4] offers a good example of transmedia storytelling; this new digital cultural genre is not only consumed as remediation of comics on the Internet but also reappropriated and transformed into different media forms such as films and video games.[5]

After trials and errors, Korean IT corporations and venture companies tried to establish a unique platform for maximizing the synergy between technology, content, and services. Kakao (i.e., the KakaoTalk corporation)'s recent media convergence clearly shows how the process of "corporate convergence" has been integrated into the new, digital phase of Hallyu. Kakao has tried to ride the Korean Wave to enter bigger and faster-growing foreign markets than Korea by focusing on webtoons, music, and other media—but in a new, dynamic way that breaks from the previous paradigm. Kakao's corporate convergence strategy has transformed the old paradigm of transnational cultural flows that primarily engage with content export. Kakao's aim is not just to explore new content but rather to develop a new ecosystem that can produce, rework, and transmit various forms of new content through a platform (or platforms) (Ramirez 2018). In so doing, Kakao plans to synergize the app economy with wider content and IT industries; its ambition might be to become a platform of platforms, hosting its portfolio services such as mobile messenger, games, webtoons, music, and videos on the one killer platform of Kakao.

Leveraging Japan's $4 billion obsession with manga and webtoon comics, Kakao in 2017 launched the webtoon platform Piccoma, which became the No. 2 player behind Line Manga, launched by Naver (Ramirez 2018).

Media convergence enables multiplication of storytelling across different channels and delivery methods. By navigating on smartphones, for example, Hallyu fans in Chile (see chapter 5) can access K-pop idols' video diaries, webtoons, and mobile games all at once on one platform. Among various aspects of media convergence, convergence of technology and content can be effectively observed in the Korean webtoon and its global circulation, as will be discussed in the following section.

THE KOREAN WEBTOON AS A TRANSMEDIA STORYTELLER

The Korean webtoon is an engaging example of digital media convergence as it diversifies the ways in which Hallyu content is generated and disseminated through various platforms. In the late 2010s, the webtoon has become a very significant cultural form representing Korean youth culture due to its convergence of digital technologies, such as the Internet and smartphones, and popular culture—manhwa (comic strips in Korean) (Jeong 2020; Jin 2015). This new form of comic format was generated in Korea by utilizing major characteristics of digital technologies—portal sites and smartphones in particular (Song et al. 2014). The webtoon is a manhwa-style webcomic that is typically published online on specific portal sites (J. O. Kwon 2014).

Webtoons allow readers to scroll vertically up and down through comics unlike traditional comics that read horizontally from panel to panel. There is no fancy cover art, no variant covers to collect, and no pages to flip in webtoons (Acuna 2016).

The webtoon is a good example of media convergence and transmedia storytelling. On the one hand, webtoons show media convergence between digital technology and content. The webtoon is distributed by Internet portals, such as Naver and Kakao, which are archetypal transmedia platforms and extensively used among Korean Internet users and global Hallyu fans. On the other hand, the webtoon is a good example of digital transmedia storytelling in that many filmmakers, television producers, and game developers in many countries have relied on webtoons as new resources for their cultural forms. Given the webtoon's two different characteristics, we have to discuss the genre as (1) individual cultural products (effectively exploiting and developing the existing convergent platforms) and (2) a transmedia storytelling resource (generating and transmitting content through different media platforms).

Webtoon as Content Integrated into Transmedia Platforms

Webtoons are becoming popular in both Asian and Western markets. Although it is not yet comparable to other cultural forms, such as K-dramas and films, in terms of market size, webtoons are gradually expanding their overseas markets. Unlike the majority of local popular culture, such as film, television programs, and music, which big cultural industries corporations dominate, webtoons have been created and exported by both big media corporations and small venture capital. Webtoon was launched overseas with the popular messaging tool LINE. Domestic webtoon platforms, including Naver through LINE Webtoon and DaumKakao, have developed their globalization strategies. These Korean webtoon providers pay attention to attract global viewers with multilanguage services. For example, as of early September 2017, Lezhin Comics provided as many as 7,000 webtoons, including 150 webtoons in English in the United States and 320 webtoons in Japan. Excluding Korea, the United States, Japan, the Philippines, and Canada were major markets for Lezhin Comics among many countries that watched webtoons during the first half of 2017 (B. S. Kim 2017; Y. J. Ju 2017).

Naver, as one of the largest media giants in Korea, has started to upload forty-two webtoons in English and fifty webtoons in Chinese through LINE Webtoon, which is Naver's instant mobile messenger, since July 2013 (Ministry of Culture, Sports, and Tourism 2014, 127). However, as of November 2017, LINE Webtoon provided 1,033 webtoons in the United States, China, Taiwan, Thailand, and Indonesia, publishing 203 English-translated

Table 3.1. LINE Webtoon's Releases in the Global Markets (November 2017)

	Current	Completed	Total
United States	108	95	203
Taiwan	135	137	272
China	153	106	259
Thailand	78	71	149
Indonesia	81	69	150

Source: Ministry of Science and ICT (2017b, 29–30)

webtoons in the United States alone (Ministry of Science and ICT 2017b) (table 3.1). As of March 2021, LINE Webtoon provides services in English-speaking countries, including the United States and Canada, as well as China, Japan, Taiwan, Thailand, and Indonesia. Like the Korean site, LINE Webtoon, the English-language version (http://www.webtoons.com/en/), is free. The Korean site and creators make money through merchandising, product placement, and subscriptions that allow users to read new chapters before they become available to everyone (Gustines 2015).

Before Naver tried to translate its webtoon content, the company realized that some webtoons were already being translated by fans and others. In 2014, due to increasing demand, LINE Webtoon adopted the use of HTML5 in several series to create sound effects and moving images as readers scrolled to add extra depth to the comics they release. They have had a few deals with intellectual property holders including Lucasfilm, which releases a *Star Wars* comic, and *BuzzFeed*, which puts out quick, daily comics. They had also gained the attention of Marvel's Stan Lee. The U.S. version of the app mixes original content along with translations of some of Korea's biggest hits like *Tower of God* and *Noblesse* (Acuna 2016).[6]

The webtoon's global popularity has continued to soar. In October 2017, for example, Naver announced that about 40 million people enjoy Naver Webtoon from many countries, including 3 million people in North America (T. G. Kim 2017). Including Lezhin Comics (10 million), Kakao (15 million), and Comico (26 million), about 100 million people around the world enjoy K-webtoons. As of September 2019, Line webtoon app alone has 60 million users who enjoy Korean webtoons. Asia is the largest market, but North America (9 million) and Europe (2.5 million) also consisted of 19.1 percent (J. Kim 2019). These webtoon platforms have greatly expanded their global penetration, both in Asian countries and Western countries (Cho et al. 2017). Again, Kakao's manhwa platform Piccoma has substantially gained its popularity in Japan. It opened its service in April 2016 and as of August 2017, 900,000 people used Piccoma to enjoy Korean webtoons (Kakao 2017). Tapasmedia, which is a venture capital firm, also opened its Korean webtoon service platform in the United States in 2012, recruiting 1,200 designers and authors, and translated 52 Korean webtoons in tandem with Kakao for U.S. customers (T. Kang 2014). Korea's webtoons have become the latest cultural content in the contemporary digital wave as part of the Korean Wave.

The webtoon has not only contributed to Korea's cultural industries. It has consequently influenced other countries' cultural industries and markets. Several countries have introduced the K-webtoon model in their comics industry, creating similar and/or new styles of webtoons (Jang and Song 2017, 181–82). For example, in France, where webtoons have been received favorably, Delitoon, a new comics company, was built in 2009 under the influence of Korean webtoons. Since 2015, Delitoon has provided forty Korean webtoons and three webtoons created by local webtoon creators. In Japan, NHK (Japan Broadcasting Corporation) Entertainment, teaming up with Lezhin Entertainment,[7] has distributed webtoons created by local webtoon creators since 2013.

The K-webtoon's contribution to transforming local comics has also been observed in Southeast Asian countries where local comics artists are increasingly participating in webtoon industries. The flourishing webtoon culture in Southeast Asian countries, as well as the aforementioned France and Japan, is partly facilitated by the policies and support of the major K-webtoon providers Naver and Daum—they do not only introduce K-webtoons to the overseas markets but also provide opportunities for local creators to become webtoon artists through contests and education. LINE Webtoon indeed holds contests to cultivate local webtoon creators, such as *Challenge League* and *Super Hero Contest* in Indonesia. Selected local creators can upload their works to the LINE Webtoon, and some of the works are reproduced as a movie or a game (Jang and Song 2017).

Webtoon as a Transmedia Resource

The surge of local webtoons in the global market has also been the result of the convergence of popular culture (comics) and digital technologies (e.g., smartphones), which emphasizes the nature of webtoons as a transmedia storytelling source. K-webtoon becomes a site where old and new media collaborate and multiple media functions are combined to create distinctive effects, stories, and genres. As Jenkins (2006a) argues, transmedia storytelling in the digital era consists of the narratives that are deployed across diverse media platforms, creating an integrated world with unique involvement from each medium. In this regard, webtoons may be one of the most significant examples of transmedia storytelling in the 2020s, as they are frequently adapted to television dramas, film, games, and theater performances. The most common transmedia production is filmic adaptation, of course (H. Cho 2016). Prominent K-webtoonist Kang Full's works, such as *Sunjŏng manhwa (Love story)*, *Iut saram* (A neighbor), *Babo* (An idiot), and *Apt* (Apartment), were made into movies. *Ikki* (Moss), the work of another popular K-webtoonist Yun Tae-ho, was made into a movie and his *Misaeng* (Incomplete Life) was remade as a television drama. For Korean filmmakers (and increasingly global filmmakers), it is no longer exceptional to keep an eye on new webtoons to get inspired. H. Cho (2016) described this process of transmedia storytelling in detail:

> Producers in the film industry often read new webtoons to find potential scenarios and offer the creator a contract even long before the serialization of the webtoon ends. After witnessing the frequent transmedia production of webtoons, consumers of webtoons also anticipate the future circulation of the webtoon narrative on other media platforms. For instance, the readers/viewers of Yoon Tae-ho's *Pain*, which was serialized on the Daum portal site from July 29, 2014 to August 14, 2015, started to predict the cinematization of this webtoon when less than one-fourth of the episodes had been published. Some readers entertained themselves by making various casting lists and sharing them with other readers through the comments sections that are available at the end of each episode of a webtoon.

In particular, as the stories of webtoons are fresh and audacious in terms of topics and expressions with vivid visual images, they provide the possibility of a transformation into diverse forms of cultural content. This remediation of Korean webtoons in the global markets has been increasingly popular (Jin 2019). With the growing popularity of webtoons, the global entertainment industries are interested in Korean webtoons, not only because of the webtoons themselves but also the possibilities of the adaptation of webtoons to make television programs, games, and film. In other words, webtoon producers and distributors have attempted to export webtoons as either cultural products or transmedia storytelling resources. Webtoon distributors have certainly utilized transmedia storytelling as a new way to penetrate the global cultural markets. LINE Webtoon has sought television and movie adaptations of its most popular webtoons. Some of LINE Webtoon's recent titles include YA series *Dents* from *2 Broke Girls* star Beth Behrs and Broadway actor Matt Doyle, fantasy romance *Siren's Lament* from *Kaitlyn Narvaza*, and the New Brooklyn superhero universe created by a group of writers and artists including *Dean Haspiel* (Spangler 2016). In March 2016, DaumKakao partnered with Huace Group, China's comprehensive film and TV media group, to bring five of its popular Daum Webtoon titles to the screens in China (beSUCCESS 2016).

In parallel with the webtoon genre's growing popularity, its pirate reproduction has emerged as a problem adversely affecting the industries and the creators. Reportedly, some webtoons have been illegally translated and reproduced. The piracy has not only damaged revenue but also resulted in the circulation of poorly reproduced and translated webtoons; when copied and translated with no legal contracts, to share and circulate webtoons as soon as possible, the quality of pirated webtoons can be deteriorating. Thus, webtoon creators and distributors have struggled with Korean and overseas pirates, whose reproduction and illegitimate circulation may discourage transmedia storytelling's successful revenue model and contribution to creative economy. Illegal sites, both domestic and foreign, have deeply affected the Korean webtoon industry. According to the Korea Copyright Protection Agency (KCPA), the amount of damages caused by the infringement of digital contents copyrights increased from 1.07 trillion Korean won in 2015 to 1.2 trillion won in 2017 (Y. S. Yoon 2018).[8]

It is undeniable that pirate markets paved the way for media industries' growth in Asia, which constituted one of the world's biggest pirated music markets (Otmazgin 2008). Asian media industries have illegally copied overseas television programs, music, and films over the past several decades. For example, Korea has copied Japanese television programs since the 1990s, and China has been copying Korean television programs in the critical transition period (Newsis 2017). Likewise, other Asian countries have plagiarized Korean webtoons in the 2010s. While it is not legal, nor desirable, what is certain is that several Asian countries have experienced a similar path in the process of industrial growth.

Pirating was also observed among Asian media consumers until recently. During most part of the twentieth century, Asian audiences had limited access to other Asian cultural materials in official markets, partly due to economic reasons (e.g., rather inert intra-Asian cultural trade and collaboration) and partly due to political reasons (e.g., the history of Japan's colonization of several other Asian countries including Korea and Taiwan). The lax state of copyright agreements between Asian countries, along with the lack of availability of legitimately imported intra-Asian pop cultural products in domestic official markets, increased the circulation of unlicensed "B-copies" often in the form of compact discs (CDs) or video CDs (VCDs) among fan audiences (Hu 2005, 172). It is undeniable that such early illegitimate reproduction contributed to expanding the fan base of transnational pop culture, in one way or another. As Lessig (2004) argues, free access and (unpermitted) reproduction potentially facilitates cultural creativity and thus contributes to participatory culture. In the early digital era, fan-driven reproduction of cultural content also accelerated certain digital technologies such as person-to-person (P2P) file sharing in the circulation of transnational media.

It is argued that Internet-driven, pirated access to cultural content accelerated the global rise of Hallyu in the 2000s (S. Lee 2015). Media fans' unpermitted access to Hallyu content through the Internet has contributed to development of media platforms, which have expedited transnational circulation of Korean media content. However, despite its creative potential, digital piracy has harmful effects on the digital media ecology in which "corporate" and "grassroots" modes of convergence coexist. As shown with the early digital "pirates" in intra-Asian cultural flows, some fans were professionally involved in profit-seeking routines of piracy and became "fan entrepreneurs" who made profits from reproduction and distribution of the content they did not produce (Lukács 2010). Thus, while fan audiences' use and modification of Hallyu content for creative activities, as shown in many K-pop parody videos, constitute Hallyu's unique participatory culture, "pirated" and poor reproductions of the Hallyu content appear to harm and restrict the creative growth of Hallyu as industries and fan practices.

Hallyu shows how technology is articulated with culture through different media forms and in so doing illustrates the ongoing media convergence and its contribution to transnational cultural flows. Hallyu has been integrated into the global mediascape through creative media convergence facilitated by its fan audiences and industries. That is, again, Hallyu shows a fruitful marriage of grassroots and corporate convergence. Among other cultural forms, the webtoon is a vivid example of digital media convergence and transmedia storytelling. Previously, the Korean cultural industries exported cultural products and digital technologies separately. However, they are now exporting webtoons as a form of independent cultural product and the resource of transnational storytelling, which is not only new but also innovative. The webtoon, which opened up the new territory of web-based comics culture, has created new added values to the cultural economy (*The Korea Herald* 2016). The globalization of Korean webtoons shows new possibilities for Hallyu as the convergence of old media and new media in conjunction with transmedia storytelling.

CONCLUSION

This chapter has discussed the emergence of the digital Korean Wave as a major part of Hallyu, which has been a new trend in the 2010s. With the rapid growth of digital technologies and social media, a handful of digital technologies and social media platforms that Korea has advanced have been globally popular. These digital technologies have sometimes closely connected with popular culture and at other times individually played a key role in the realm of Hallyu. Digital technologies provide platforms and vehicles through which Korean media content is disseminated extensively and intensively. Moreover, the rapid growth and flows of Korea-developed digital technologies and relevant services in the global markets constitute an important part of contemporary Hallyu.

The digital phase of Hallyu involves dynamic processes of conjunction and synergy between digital technologies and cultural content. In the rise of Hallyu, digital technologies themselves have become the major part of contemporary Hallyu. Locally created digital technologies, including smartphones, digital games, both online and mobile games, instant mobile messengers (e.g., Kakao and LINE), and webtoons, have attracted global consumers. For example, overseas fans use Korean-produced apps to access and enjoy Hallyu content, such as K-pop fans' communication with their favorite idols.

Hallyu has deeply engaged with digital media convergence practices, through which cultural industries, technology, and audiences synergistically and continuously engage with storytelling. Korea-developed apps and social media are increasingly adopted by overseas K-pop fans to share their stories. Webtoons are increasingly accessed by international audiences and remediated and remade to other media genres such as films and TV dramas, while facilitating transnational and transmedia storytelling. Media convergence in Hallyu is still evolving, and one cannot fully understand what it will bring in the future and how this will shift the direction and movements of Hallyu. Nevertheless, it is obvious that digital technologies and social media platforms have already made a great contribution to the rise of the digital phase of Hallyu and will further transform the transnational cultural flows.

Digital technologies enhanced the global circulation of Korean popular culture. Digital technology especially enables a new form of cultural circulation that transforms Korea's music industry and accelerates its global reach; as a result, a new economic system, including the social media-driven revenue model, has been established (Oh and Lee 2013). Social media is especially becoming an effective platform for promoting Hallyu through word of mouth and virally circulating cultural content without reliance on broadcast media (Jin and Yoon 2016). In light of the importance of digital environments in Hallyu, the following four chapters provide details on how global audiences access, use, and make meanings of Korean digital and popular culture. The audience studies will offer insights into how transnational Hallyu is evolving and integrating into the diverse geocultural contexts.

NOTES

1. Esports (electronic sports and the leagues where players compete through networked games and related activities) saw its first league in Korea in 1998 when StarCraft became popular. With the growth of PC *bangs* (Internet cafes), esports has become one of the major activities among teens and those in their early twenties.

Since then, several dozen online game leagues have burgeoned in Korea, while a handful of major corporations have invested in esports as one of the new media and/ or cultural businesses (Jin 2010). Partially due to the popularity of esports in Korea, global youth have also started to enjoy esports and the World Cyber Games (WCG) has been getting bigger and popular, including after its revival in 2019. As Taylor (2015, 19) writes, "The story of South Korea holds an interesting place in North American and European pro gaming because it is regularly held up as a model for the future of esports worldwide."

2. The mini-hompy was a small cyberspace that users got when they became members. Through their mini-hompy, which could be decorated by virtual items and play soundtracks, users expressed themselves to others and, moreover, made family-like virtual networks (known as *Il-chon*) (J. H. Choi 2006).

3. Cyworld attempted to become a global social network site by extending its services to consumers beyond Korea, including the United States, Germany, China, and Vietnam. Cyworld U.S. launched in August 2006. In the hope of benefiting from Hallyu, Cyworld tried to attract overseas users making content available regarding Korean music groups and actors and interviews with celebrities as part of its marketing strategy (Kim and Sohn 2014). However, Cyworld's global market penetration was limited to only a few overseas countries and did not last long. Cyworld's international services lasted only between 2011 and 2014.

4. As will be addressed in a later section, the term "webtoon" is the neologism combining Web and cartoon—meaning comic strips distributed via the Internet originally, but now via the smartphone (Jin 2015; S. Park 2013). They were invented in Korea in the early 2000s as a web-based comics genre, and it has since rapidly grown as a major genre of the new Korean Wave.

5. In this book, we define transmedia storytelling as a process of making cultural content available on different media platforms "without causing any overlaps or interferences, while managing the story experienced by different audiences" (Giovagnoli 2011, 8; see also Jenkins 2006a; Jin 2020).

6. *Tower of God* is a Korean webtoon (fantasy) written by Lee Jong-hui, known by the pen name SIU. It was started in 2010, and later translated into Japanese and English. The same title was transformed into a mobile game in 2016 (BizFact 2016).

7. Lezhin Comics is a premium webtoon platform operated by Lezhin Entertainment.

8. In order to control the piracy issue, in April 2018, the Korean government announced a "joint countermeasure for overseas websites distributing pirated content." The government started the development of technology that blocks illegal reproduction and distribution websites, like *The Night of the Rabbit* that distributed webtoons through servers in a foreign country (Y. S. Yoon 2018).

Chapter 4

Social Media, Digital Platforms, and Hallyu in North America

INTRODUCTION

For Hallyu industries, the United States has been estimated not only as one of the largest single cultural markets but also as an important gateway to other overseas markets. Most of all, BTS and Bong Joon-ho (with the movie *Parasite*) have been new leaders who have rapidly emerged in the United States and consequently accelerated Hallyu's global media attention and market penetration. In October 2018, BTS became the first Korean artists to perform a U.S.-stadium show, when the group appeared in New York's renowned Citi Field, among other global venues. Surprised by the increasing number of devoted young K-pop fans in the United States, several U.S. network and local news media reported the fever around BTS's North American concerts, even comparing the group with the legendary band the Beatles' "British invasion" (*CBS San Francisco* 2018). BTS has also performed at several U.S. network TV shows and award ceremonies, such as the American Music Awards (2017) and the Grammy Awards (2020). The group's rise in the United States is significant as this market has often played a gateway role to other markets of the world, as shown with the *Gangnam Style* phenomenon, in which U.S.-based media platforms provided a tipping point for the song going viral (Jin and Yoon 2016a).

The impact of U.S. media and market in the global rise of Hallyu can be observed by another recent example—the surprising 2020 Oscar nominations and wins of the Korean film *Parasite*, which boosted the film's global box-office revenues and furthermore contributed to increasing global demands for other Korean films in streaming video markets. While the director of *Parasite*, Bong Joon-ho, wittily described the Oscars as a "very local" film festival in an interview prior to the Oscar season (E. A. Jung 2019),

Parasite's wins at the Oscars undeniably helped the film and the director obtain an extensive audience far beyond the U.S. market. For example, this film's box-office numbers at UK cinemas the day after the Oscars ceremony increased by 213 percent against for the same day from the previous week (McClintock 2020; Pulver 2019).

BTS and *Parasite* are among many examples illustrating the importance of the U.S. media and its market. The U.S. market has been the headquarters of large media corporations and the home for celebrity culture, as represented by Hollywood. The U.S. media and cultural industries have dominated traditional media and cultural markets and more recently have also extended their global influence through social media platforms (Jin 2013). Furthermore, the rise of Hallyu in North America may benefit from the region's technological infrastructure, which includes not only global media platforms but also venture media companies, some of which were established by Asian American personnel.[1]

While the United States has been the largest overseas market for Hallyu industries, the country's northern neighbor Canada has also emerged as an important overseas Hallyu fan base. K-pop is considered to be a facilitator in the expansion of Korean language programs at major Canadian universities (Shahzad 2017), and major K-pop concerts have been successfully held in several major Canadian cities. Canadian media excitedly described Vancouver as an emerging site of Hallyu when K-pop idol group TWICE shot its new song Likey's music video in Vancouver (Nair 2017). K-pop's rise in Canada was described as an "invasion" when three BTS concerts (12,000 seats each) were sold out in about an hour (Rockingham 2018).

Meanwhile, grassroots fans have increasingly participated in, or organized, local Hallyu events, such as K-pop events and an annual K-pop competition hosted by the Consulate General of Korea in Vancouver. Several movie theaters in Vancouver have regularly screened Korean films, including *Along with the Gods: The Two Worlds* (2017) and *Parasite* (2019). It is sometimes observed on campuses or in public places in Vancouver that a group of young people gather to play some games that they learned from Korean reality shows, such as *Running Man*.[2]

It is intriguing that cultural content and digital technologies made in Korea are thriving in North America, which has been considered as a model for political, economic, and social advancement throughout the modern history of Korea (Y.-J. Kim 2005). For the second half of the twentieth century, commodities and cultural products labeled as "made-in-the USA" represented high-quality materials and a "global standard" while their Korean counterparts were often perceived as imitations or knock-offs (C. Choi 1995). Even today, the sizes and infrastructures of cultural industries in Korea and North America are significantly different. The North American (the United States and Canada) box-office market is nearly seven times bigger than that of Korea (UNESCO 2017).

North America has become a region that plays a key role in spreading Hallyu beyond Asia. In the 2010s, Hallyu in North America was led by the success of K-pop musicians, as well as the global popularity of Korea-created digital games, both online and mobile. From television dramas to digital games to popular music, North America is the largest cultural market. As success in North American markets is often considered a barometer for the global penetration of a non-Western cultural form, the Hallyu industries vehemently target the North American market. Several K-pop idol groups, such as Wonder Girls, Girls Generation, and BTS, have made their U.S. debuts and North Americans started to know K-pop, K-drama, and K-variety shows.[3]

The recent Hallyu phenomenon in North America may be shaped by several forces, such as the Korean cultural industries' continuous effort to penetrate Western markets after their initial exploration of Asian markets and Korean diasporas in North America that have developed ethnic and diasporic media channels through which Korean media content is circulated (Ju and Lee 2015; Yoon and Jin 2016). Notably, North America's new media environments have influenced the ways in which Hallyu is translated into digital, viral, and participatory cultural consumption in the 2010s. The rapid global circulation of Hallyu content has been facilitated by the U.S.-based giant media platforms (old and new), such as network television channels, video-streaming services (e.g., YouTube), and social media (e.g., Twitter and Facebook). In particular, the recent phase of Hallyu, known as either Hallyu 2.0 or the New Korean Wave, could not be explained without considering the increasing role of digital media and audiences' responses to digital media. Social media indicates a shift from the model of the rather static Internet web page toward a social web model by means of which the possibilities of users interacting with the web have multiplied, eventually facilitating sociality (Terranova and Donovan 2013, 297).

In this regard, this chapter explores how the Hallyu phenomenon is integrated into a social media-driven cultural landscape, which has been termed as the *social mediascape* (see Jin and Yoon 2016a) in the North American context as a birthplace of several major social media platforms. By the term social mediascape, we address not only political economic infrastructure surrounding social media (many of which originated and are owned by the U.S. corporations) but also technological affordances of social media, which frame "the possibilities for agentic action" (Hutchby 2001, 444).[4] We also emphasize the role of offline socialities among the fans in transnational Hallyu. Thus, drawing on the fan audiences' narratives, we explore how media content, technology, political economy, and fans are interwoven with each other in the transnational circulation of Hallyu.[5]

HALLYU AS HYBRID CONTENT

The hybrid nature of Hallyu has been identified as a key reason for its global circulation, especially in the phase of Hallyu 2.0. While some K-dramas popular in East Asia in the earlier period of Hallyu (Hallyu 1.0) appeal to Asian audiences by their "Korean" characteristics, which were evident in the historic genre (e.g., *Dae Jam Geum*, 2003–2004) or in nostalgic romance (e.g., *Winter Sonata*, 2002), increasingly post-national, if not cosmopolitan, atmospheres seem to define the recent phase of Hallyu (Hallyu 2.0); various cultural styles are intermingled and thus the myth of authentic Koreanness is constantly questioned in recent Hallyu content.

Hallyu fans interviewed for this chapter tended to consider recent Korean pop culture texts as a mixture of different styles and influences. Several fans of Korean culture were hesitant to answer when asked to point out anything particularly Korean in the Korean Wave and in particular K-pop. For them, as far as recent idol pop is concerned, Hallyu is not a cultural trend that represents something uniquely Korean, but rather a new cultural trend including appealing factors—such as various stylistic bricolages and visualized (choreographed) musical experiences. These attractions of Hallyu are especially visible when this cultural trend is compared with other non-Western cultural forms. For example, Samantha, an eighteen-year-old Canadian fan, who also listened to J-pop, compared K-pop with Japanese pop music (J-pop); for her, J-pop is "a bit isolated in what they do" without sufficient global circulation, while in K-pop "there are some parts of it that are similar to what Western artists are doing." Indeed, the recent waves of Hallyu have been recognized for its hybrid style, in which different cultural forms are intermingled and generate a "third space" (Bhabha 1994; Jin 2016; Ryoo 2009). Among other Hallyu genres, K-pop visibly illustrates the hybridity of recent Korean popular culture. K-pop has increasingly embraced different cultural influences and developed the genre as post-national, hybrid content, which moves beyond the boundary of Korea-based pop music. It often uses English mixing partly for appealing to global audiences, while diligently recruiting overseas talent.

Many Hallyu fans identified English raps or refrains in K-pop songs as an important attribute of the genre. They felt that the English part might not always be relevant and harmoniously integrated into Korean song lyrics; nevertheless, English mixing in K-pop lyrics was considered a playful attribute that attracts overseas fans and allows non-Korean-speaking fans to easily sing along with some parts of K-pop songs. Alice, a twenty-year-old Canadian fan, noted: "I noticed a mix of Korean and English a lot [in K-pop]. I think it does influence my liking and following K-pop. It makes it easier for me to follow and understand, and I can sing along to the chorus and remember songs better."

The increasing formula of English mixing in K-pop shows the genre's strategy to reach global fans and to present itself as a global cultural form. However, the use of English does not necessarily represent Westernization and Western modernity, as North American fans considered the formula as a resource for playful participation (such as the practice of singing along). The fans even felt that K-pop's English lyric parts were unclearly pronounced, inaccurately composed, or irrelevantly incorporated into the theme of the song. The playfulness of English mixing in K-pop characterizes the way in which K-pop is appropriated by North American fans. They may consider the "unauthentic" or "inaccurate" English lyrics of K-pop as a gesture for reaching out to, and communicating with, overseas fans. What is important here is not necessarily that English is written and pronounced like that of native speakers but rather that English is a playful tool for singing and enjoying together beyond nationalities.

The recent Hallyu phenomenon is characterized by its fan practices that often bypass the conventional media platforms (such as broadcast media) and playfully engage with the original text. The fan activities question the discourse of quality suggested by media critics and academics in the earlier period of the Korean Wave. The quality-oriented approach to Korean pop culture not only narrowly defines the cultural practices of the Korean Wave in terms of a Western standard of "quality" (Hong-Mercier 2013) but also fails to pay due attention to an emerging environment of the social mediascape. In the social mediascape of Hallyu, media texts may spread for reasons other than their quality. Some fans were uncertain about the quality of Korean pop culture although they enjoyed it very much. For several fans, K-drama characters and plots were often too stereotypical and predictable. However, for some of them, K-dramas were "highly addictive." In this manner, "omnivorous audiences" (Hong-Mercier 2013) are increasingly engaging with the viral pleasure offered by the Korean Wave. In comparison, for some respondents who were enthusiastic about K-pop in particular, the room for engagement with the original texts, especially via YouTube and Facebook, was an attractive feature of Hallyu. Users share, post, and remake what they like, as exemplified by the numerous parodies of the original video text of *Gangnam Style* (Lee and Kuwahara 2014).

Another aspect of the hybridity of Hallyu can be seen in the Korean cultural industries' increasing recruitment of overseas talents. Korea's major entertainment companies have recruited global talents for their K-pop idol groups (i.e., boy and girl bands). For example, a popular nine-member girl group, TWICE (2015–present), includes four non-Korean members (three Japanese and one Taiwanese members) and has successfully penetrated East Asian markets. In addition, national audition programs, such as *Survival Audition K-Pop Star* (aired on SBS between 2011 and 2017) and *Superstar*

K (aired on cable channel Mnet between 2009 and 2016), have widely recruited international talent. Indeed, a large number of foreign nationals have been introduced to Hallyu industries, while many of them were ethnic Koreans (or half-ethnic Koreans) who were born and raised in Western countries. To name a few, Jay Park, Eric Nam, Ailee, and Jessica (Girl's Generation) have been popular idol stars in recent K-pop industries. Their bilingual literacy and overseas experiences may show an aspect of increasing global and hybrid nature of K-pop industries.[6]

Hybrid content in recent Hallyu, observed in the aforementioned examples, such as frequent mixtures of languages and styles, and the increasing recruitment of international talents can be compared to the findings of earlier studies, in which several themes, such as pure love and traditional family norms, were considered by overseas fans as appealing Korean characteristics of the K-dramas especially in the early 2000s (Lee and Ju 2010). Most respondents enjoyed Korean pop culture not because of its alleged Korean or Asian sensibilities but because of its mixed textual aspects. For many Hallyu fans, Korean pop cultural forms were appealing largely because of their mixture of Western and local cultures. Hallyu was perceived as "Western-inspired" pop culture, on the one hand, and "different" (i.e., different from American culture) on the other. Margaret, a twenty-one-year-old fan, noted: "[The recent Korean pop culture] is a mixture of Eastern and Western cultures, so it allows people to be exposed to both cultures. It's not too traditional, not too unfamiliar." The ambivalent, or even contradictory, perceptions of recent Korean popular culture imply that Hallyu might be a set of various intangible cultural forms rather than a particular genre or style that can be easily defined. As Stella, a twenty-three-year-old fan, noted, "There is always something to suit a variety of tastes in K-pop."

For the Hallyu fans, Korean media content did not necessarily represent an authentic, pure, traditional culture of the other but rather implied a hybrid cultural form that is open for audiences' reappropriation and participation. Thus, some fans were not exclusively loyal to Korean pop culture, while omnivorously navigating different pop cultural tastes. Despite their self-identification as fans of the Korean Wave, many interviewees were not necessarily exclusively enthusiastic about Korean pop culture. For instance, Ellie, a twenty-four-year-old American fan, did not deny the probable temporary nature of her taste for Korean pop culture when she noted, "The idea of different cultures is exciting for me, and I feel that Korean culture is currently my phase."

The recent wave of Hallyu appears to be relatively spreadable due to its textual and contextual hybridity. In their discussion of transnational media flows, Jenkins et al. (2013, 263) claim that the "unexpected mixing and mingling of cultural materials" appeals to multiple audiences beyond national boundaries, and thus, hybridity media forms are more spreadable. Of course, textual attributes alone do not accelerate transnational media flows. Media content, best customized for and exploiting social media, may continue to be appealing and noticed. Some Korean cultural industries have rapidly developed the social media-based revenue model (Oh and Park 2012). The recent phase of Hallyu proves that social media-driven practices can attract large audiences even without conventional media gatekeepers such as global network TV. Hallyu has effectively been integrated into social media platforms, such as YouTube, streaming sites, and Twitter, as further discussed in the next section.

TECHNOLOGICAL AFFORDANCES

Social media environments allow K-pop, K-drama, and other Korean pop culture genres to be virally circulated and translated, and thus significantly reduce cultural discount—the tendency in which cultural products made overseas are likely to have limited value and appeal in another cultural context due to cultural distance (Hoskins and Mirus 1988). For example, numerous K-pop video segments on YouTube are often accompanied by fan-produced English subtitles and/or the official translations. Hallyu content has increasingly been translated into English by its fans on YouTube and other social media platforms. Even if the subtitles are not available, social media's comment function or real-time chatting allow the viewers to ask other viewers for partial translation. It is not rare in the social mediascape of Hallyu that one viewer asks, and talks with, other anonymous viewers. While numerous languages are circulated in cyberspace, English is the most commonly used language of communication in the comments section of many popular YouTube K-pop videos. The fan interaction on YouTube (often via English) reveals that Hallyu is not free of U.S.-based hegemonic platforms. In this regard, as will be discussed in chapter 5, non-English-speaking fans often have to rely on English translation, or, otherwise, have to wait longer for English subtitles to be translated further into their local languages (S. Sohn 2012).

The way in which social media evolved in regard to fan practices was well observed in the accounts of several interviewees whose engagement with Hallyu had already begun during the pre-social media era. For instance, Claire, a twenty-four-year-old Canadian fan who had been a fan of K-pop for over nine years, recalled the emergence of social media in her cultural practices. She initially learned of BoA (a K-pop singer who performs in both Korean and Japanese) and her Japanese songs through her friends. However, it was YouTube that substantially increased her interest in, and knowledge of, Korean pop culture. During our interview, she noted: "I stumbled upon

Korean songs on YouTube through various situations. . . . This all happened around 2005. It snowballed into something larger as YouTube expanded and Korean music videos flourished. My exploration led me from one thing to another, and I was completely hooked." This account reminds us that the major social media technologies, including Facebook (2004), YouTube (2005), and iPhone (2007), appeared between 2004 and 2007; thus, in the early stage of the Korean Wave (i.e., Hallyu 1.0), fans were unable to use these social media platforms. Therefore, it is not difficult to contend that at the center of the new Korean Wave is the development of new media technology. The Hallyu fans in this book were immersed in the social mediascape through which the Hallyu content was increasingly available and spreadable. According to Lucas, a twenty-one-year-old Canadian, "The growth of the Korean Wave is substantially a direct result of social media." He noted, "I don't think there's any other medium in which information can travel and grow this exponentially."

For Hallyu fans, social media was considered as a main reason for Korean pop culture to be globally circulated, compared to other Asian pop culture. Making a comparison between Korean and Japanese pop culture, Jackie, a twenty-four-year-old Canadian fan, addressed the extensive availability of Hallyu content on YouTube: "It's difficult to find Japanese stuff, especially with English subtitles. In comparison, Korean drama and K-pop are all over YouTube, and they're accessible in countries all over the world. Subtitles are also easy to find." This account resonates with critics' analyses of Hallyu 2.0, in which the recent global popularity of K-pop is attributed to its high availability and viral diffusion on YouTube (Lee and Kuwahara 2014).[7]

North American audiences' access to, and consumption of, Hallyu content is deeply integrated into the environment of media convergence, in which various media are articulated with each other, and their users are likely to appropriate forms of media without a clear sense of boundaries between these media (Jenkins 2004). Most Hallyu fans did not necessarily utilize a singular form of traditional media, such as television, radio, or film, to access the Korean content that was circulated via multifaceted yet converged media platforms. In particular, social media, which allows for the users' transnational access to Korean pop culture content, seems to rapidly replace the role of the traditional media. As Naomi, a twenty-year-old student, noted, "Social media brings together like-minded individuals to enjoy K-pop together. We follow similar blogs on Tumblr or socializing with people who watch the same drama on Twitter." The lack of availability and presence of Korean pop culture content in mainstream North American media may have triggered the emergence of the social mediascape of Hallyu.

Hallyu audiences interviewed in North America often noted that reliance on social media was inevitable since broadcast and cable media channels have not programmed Korean content on a regular basis, with the exception of a very limited number of satellite or cable channels. Of course, some areas of North America, populated by Asian and Korean ethnic communities, have had access to Korean media content even prior to the Internet era (S. Lee 2015), which can be compared with other areas of North America and other countries outside Asia where access to Korean media has been extremely limited until recently.

The interviewees accessed Hallyu content through video-streaming services or file-sharing sites.[8] Whereas early access had involved file-sharing sites due to the limited number of streaming services, video streaming services, often along with social media, became popular tools for accessing Hallyu content. Alice, the aforementioned twenty-year-old Canadian fan, described how she accessed K-pop and K-dramas: "I usually enjoy them on Facebook. My friends share links or talk about Korean music and dramas. I also watch music videos on YouTube. On other online streaming sites, I watch Korean dramas and movies." The interface or design of social media seemed to frame the ways in which they enjoyed new Korean Wave content to some extent. As Kelly, a twenty-one-year-old American, commented, "I usually just search on YouTube, where I get updates on my feed from artists I have already subscribed to." She became familiar with the latest Hallyu content by watching "whatever shows up on Viki.com."

The Hallyu fans considered the social mediascape as a user-friendly and user-oriented arena. For example, Julie, a twenty-one-year-old American who had been enthusiastic about Korean movies, dramas, and pop music for over two years, described social media as a user-customized channel to enable fans to consciously choose and access the content:

In social media, I have to click on things myself and consciously decide to watch and listen to certain things, in which case I can actively choose not to. In traditional media [such as TV], I see advertisements or hear music playing even if I did not click to play it. [In social media,] I like that I can be exposed to things and feel more connected to the culture while also knowing I haven't abandoned myself in the process.

The rapid circulation of music videos, drama clips, and information about K-pop and K-drama stars on the social mediascape seemed to transform the nature of cultural consumption. For the respondents, consuming pop culture did not mean the possession of materials; rather, it implied participatory processes, such as searching, accessing, enjoying, and reworking. In particular, searching and surfing the web serendipitously introduced some respondents to Korean pop culture. Amy, a twenty-one-year-old American college student, described how her interest in Hallyu began: "In high school,

I accidentally stumbled upon a drama title, *Full House* while browsing YouTube. And then, I was searching for the American show of the same title, but the Korean one kept popping up. So, one day, I decided to give it a try and ended up watching the whole series." This initiation process of becoming a fan suggests that technological affordances may be increasingly influential in the dissemination of Hallyu. There may be no better example than the *Gangnam Style* phenomenon (2012) in explaining the importance of a technology dimension in Hallyu 2.0. The viral circulation of the *Gangnam Style* video in global markets was possible mainly because of YouTube and Twitter. In particular, the phenomenon was seemingly ignited by the initial Twitter mentions made by two popular users—an overseas K-pop fan (@ WeLoveDara) and an influential entertainment manager, Scooter Braun, who discovered Justin Bieber (Billboard 2012). Of course, the phenomenon does not only benefit from social media but also from traditional media, including television and radio.

After the social media success of *Gangnam Style*, traditional media, such as NBC's *Today Show*, introduced Psy to Western audiences, and this media convergence of traditional and new media expedited the global sensation of *Gangnam Style*. In this manner, digital media does not simply replace conventional, "old" media, but new and old media converge and feed each other. BTS's recent global rise indeed benefits from the fans' active role on social media, which is compounded by conventional media's reporting on network TV and in print media; the conventional media's attentions are again circulated on social media, and further excite and solidify fans. Social media's technological affordances, which constantly connect audiences and might transfer audiences/users into a "networked public" (boyd 2014), are suitable for facilitating the connection of different (new and old) media forms and viral circulation of fan culture.

FAN SOCIALITY

The circulation of Hallyu in the social mediascape enhances, and is enhanced by, participatory cultural practices. Most Hallyu fans started to enjoy Korean pop culture through user-generated content on YouTube or other digital platforms, after they learned about the popularity of several cultural forms from their friends on Facebook and Twitter. While the technological affordances of social media distinguish the recent Korean Wave from its earlier iteration, this does not mean that the fans' practices are determined by the technological aspect of social media. Social media can constitute a meaningful cultural economy of fandom only when it involves users' engagement and participation (Jenkins et al. 2013).

North American fans commented on the ways in which social media contributed to networking and sharing with peer fans. Most respondents who could not speak Korean sought the prompt translation of the Korean content; therefore, the peer production of subtitles and translations played a crucial role in the rapid circulation of the Korean Wave. While the mainstream media was unable to provide North American fans with the prompt cultural and linguistic translations of Korean content, the fans kept translating and circulating Hallyu materials, especially via participatory online social networking or video-streaming portal sites, such as YouTube and Viki. Once translated by bilingual fans, the original content tended to be revised, recommended (or disapproved), shared, reframed, and remixed by numerous, often anonymous, participants. Social media facilitates the process of retranslation in that it transforms hard media content, which is contained in a traditional media form, into soft, remixable, and spreadable forms. For instance, TV programs quickly become available on YouTube or Viki, among many other websites, and are shared among fans while being integrated into their Facebook timelines.

With the case of fans' K-pop reaction videos on YouTube,[9] D. Oh (2017a) points out that the YouTubers likely seek the meanings to empower their marginalized fan identities. In other words, they actively work to interpret the meaning of the music video apart from the song with stated intentions of later matching it to the lyrics when English translations become available. Because of their inability to understand the language, the visual readings of the texts are important to global fans' interest in K-pop (Ono and Kwon 2013). The viral speed and scale of the translation and circulation of Korean pop culture in the social mediascape imply that a wide range of media users are potentially "shaping, sharing, reframing, and remixing media content in ways which might not have been previously imagined" (Jenkins et al. 2013, 2).

Sharing practices not only included the uploading/downloading of cultural materials but also the sharing of information, opinions, and feelings. As Jacob, a twenty-four-year-old Canadian, explained, social media enabled users to exchange their comments on Korean pop culture:

> Facebook has helped to promote the [Korean] culture shared by friends. In addition, YouTube has a big impact based on the number of subscriptions and views. The comments posted by many users from around the world encouraged other people to become more aware of the culture. . . . Social media has definitely played a major role in promoting the Korean Wave. People around the world can share, post, and provide countless feedback.

Hallyu fans' practices of sharing can be understood in the wider context of the emerging digital-sharing culture, which is driven by the collaborative creation and consumption of popular cultural texts and challenges the dominant notion of ownership, authenticity, and creativity (Denison 2011). As original materials can be easily recreated and owned in many different ways in the social mediascape, the very notion of authenticity is questioned by fans' creative practices. For instance, as exemplified by the ongoing phenomenon of the fansubbing[10] of K-dramas on the Internet, fans do not value "authentic" or "accurate" translation but rather appreciate the creative aspect of engaging with texts through voluntary translation and interpretation (Dwyer 2012). The participatory culture of Hallyu fandom emerged and flourished via sharing practices on social media. In this respect, Daniel, a twenty-year-old Canadian man, raised an intriguing point:

> Korean stuff is shared, and it changes what I am exposed to and what I may like in the future. If it is not shared, I may never have checked out that Korean restaurant or listened to the new K-pop single. In particular, sharing on social media changes who I enjoy it [the Korean stuff] with. Social media is completely changing my experience through my peers, as I know only few who regularly immerse themselves in Korean culture.

Based on this account, the social mediascape is a means to connect a fan to a wide range of other fans and even to shape his or her cultural tastes by managing his or her virtual fan networks. This networking process via social media seemed to offer a platform for discussions and deliberation, as Arabella, a twenty-one-year-old Canadian, noted: "I think social media provides the opinions and reviews of others around me, which then shapes my own opinion of a certain Korean TV show or K-pop band." For her, the social mediascape seemed to be a form of public sphere in which individuals share their opinions.

The sociality of Hallyu's social mediascape implies political moments in which fans are networked and questions the structural powers behind the flows of Hallyu, such as traditional media institutions. While acknowledging the significance of instantaneous accessibility and data sharing provided by social media, several fans also believed that social media played a key role in providing uncensored and uncontrolled cultural content. Most fans enjoyed social media-driven consumption of Korean content. By accessing and consuming foreign content outside the conventional media outlets, ones not strictly controlled by any third parties, they seemed to feel empowered to certain extent. As Ivy, a twenty-two-year-old fan, stated, "To international fans, social media is the easiest and is somewhat less controlled and/or filtered." For some fans, the social mediascape of Hallyu meant a space in which young people can freely access and consume Korean (and sometimes other Asian) cultural content. John, a twenty-two-year-old fan, claimed: "Sometimes it is for me to avoid censorship through social media platforms, like Facebook and YouTube, because some contents that seem sensitive in Asia would be available to North America and is still perfectly acceptable with the culture in North America." In the same vein, Hailey, a twenty-three-year-old fan, stated, "Traditional media are highly controlled by third parties, such as the government and corporations." In this manner, to international fans, social media are less controlled and/or filtered. By using social media, the Hallyu fans seemed to feel freedom from both the government and corporations (e.g., both cultural producers and advertisers). Unlike traditional media, where the government through legal measures and corporations through advertising control the nature of cultural content, fans believe that social media is a censor-free platform. They understand that social media as a new platform for popular culture provides a space in which local culture can be seen and spread with no control.

The fans' desire to avoid censorship by accessing the social mediascape of Hallyu may imply their pursuit of negotiating technological environments. In the digital era, media audiences increasingly participate in media environments, seeking the right "to be part of decisions and to govern and control the structures that affect them" (Fuchs 2014, 57). For North American fans, social media-saturated consumption of local culture is the most desirable cultural activity because they put themselves, neither the government nor corporations, as controllers of cultural activities (Jin 2018). Global fans of Hallyu do not want to be controlled by institutional gatekeepers—such as public censorship and corporate intervention through advertising—which are default settings of traditional, conventional media, such as network TV. In so doing, the fans seemed to engage with particular *networked power*, through which social actors assume power over other actors (such as traditional media institutions) (Castells 2011). Hallyu fans appear to increasingly resignify participation as a networked and agentic process through social media.

POLITICAL ECONOMY OF SOCIAL MEDIASCAPE

As discussed in the previous sections, the marriage of Hallyu content and social media has effectively attracted overseas fans, while providing them with virtual space for self-expression and fan sociality. An increasing number of "free" music videos and user-generated content on YouTube allows online media users to easily engage, navigate, and participate in the fan world of Hallyu beyond national borders. Through social media platforms, Hallyu seems to offer some young fans—as also discussed in following chapters— who otherwise remain marginalized the opportunities to constantly feel connected and express their identity.

Despite the enhanced availability of Hallyu content and a sense of participation in the social mediascape, some overseas fans are aware of side effects of social mediascape, especially those derived from the political economic restriction of social media as a tool of corporate-driven convergence. They are critical of the ways in which Hallyu content and fan culture are seamlessly immersed in the commodification of popular culture in social mediascape. A few interviewees seemed to feel that both K-pop stars and fans were extensively exposed to social media's attention economy[11] to become celebrities. Indeed, an increasing number of K-pop fans seek to become YouTube stars, which have been named "micro-celebrities" (Duffy 2017).

Acknowledging the limitations of social media-driven media consumption among fans, Sera, a twenty-three-year-old Canadian, expressed her concern about the excessive attention economy among K-pop celebrities and fans:

> K-pop stars and fans are so active on social media. Anytime I go on my social media that's all I see, I'm like, it's too much. . . . if you need to be a singer, a dancer, an actor, a model, you need to know how to be constantly on social media, and you need to use all these little things that make you into this person that people are going to want to pay attention to.

In this manner, some fans felt overwhelmed by constant connection, information, and attention on social media. Moreover, constant access to the seemingly free Hallyu content implies ongoing exposure to commercial materials. The interviewees initially enjoyed increasing "free" content on social media but gradually realized it is not free at all, and were annoyed by commercials they had to encounter to access "free" Hallyu content on social media and streaming sites. Angie, a twenty-year-old Canadian student who enjoyed watching K-dramas and TV shows, noted:

> Whenever I watch Korean content on streaming sites, like every 10 minutes or every 5 minutes there will be a commercial. And it's not even a Korean related commercial. It's extremely frustrating, so I don't really have a platform that I would like to enjoy to go to anymore. But because I wanna watch that specific show or drama, I have no other choice.

Angie's comments resonate with critical media scholars' claims that social media's "free" content and platform hail the seemingly autonomous audience as commodity through various implicit profit-seeking strategies (Fuchs 2014; Scholz 2013). While this process of exposure to commercials to access content "for free" is not unique to the social mediascape of Hallyu, the overseas fans' reliance on free content may increase the fans' awareness of precarious "free labor" (Terranova 2000). Thus, the fans may notice that networked power is not free of media convergence operating at the level of platform corporations. In this regard, the global circulation of Hallyu can be examined in relation to the way in which fans' grassroots transnationalism interplays with top-down, corporate transnationalism.

Hallyu in the North American social mediascape shows that the transnational cultural wave has found its way to the West and other regions through constant appropriation of hegemonic communicative tools and resources, such as American-based YouTube and Facebook, which are arguably designed to reflect Americans' socialities and linguistic patterns (Kraemer 2014) and commercial interests (Fuchs 2014). In the early period of social media, Jin (2013) found that most major online media platforms (98 percent) were for-profit, which was sharply contrasted with the small amount of nonprofit platforms (2 percent), and thus, he warned about the increasing commodification of digital platforms, which are dominated by several major corporations. In a similar vein, Fuchs' (2014) political economic analysis revealed that social media platforms tend to exercise Western cultural and economic interests.

The social and digital media environments of Hallyu show that whereas this cultural trend originated in Korea, industries and business of Hallyu are not entirely controlled by Korea. English-language Hallyu content and platforms have increasingly been acquired and managed by giant, multinational, or U.S.-based corporations. Furthermore, non-Korean Hallyu platform providers tend to merge and acquire different media regarding Hallyu for synergy and horizontal concentration. For example, K-drama-streaming service Viki was sold to Japanese media giant Rakuten, which ran Viki as its subsidiary company based in the United States in 2013. After purchasing the Hallyu content services of Viki, Rukuten acquired popular English language K-pop news sites Soompi (https://www.soompi.com/) in 2015. Soompi has been one of the oldest English K-pop fan/news sites, which is popular among overseas Hallyu fans, since its establishment by a Korean American web developer in 1998. After being sold to a Korean IT company in the early 2010s, it was purchased by Viki. As shown in this example, multinational corporations and U.S.-based platforms have increased their power in the global circulation of Hallyu. In particular, North American-based digital platforms have affected the way in which Hallyu is produced, diffused, translated, and enjoyed. Given the context, it is important to ask how Hallyu has arrived and begun to flourish in North America in relation to this region's social media and digital platform environments.

Some Hallyu fans in North America constitute an early adopter group of this cultural trend by deploying extensively social media platforms, many of which were designed and established in the United States. While social media have been extensively appropriated by global Hallyu fans, it is undeniable that the strong media infrastructure in North America may generate the powerful synergy between traditional and new media through various participatory fan practices. However, social media may increase the com-modification of fans' participation in cultural activities. Indeed, some inter-viewees were highly dependent on the algorithmic processes of social media; therefore, their online fan practices appeared to oscillate between interactivity and interpassivity (Taylor 2012). Consequently, it is still questionable how the participatory culture of Hallyu in the social mediascape is challenging the hegemony of the corporate-led, profit-seeking nature of social media. While the social mediascape enables the global fans to spread the wave, the nature of the participatory culture emerging through the social mediascape may require further investigation.

CONCLUSION

This chapter has shown how and why Hallyu is meaningfully incorporated into North American fans' social media-saturated everyday lives. The fans' accounts revealed that the social mediascape of Hallyu comprises several interacting dimensions—(a) a content dimension, in which the hybrid nature of media content accelerates its global circulation, (b) a technology dimen-sion involving certain affordances that frame users' actions, (c) a sociality dimension addressing the participatory cultural atmosphere that is facilitated by fans, and (d) a political economy dimension revealing top-down, corpo-rate convergence and its effects on media user behaviors. Hallyu in North America vividly shows how social media are becoming the default media for transnational cultural flows, and how Hallyu reaches out to global audiences by bypassing (or articulating) conventional media systems.

The social mediascape may open a door for comfortable access to different cultures that are otherwise not available. The extensive and multidirectional cultural flows of Hallyu through social media, however, do not necessarily mean that the tensions and barriers to transcultural flows are rapidly disap-pearing. In this respect, Hallyu as a new transcultural phenomenon requires more contextualized studies revealing the tensions and blocks implicated in cultural circulation. For example, there are ongoing tensions between bottom-up fan experiences of transnationalism and top-down forces of transnational media convergence led by corporations.

The technological affordances of social media and fans' sociality interplay with each other and rapidly spread Hallyu as a set of hybrid cultural forms. However, social media's technological affordances may not universally direct overseas Hallyu fans as media audiences access, consume, and negoti-ate transnational culture in their own particular local contexts (S. Sohn 2012). Thus, the social mediascape of Hallyu in different regions may reveal dif-ferent global-local conjunctions. The North American fans' practices offer a reference point to be compared with fan practices in other contexts, such as Asian contexts in which earlier Hallyu (Hallyu 1.0) emerged, and other non-Asian regions (to be examined in the following chapters). In this regard, the next chapters will show how Hallyu's social mediascapes engage differently with fans in Chile, Germany, and Spain.

NOTES

1. Venture media companies established by Asian Americans, including the U.S.-based Korean TV streaming services, such as Viki (2007–present) and DramaFever (2009–2018), have rapidly expanded their subscriber bases in North America and elsewhere. Viki was launched in 2007 as a U.S.-based start-up IT business by three young people, including two Korean Americans, as a university team project. Viki specializes in streaming Korean and other Asian media content on a subscription basis. The site has been known for its active incorporation of fan culture elements (such as fans' contribution to and comments on translation) and audience participation into its platform. In the midst of the increasing popularity of streaming services in the United States and elsewhere, Viki was acquired by the e-commerce giant Rakuten in 2013 and became its subsidiary company located in San Francisco (Wee 2014). In comparison, launched in 2009 by two Korean Americans, DramaFever was initially a venture business known for its streaming services of English-subtitled Korean TV dramas. The service, which was sold to the Japanese corporation SoftBank in 2014, was later acquired by the U.S.-based media giant Warner Bros as part of its online video strategy in 2016. According to a recent survey conducted by the data analytics company comScore, DramaFever had 2.4 million unique visitors in November 2016 alone (Bai 2017). However, in October 2018, Warner Bros abruptly announced that DramaFever would be shut down "due to business reason" (Spangler 2018). While both services were later acquired by media conglomerates, they initially drew on Asian American Hallyu fan subcultures. For example, it is estimated that 30–40 percent of the content's subtitles on DramaFever are created by fans (S. Lee 2015, 183).

2. *Running Man* (*reoningmaen*) is the Korean network TV SBS's Sunday variety show (2010–present). In this popular reality show, the MCs and guests competitively yet comically complete missions to win the race in an urban landmark. As the show has been one of the most popular Korean variety shows, the games played in the show have been popular among young people in Korea and elsewhere.

3. In particular, the United States has been the central market for KCON, the world's largest K-pop convention held in North America, Latin America, Middle East, Europe, and Asia. The United States, along with Japan and China, is among the three largest K-pop concert-hosting countries, which makes it the top country outside Asia; between 2013 and the first half of 2016, 102 K-pop tour concerts were held in the United States (Benjamin 2016).

4. The notion of "mediascape," popularized by Appadurai (1990), often addresses the images of the world shaped by the global distribution of media. By extending the currency of the term to social media-surrounded environments, we

propose the notion of the social mediascape to address the mediated space enhanced by the global distribution of social media. Our definition of social media refers to media forms in which the participatory culture of "ordinary" users is facilitated (Murthy 2012). While pointing to social networking sites (e.g., Facebook), user-driven online platforms (e.g., YouTube and Instagram), and microblogs (e.g., Twitter), the term also addresses those media forms' interactive processes that enable participants to productively collaborate.

5. We introduce and discuss the framework of social mediascape of Hallyu in detail in this chapter primarily because North America has been the home for major social media platforms and functions as a gateway to the non-Asian overseas market for Hallyu industries. However, this framework should not be exclusively applicable to the North American context. As is evident in the following chapters on Chile, Germany, and Spain, social mediascapes are increasingly observed in various reception points of Hallyu. Depending on particular local contexts, there may be variations in terms of components that constitute a social mediascape.

6. As a result of the Hallyu industry's ongoing global recruitment, an increasing number of non-Korean young people have joined K-pop idol groups. However, those overseas talents recruited and successfully integrated into K-pop groups were often either racially Asians or Western-educated people of Korean origin. Moreover, "global" talents of Korean origin in K-pop industries tend to be recruited primarily in North America rather than in any other region. These tendencies imply that postnational elements of Hallyu may draw on racial or ethnic proximity and are not free of American hegemony in global media industries.

7. This interviewee's account reveals a succinct comparison between Korean pop culture and Japanese pop culture in the global digital mediascape. Japanese cultural industries have not diligently made efforts to circulate their products and content globally (Iwabuchi 2002; Lukács 2010). With a few exceptional examples of cultural content, such as anime, Japanese cultural industries have focused primarily on the domestic market rather than actively exploring overseas markets, mainly because the efforts to penetrate the global market have not been considered by the industries to be profitable. In comparison, the Hallyu industry did not remain domestic, as it quickly resembled the nation's export-oriented industrial development model. As Korea's domestic cultural market is not as large as Japans', a significant portion of Hallyu content has been produced for overseas markets.

8. Only one respondent still preferred using the traditional media forms of network or cable TV to access Hallyu content. The unpopularity of traditional media among the Korean Wave fans may reflect a general tendency of young North American audiences who have been turning to the web, instead of traditional media, for information and entertainment. For young Americans, television is a medium that is relatively easy to give up in comparison to the Internet, as shown in a survey in which only 12 percent of young Americans aged eighteen to twenty-nine agreed that television would be very difficult to give up (Fox and Rainie 2014).

9. Reaction videos are videos in which people react to texts, things, or events. Typically, reaction videos show ordinary viewers' emotional responses while watching TV, movie, and music video clips. Overseas fans' reactions to K-pop have

emerged as a popular form of fan-generated content of social mediascape of Hallyu. Some fans are recognized as micro-celebrities.

10. Fansubs mean fan-created subtitles. While various forms of fansubs exist, the fan-generated subtitles are prevalent in the transnational circulation of bootleg content. In particular, American fans of Japanese anime have relied extensively on fansubs because licensed import of Japanese content has been limited even in the United States (especially in contrast with dedicated fans' extensive demands), and thus, translations via official channels are not always available. For further discussion about recent fansubbing practices on social media platforms, see Dwyer (2012).

11. A political economy of the attention economy emphasizes the ways in which "the audience labor of paying attention is capitalized." Attention economy highlights how cultural industries "seek to gain power over attention by determining the conditions under which audience practices of consumption can occur" (Nixon 2017, 4719).

Chapter 5

Participatory Translation of Hallyu in Latin America

INTRODUCTION

The popular Korean TV music show *Music Bank* held its thirteenth world tour concert in Santiago, Chile, in May 2018—six years after the program's first-ever overseas tour concert, which was also successfully held in Chile (Viña del Mar) in 2012. The 2018 concert seemed successful as the venue was filled with enthusiastic, chanting young fans, who passionately welcomed, and sung along with, major K-pop idol groups, such as B.A.P, TWICE, and Wanna One. However, the enthusiastic atmosphere ended up with some audience members being injured while rushing to a limited number of special seats for photo shooting (cooperativa.cl 2018). The fervent atmosphere and the lack of organization, which might have caused an accident, may illustrate how Hallyu has begun to emerge and evolve in Latin America, including Chile. That is, Korean popular cultural content has rapidly attracted fans via social media despite the lack of availability in mainstream media. The Latin American fans, introduced to K-pop primarily via social media, had sought to meet with Hallyu stars in their local arenas for many years, and thus, when the rare opportunity of attending a live K-pop concert came, the fans fervently responded.

Hallyu in Latin America with our emphasis on Chile offers an interesting example of how a non-White/non-Western cultural form is introduced, consumed, and negotiated in relation to the dominant White culture, in which social elite groups strongly identify their nations as being White (Goebel 2016). Then, who are Hallyu fans in Chile? A few recent studies of Hallyu in Latin America have revealed that young people of lower-middle class or low-income families tend to enjoy Korean popular culture as a way of seeking escape from their present environments (Carranza Ko et al. 2014; Madrid-Morales and Lovric 2015; Min 2017). Similarly, in a study conducted in Chile, Min (2017) also finds K-pop as an emerging cultural trend among working class youth. As seen in the 2019–2020 anti-government demonstrations in Santiago, social inequality and polarization have been serious issues in Chile (Laing 2019). K-pop's integration into youth culture in low-income neighborhoods may imply its subcultural aspect that questions and challenges the mainstream culture.

What are the probable barriers and facilitators of Hallyu in Latin America and how do the young fans engage with Korean popular cultural forms despite ongoing racialization of Asians and Asian cultures? To answer these questions, this chapter addresses how young Chileans understand, interpret, and reappropriate Korean popular cultural content in their own local contexts. We explore how Korean popular cultural content is consumed among young Chileans through social media, and potentially moves beyond (or reproduces) the racialization of non-White cultural forms in the country. In so doing, we examine how Hallyu in Chile may facilitate, and be facilitated by, bottom-up transnationalism led by audiences. Furthermore, by extending the notion of social mediascape, we explore how social media is integrated with participatory youth culture and how online and offline contexts are articulated with each other in the Chilean Hallyu fandom. We do not claim that Chile represents Latin America, but rather we focus on a segment of Hallyu fans in urban youth culture settings in Chile, in which we can observe a vibrant and emerging Hallyu fandom. In that way, we propose that Hallyu subculture in Latin America could be conceptualized as a participatory, bottom-up mode of transnationalism.

GEOPOLITICAL MEANINGS OF HALLYU IN LATIN AMERICA: A CASE OF CHILE

While there are several different forms of Hallyu content, K-pop has rapidly been visible in Chilean youth culture, and in general Latin American culture, over the past few years, especially due to the dedicated fans of several major K-pop idol bands—BTS in particular. The 2017 BTS concert, which was sold out in just two hours, was filled by a dedicated audience and held in Movistar Arena, Santiago's biggest indoor arena. Reportedly, the audience's sing along and chanting were far beyond any other concerts. According to the concert's promoter, the audience's screaming was as loud as an ear-splitting 127 decibels, a noise level that can cause permanent hearing loss (Benjamin 2017). American music magazine *Rolling Stone* described how BTS members were received by Chilean fans: "When their airplane landed in Chile, they were greeted with Beatles-esque pandemonium" (*Rolling Stone* 2017). The K-pop fan base in Chile is recognizable by the enthusiastic fans in recent K-pop concerts, as well as an increasing number of young people who dance to K-pop in urban spaces (Min et al. 2019).

Of course, K-pop alone does not fully explain the recent rise of Korean popular culture in Chile, as an earlier wave already arrived in the country a decade ego. Hallyu has not been exclusively reliant on social media and the Internet. As in other parts of the world, Hallyu in Chile started with a few television dramas. For example, several K-dramas have been broadcast on mainstream platforms and have appealed to the public since the mid-2000s. In 2006, the Korean drama *Stairway to Heaven* was aired by the Chilean public television broadcaster, TVN. K-dramas began to attract a relatively high viewer rating in Chilean broadcast media in 2012 when *Boys over Flowers* (Spanish title: Los chicos son mejores que las flores) was released by Mega TV, one of the major Chilean TV channels.

While K-dramas have been gradually introduced to Chilean viewers, K-pop idol groups' popularity has arisen more quickly. Due to the passionate fan culture, as stated above, Chile was chosen to be the first overseas venue of *Music Bank* in 2012. Yet, Chilean Hallyu fans are more than dedicated consumers of Korean popular culture products. They are also known for their participatory fan culture (Min et al. 2019). Some K-pop fans who cover dance[1] have become famous among local Hallyu fans. For example, fan-based Chilean girl group Rough Bunnies, which was initially formed as a tribute to the K-pop band B.A.P, has become popular among Chilean K-pop fans (*South China Morning Post* 2018). Given the limited opportunities to go and see K-pop tour concerts, it might be a feasible option for local K-pop fans to "cover" and "do" K-pop music videos by themselves and for their peer fans. K-pop's fan practices, such as dance cover, have contributed to the growth of local youth groups enjoying and practicing K-pop together in their own local contexts such as urban spaces where they can dance together or participate in flashmobs. It has been estimated that nearly forty Hallyu fan clubs operate in Chile (Korea Foundation 2017a). BTS's Chile-based Facebook fan group, BTS Chile, has 109,912 followers as of October 30, 2018.[2] In our interviews, the fans claimed that there seem to be hundreds of K-pop fan clubs in Chile, both online and offline. This claim seems to be corroborated by a Korean news report that has estimated 200 K-pop fan clubs with a total of 20,000 members in Chile (KBS News 2012).

Hallyu arrived and emerged in Chile without close geocultural connection with the wave's country of origin. Young Chileans have been familiar with several music genres, such as Latin music, hip-hop, reggaeton, and American pop music, while other cultural forms such as Asian popular culture have been marginalized in the existing racial hierarchy, associating Whiteness with higher sociocultural status (Webb et al. 2018). Moreover, given the small Korean ethnic population and cultural presence, even compared with a few other Latin American countries cited as major Hallyu sites, the evolution of Hallyu fans in Chile provides an important perspective on how and why audiences transnationally translate and engage with pop culture originating in a country far from their own. Compared with North American contexts, in which Asian American youth have played a significant role in exploring and spreading K-pop and other Hallyu content (J.-S. Park 2013), the rise of Hallyu in Chile (as well as in other Latin American countries) does not seem to draw directly on Asian diasporic communities. As of 2017, the number of Koreans (including Korean nationals residing in Chile and Chilean nationals of Korean heritage) in Chile was 2,635, which is much smaller than in other major Latin American sites of Hallyu—11,673 in Mexico, 23,194 in Argentina, and 51,534 in Brazil (Korean Statistical Information Service 2018). Rather than being ignited by Korean or Asian diasporic communities, Hallyu in Chile might have emerged through social media-savvy young people and from below, especially in its recent phase.

Chile has been addressed as an important Hallyu site that reveals its vibrant fan cultures from below (Min 2015, 2017; Min et al. 2019). Hallyu's relatively early arrival in Chile, compared with other Latin American countries, may be indebted by the country's relatively strong consumer culture and Internet penetration rate. First, Chile is considered one of the most globalized countries in Latin America, as the first South American country that became a member of Organization for Economic Co-operation and Development (OECD). Chile became Korea's first Free Trade Agreement (FTA) partner in 2004. As of 2018, its national economy has the highest GDP per capita among South American countries—US$25,222 as of 2018, which is followed by Uruguay, Argentina, and Brazil (The World Bank 2019). However, along with the lengthy anti-government protests starting in 2019, Chile's economic growth rate has lowered (Esposito and Ramos 2019).

Second, the country has been equipped with good, if not great, new media infrastructure, which is estimated to be more advanced than most other Central and South American countries. In particular, 86 percent of the eighteen to twenty-four age group used the Internet as of 2010 (World Internet Project-Chile 2011). In the early 2010s, Facebook estimated Chile as one of three most rapidly growing national markets, along with Venezuela and Turkey (Fisher 2012). The country has been ranked as one of the most wired South American countries as demonstrated by several indicators such as Internet and personal computer users per capita (NationMaster 2020).

The economic and technological condition alone cannot explain the recent rise of Hallyu in Chile, especially given that there have also been barriers that might have obstructed the influx of Korean popular culture, such as racism against non-White populations. Historically, many Latin American countries embraced European influences, while social elite groups in the region attempted to "white" themselves by strongly identifying themselves as European descendants. Due to its significant European migration and influences, Chile has majority White populations. According to the 2000 census, in which 63 percent of the national population self-identified as White, Chile was one of the highly White Latin American countries, along with Argentina and Uruguay (Telles and Flores 2013). Therefore, the influx of Hallyu content in Chile has been closely connected with local geopolitics, which makes the popularity of Hallyu unique and unprecedented.

KOREAN POPULAR CULTURE IN LATIN AMERICA

Due to Hallyu's short history in Latin America, there has been limited information about who Hallyu audiences are in this region (i.e., the demographics and characteristics). According to recent studies (e.g., Regatieri 2017), Hallyu tends to be popular among young people of a lower social class in Latin America. K-pop consumption among working-class youth in Brazil reportedly "fosters hope and fantasy" and sublimates "socio-political tensions that are so present in a developing yet extremely unequal country" (Regatieri 2017, 518). This tendency has also been observed in previous studies conducted in Latin America (B. Han 2017; Min 2015, 2017). Thus, as B. Han (2017) suggested, K-pop fandom in Latin America might be a form of "class struggle that resists the hegemonic class hierarchies" in contemporary Latin America (2265).

Hallyu in Latin America is particularly enjoyed by female fans. According to Carranza Ko et al.'s (2014) survey on Hallyu reception in Latin America, the majority of the respondents were female (over 90 percent).[3] Hallyu's special appeal to Latin American women is attributed to the "soft" masculinity portrayed in Korean pop culture. As Carranza Ko et al. (2014) claimed, while conventional Latin American heroes (as portrayed in typical telenovela content) are protagonists "involved in a high level of sexual exposure and violence," male Hallyu stars are recognized by Latin American fans for their "soft look, cuteness, gentle manners, and sweetness" as "an alternate image of the over-masculine Latin American male" (321). These demographic attributes of Latin American Hallyu fans are also found among the Chileans interviewed for this book. In our field study conducted in Santiago, the capital city of Chile, most Hallyu fans whom we met were young women. In addition, given their residential areas, they seemed to be lower middle class or working class.[4]

Hallyu has been emerging in Chile but is not yet fully integrated into the mainstream pop cultural repertoire. This cultural trend is rather new and subcultural, while being enthusiastically received primarily among groups of young people. The subcultural nature of Hallyu fandom may not be unique to the Chilean context, as it has been reported in other Latin American contexts (B. Han 2017; J. Choi 2014). The Hallyu fans negotiated the pervasive stereotyping of Korean popular culture within Chilean society, on the one hand, and explored different methods of accessing and translating the Korean materials, on the other hand.

Hallyu and its fans are subject to public gazes in Chile. During their interviews, the fans often recalled how their tastes for Korean popular culture were negatively received by their peers, families, and the public. Korea and its popular culture have been insufficiently recognized for many years in Chile, not unlike in most other Latin American countries. Despite the history of Asian immigration in Chile, which already began in the nineteenth century, Asian communities, including Koreans, are relatively small, and Asian culture has not been particularly popular in this country. Asians and Asian cultures are stereotyped with derogatory terms such as *chinitos* (literally referring to "Chinese people"), which are still used even in public.

The lack of recognition of Asian culture seems to extend to Hallyu, which was often racially recognized as part of Asian culture by mainstream Chilean audiences. According to young Hallyu fans in the interviews, such racialization of Korean popular culture among mainstream audiences discouraged the fans to express in public their enthusiasm about Hallyu. Several K-pop fans addressed how they were negatively identified by others. Elias, a twenty-six-year-old man even stated that "almost the whole Chilean society considers K-pop fans weird," while adding that "however, each person has his (her) own life. I don't care what others say." Similarly, Miguel, a twenty-six-year-old man, stated, "Nobody in Chile likes us K-pop fans." As Laura, a twenty-year-old woman, noted, "Chilean society thinks K-pop fans are nerds—people who don't have any friends." Even in the family, the young fans' penchant for Hallyu seemed to be disregarded, as their parents were often unhappy about their taste for Hallyu: "My mom scolds me all the time because I spend most of my time listening to K-pop. She says my head is packed with *chinitos*. My dad doesn't say anything to me, but I know that he doesn't like that I like K-pop either," stated twenty-two-year-old Juliana.

Stereotypical representation of media fans as nerds is not new (Jensen 1992). However, Hallyu in Chilean society is doubly marginalized as it is easily associated with the influential stereotyping of East Asian people and culture, derogatorily referred to as *chinitos*. While North American fans of Korean popular culture interviewed for chapter 4 pointed out their experiences of public's discriminatory gaze on their cultural tastes (see K. Yoon 2017), Chilean fans tended to more strongly and frequently experience public prejudice against their interest in Hallyu.

In this regard, it is intriguing to examine how Hallyu flows into youth subcultures in Chile, despite the ongoing misrecognition and stereotyping in public. Due to the lack of integration into mainstream media, Hallyu in Chile is consumed primarily through subcultural networks, which often involve extensive use of social media and "cultural translation from below" (K. Yoon 2017). Young Chileans dancing to K-pop songs at GAM Cultural Center in Santiago show how Hallyu is interpreted and appropriated by the young people who creatively translate the unfamiliar cultural form into a familiar and relatable cultural resource. Hallyu fandom in Santiago, which is over 18,000 km away from Seoul, implies that Hallyu is actively resignified by young people regardless of the geographic location of its reception points and pervasive racialization of Asian culture (B. Han 2017; K. Yoon 2017). K-pop is a good example to show how Hallyu is culturally translated by fan audiences in the social mediascape. K-pop does not require literal translation but is consumed through multisensory and transmedia (i.e., mediated and remediated through different forms of media) experiences. For most fans we interviewed, the affect and feelings of the genre and idols, rather than lyrics, were the primary appealing components of K-pop.

SECONDHAND TRANSLATION OF HALLYU

Hallyu fans in Chile do not only negotiate the public stereotyping and racialization but also encounter difficulties translating Hallyu into their own language and everyday life contexts. The influx of Hallyu in Latin America seems to be influenced by its North American counterpart as the U.S.-based and English-speaking overseas fans often play the role of early adopters and early translators of Hallyu, especially outside Korea and Asia. In this regard, cultural flows of Hallyu in Latin America can be characterized as what we would like to call "secondhand translation." In our field studies, Chilean fans' access to Hallyu content was not free of the influence of North American, English-based fans' infrastructure and knowledge.

Hallyu fans in Santiago encountered substantial cultural barriers, especially compared to Hallyu fans in Los Angeles or New York, at least during the initial phase. Compared with the high availability of English translations (due to prompt fan translation between Korean and English), Spanish translations of Hallyu content are still scarce. Clara, a twenty-four-year-old woman who is a K-pop fan club manager, noted her participation in fansubs (fan-created translation and subtitles, as addressed in chapter 4): "Since I am a BTS fan club manager, I'm responsible for updating the social media of our club, such as Facebook, Twitter, etc. I translate news in English to Spanish and post the news on the social media since most of the fans don't know English." Another nineteen-year-old fan, Irene, lamented the lack of availability of Spanish translation of K-pop: "I find the meaning of lyrics through Google translator. Most of the translation is in English. The Spanish translations are really weird." To appeal to Latin American fans, several K-pop songs had Spanish-mix parts. While a few fans positively considered such Spanish parts in K-pop lyrics as an effort to communicate with Latin American fans, other fans did not find Spanish mix particularly appealing. "When *Big Bang* sang 'Uno, dos tres . . . [i.e., one, two, three . . .]', I giggled. Sometimes an English and/or Spanish interruption might help to guess the message that songs transmits," stated Malena, a twenty-six-year-old fan.

In Anglophone contexts, K-pop, K-dramas, and K-variety shows are extensively translated by fans and/or streaming services. In particular, bilingual Korean American youth fans have contributed to the vibrant culture of creating and sharing fansubs (Jin and Yoon 2016a). Due to the lack of official or fan-based Spanish translations of Hallyu content, the Chilean fans tended to rely on secondhand translation (i.e., Spanish translations of English versions). Twenty-one-year-old Juliana stated: "Most of the translations are from English to Spanish. There are several American girls who post subtitles on YouTube. Whenever a new song is released, my friends exchange information the very next day. Sometimes we translate from English to Spanish. Most of the K-pop fans in Chile don't know English."

This process of translation implies that Latin America is not only geographically distant from the origin of Hallyu but might also be left relatively behind in terms of timely exposure to Hallyu. Several fans complained that Hallyu-related merchandise available in Chile are often pirated rather than original. This time lag in linguistic translation and available merchandise of Hallyu may offer an interesting point for discussion about the nature of pop cultural transnationalism of Hallyu. The industries of Hallyu have been deeply influenced by their American hegemon (i.e., American giant cultural industries) and have been eager to penetrate the central market. Hallyu productions of K-dramas, K-movies, and more visibly K-pop have tried hard to gain recognition in the North American market first because the market is considered as a cornerstone of global circulation. For this reason, Latin America has remained undersupplied with Hallyu content, and more importantly, the infrastructure of cultural circulation—such as channels for accessing Hallyu materials and availability of Spanish translation—has remained underdeveloped, especially compared to the North American context. The insufficient infrastructure may cause the time lag (even if minimal) between Latin America and the centers of transnational Hallyu.

The notion of "center" of Hallyu here may bring another debatable question. Where are the "centers" in transnational Hallyu? On the surface, Korea is undeniably the origin and center of this wave. However, when it comes to the wave's global circulation (outside Korea), two Asian consumer capitalist giants—Japan and China—have played major roles; as discussed earlier, the very term Hallyu, or Korean Wave, was coined and began to be popularized by Chinese and Japanese media and media markets. In addition, as discussed, American cultural markets and media have been important sites through which Hallyu is circulated in non-Asian contexts (and Asian contexts, as well).

One would argue that, given the significant role of digital and social media, the physical sense of "centers" may no longer be valid in the global circulation of Hallyu. It is arguable whether Hallyu flows from the centers to other areas, given the extensive use of different social media platforms. As shown in the rapid rise of Hallyu fandom in many different countries and regions, the new Korean Wave often seems viral and simultaneous. However, despite the viral transnationalism of Hallyu, the existing infrastructure and hegemony of cultural gatekeeping may remain important. In particular, the export-oriented economy of Hallyu has relied on English language and American formats for the content's rapid circulation. In this regard, we should avoid a technological deterministic perspective on social media in Hallyu. As discussed in the previous chapter, social media neither works in isolation nor determines how culture is shaped and circulated. Rather, the technology of social media is a product of economic, social, and cultural structures and is constantly negotiated by its users.

The secondhand translation of Hallyu in Latin America may not necessarily be disadvantageous, as the process can be an opportunity for the fan audiences to explore their own strategies to engage with Korean popular culture—for example, some fans became keenly aware of the context in which they consume Hallyu, sometimes by retranslating the content via the United States. Twenty-five-year-old Josefina, who was a longtime Hallyu fan since the mid-2000s, critically captured the way in which the global circulation of Hallyu is gatekept by American media and industries: "You can find tons of K-pop music videos subtitled in English on YouTube. I think it is too American-centered. Furthermore, the translation is wrong. They put subtitles for international fans, but it's really only for English-speaking fans. It's a kind of racism. Maybe the Asian fans can understand the weird translations better." For Chilean fans, being in the noncentral (or peripheral) location of Hallyu may encourage them to generate their own framework for interpreting and reworking Korean popular culture texts. Moreover, the process of secondhand translation, even unintentionally, allows the Chilean fans to question American fans' hegemonic position in the international fan community of Hallyu.

Hallyu in Chile is not free of structural barriers that may restrict transnational flows of cultural texts and practices. Especially compared with their North American counterparts, Chilean fans encounter geographical barriers (distance), a lack of diasporic connection (through Koreans in Latin America or Latin Americans in Korea), and linguistic differences (i.e., scarcity of linguistic transactions primarily between Korean and Spanish). These barriers may make Latin America seemingly the margin of transnational Hallyu. However, as illustrated in K-pop and its fandom, the restrictions can be transcended through affective connection and cultural translation from below, which involves unique participatory culture (B. Han 2017; K. Yoon 2017). Moreover, secondhand translation processes allow Latin American fans to critically think about American hegemony and explore probable strategic consumption without relying on the hegemonic cultural market.

HYBRIDITY OF HALLYU

What we refer to as the secondhand translation of Hallyu in the Latin American context is rather metaphorical. The "secondhand" in the phrase does not mean a second-grade or inferior translation, which is hierarchically positioned below the "firsthand translation" available in North America. Instead, it means the process involving a temporal delay in translation and retranslation (of English translation of Hallyu content). The process of retranslation could entail "misunderstanding" of the original text but also includes efforts to appropriate the original text through the firsthand translation (i.e., English translation of Hallyu content). By translating and retranslating, Latin American fans engage with the multilayers of transnational Hallyu and renegotiate different versions of Hallyu texts. In particular, this secondhand retranslation generates a highly hybrid mode of cultural consumption, in which the meanings of the original text are not fixed but rather diversified. By being exposed to firsthand translation (i.e., American translation of Hallyu) and secondhand translation (i.e., translation of American versions to Spanish, by Latin American fans who can speak English), Chilean fans are given opportunities to access different interpretations and versions of Hallyu. In this regard, it is important that Hallyu is often considered by its Latin American fans as a set of hybrid texts and practices.

What does Hallyu mean to the young Chilean fans? How is Hallyu signified in its secondhand translation process? How do the young fans appropriate Hallyu as a set of cultural texts and practices, which can be differentiated from mainstream cultural forms such as American and Latin American pop culture? The cultural meaning and usefulness of Hallyu among the young Chileans, to some extent, seem to be related to their previous cultural experiences.

As K-pop is the most popular Hallyu genre among the young Chileans, it is important to examine how K-pop is interpreted and negotiated as a set of cultural texts among the young people. According to the fans, K-pop is considered cultural content that is potentially alternative to mainstream American pop music. For them, K-pop is "a kind of imitation of American pop music" (Olivia, a nineteen-year-old fan) but "an evolution of American pop music" (Paulina, an eighteen-year-old fan). While several Latin musicians—most recently Luis Fonsi—have been globally popular, American music tends to be the predominantly influential foreign cultural text in Chile.[5] For the Hallyu fans, K-pop appeared to be a substitution text (or sometimes a complementary text) to American pop music. Despite its perceived similarity with American pop music, K-pop was also recognized by difference. K-pop was often associated with forward-looking and alternative cultural practices among the young people, owing to its perceived attributes as a young, participatory, and perfectionist pop cultural text, compared with American mainstream pop music, which seems "repetitive" (Irene, a twenty-year-old fan). In the fans' narratives, K-pop and its idols were also distinguished from their counterparts. Laura, a twenty-year-old fan, expressed her feelings about K-pop idols:

> K-pop idols, especially the male idols, are much cuter and more handsome than Chilean guys. They have a different masculinity that I don't see among Chilean guys. Chilean men talk too much. Not true for all of them, though. And they are really stuck up. Chilean men talk about anything. They are born to be talkers. Korean men look more serious and honest.

Laura, as well as several other fans, compared K-pop idols' "absolutely different style and different type of masculinity," which is "so cool." As suggested in previous studies, K-pop's "soft masculinity" (S. Jung 2011) has been contrasted with conventional or hegemonic masculinity often reproduced in mainstream media content, and thus especially appealed to young overseas female fans.[6]

Case studies of Hallyu—those conducted outside Asia in particular—have often emphasized K-pop's hybridity and suggested overseas fans might be attracted to K-pop's "post-nationality" (or lack of national flavor, in which the essentialized national signifier of "K" in K-pop has been diluted) (Jin and Ryoo 2014; Lie 2012; S. Jung 2011). However, Hallyu in Latin America is not free of the national signifier. While Korean popular culture is often a racial signifier for mainstream audiences and media (as a part of *chinitos* culture, as discussed earlier), the young Chilean fans who enjoyed and consumed Hallyu content—K-pop, K-drama, and K-variety shows in particular—seemed to associate the content with a kaleidoscopic world equipped with techno-savvy youth and popular culture. For example, a few fans in the study described Korea as an example of late-developed, open society. Francisco, a twenty-two-year-old man in the workforce noted: "Korea has become a kind of model for me to follow—there the President has been impeached but the country still goes well; people join the protest but then they go to work the next day; people clean up the trash after the protest, and/or events—these kinds of things would never happen in Chile."

For these fans, admiring Korea as a place of alternative modernity, the high level of hybridity of K-pop was not necessarily contributing to Hallyu. For example, the use of foreign languages styles in K-pop was not positively received. With respect to the language use of K-pop, while some enjoyed the partial use of English or even Spanish in K-pop lyrics, others did not enjoy the irrelevant addition of Spanish phrases in several K-pop songs. A few K-pop songs have Spanish refrain in their lyrics, which is comparable with English mixing in a large number of K-pop songs. The popular K-pop girl group GFriend's hit song has a Spanish title and refrain—"Me gustas tu" (literally meaning "I like you"). The Spanish part of K-pop lyrics can be considered an example of Hallyu's hybridity. As Rafaela, a twenty-one-year-old student, pointed out, Spanish mixing in K-pop lyrics "sounds unnatural, although it might help to connect the foreign fans to K-pop." Thus, she did not like the increasing English or Spanish mixing in K-pop.

The intent of the use of Spanish in this song might be for an exotic atmosphere of the song and the band, rather than aiming to addressing Spanish audiences. In fact, GFriend has not performed in any Spanish-speaking countries, whereas its main overseas target audiences are in Asia. This exoticization of Spanish culture and language in a few K-pop songs may explain why Spanish mixing is not particularly welcomed by the Spanish fans. Carlos, a twenty-six-year-old student, was concerned about K-pop's increasing English or Spanish mixing and hybridity: "K-pop has been losing its 'Koreanness'. Many idol groups have foreign members and include lyrics in English and/or Spanish. I think that makes K-pop lose competitiveness. What's the difference compared to American pop?"

LOOKING FOR ALTERNATIVES

The appeal of the hybridity of Hallyu content is not necessarily in its adoption of and assimilation to Americanized styles but in its alternativeness to American pop culture. By seeking alternative cultural resources, Hallyu fans in Chile distinguish their cultural tastes from those of mainstream youth. The Hallyu fans might attempt to detour the hegemonic American media by exploring non-Western cultural repertoires. Chilean media industries have been under extensive American influences. Thus, Chile has been considered a primary example of the cultural imperialism thesis or dependency theory (Dorfman and Mattelart 1975). Indeed, the Chilean media industry has been affected by the American system in media content and production, while insufficiently developing competitive national media industries. This context of American influences and the nascent media infrastructure may explain why Hallyu has recently emerged as appealing cultural content especially among young people who seek content that is neither American nor domestic.

In this regard, the young Hallyu fans' previous (and ongoing) exposure to East Asian pop culture is particularly revealing in that it illustrates the transnationalism of Hallyu among young Latin Americans: they seek alternative cultural resources in geographically distant, imagined worlds and, in so doing, detour (if not resist) the global hegemony of the West. Nearly half of the fans interviewed had been exposed to Japanese pop culture prior to their interest in Hallyu in our field study in Chile. Pablo, a twenty-four-year-old student, pointed out, "Those who like Japanese culture also like K-pop." Indeed, most interviewees had been introduced to Korean pop culture via their earlier interests in Japanese anime or any other Japanese pop culture texts. This tendency seems to resonate with the previous studies on K-pop fans in Latin America (J. Choi 2014) and Europe (S. Sohn 2013), whose earlier exposure to Japanese pop culture contributed, to some extent, to the rise of K-pop fans. Given that many young people around the globe have grown up with manga and anime, and thus have been called the "Pokémon Generation" (Allison 2003), it may not be surprising that several K-pop fans recall that they "liked Japanese *manga* like any other kid at that time" (Carlos, the aforementioned twenty-six-year-old fan). Francisco, the aforementioned twenty-two-year-old fan, was introduced to Hallyu largely because of his familiarity with and exposure to Japanese pop culture. He even thought that some of the K-pop songs to which he initially listened were J-pop.

> I listened to *Girls' Generation* by chance on Spotify [an online music streaming site] and I liked it a lot. It was the Japanese version. All of the group's K-pop music on Spotify was the Japanese version at that time. I found out that *Girls' Generation* was a Korean group, so I began to look for other K-pop groups and then I searched for the Romanized form of the lyrics.

A coexistence of enthusiasm for Hallyu and Japanese pop culture among Latin American K-pop fans seems comparable with North American K-pop fandom. While cultural hybridity was considered as a key appeal of K-pop among American Hallyu fans, Latin American fans tended to consider K-pop as a new breed in their Asian cultural repertoire, through which they engaged with bottom-up transnationalism and explored the strategy of detouring Western popular culture. This appropriation of an Asian cultural repertoire as a resource for bottom-up transnationalism is succinctly narrated by Carlos, the aforementioned twenty-six-year-old university student: "In my generation, kids started to have interest in Japanese manga, J-pop and visual art. But we've never been the mainstream. K-pop and J-pop fans like that kind of music because of particular images. Asian cultures are for the outsiders of society."

For some Chilean fans, K-pop is new cultural material through which they imaginatively explore a new form of transnationalism, which was once (and still is) experienced through the *otaku*[7] world. "I think K-pop has been taking over the otaku world," stated Maximiliano, a twenty-one-year-old man. For a few K-pop fans, Japanese manga and K-pop seem complementary, although they are sharply different cultural genres. Alejandro, a seventeen-year-old man, noted, "K-pop is dynamic and strong, and Japanese manga is quiet or serene, so both are complementary." Some fans noted that otaku culture paved the way for Hallyu fandom. For example, Josefina, the aforementioned twenty-five-year-old student, assumed:

> Japanese culture was really popular about 10 years ago. I think that popularity was one of the reasons why K-pop has become popular today. I don't know why and how. The Gothic group, or very enthusiastic otaku[8] was born at that time [i.e., 10 years ago]. If Japanese culture hadn't been so popular, then people wouldn't have heard about Asia. During the 80s, there were the Japanese manga fans, during the 90s the J-pop fans, and since 2000 the K-pop fans. It's a niche taste. K-pop is more familiar to the younger generation.

Hallyu may constitute a new cultural trend, which detours the Western-oriented media infrastructure. However, Chilean fans' consumption of Hallyu as a new breed yet as a part of exotic Asia implies an irony of Hallyu fandom. That is, Hallyu fandom can be seen as a new form of Latin American con-sumption of the Orient on the one hand and as an alternative to (or hybrid of) Western culture on the other hand.

Korean popular culture—K-pop in particular—has been adopted and appropriated by young Chileans as an object for fantasizing about alternative society and as a probable antidote to mainstream cultural forms with which they could not find a strong sense of identification. The Chilean fans' engage-ment with K-pop as a cultural resource for alternative society has increasingly been noticed by the Chilean government. During the massive public protests in 2019–2020, which occurred in response to the increased cost of living and inequality, K-pop was identified as one of the factors that might have encouraged Chileans' participation in anti-government movements (CNN Chile 2019). Although the government later announced that the report does not represent its official view, the report reveals that K-pop is consumed by Chileans who are not satisfied with the dominant social order and thus seek-ing an alternative social system.

FAN SUBCULTURE OF BOTTOM-UP
TRANSNATIONALISM

Young Chilean Hallyu fans are foot soldiers of bottom-up transnationalism, as they culturally translate and appropriate the hybrid content of Hallyu as a cultural resource for exploring, and appealing to, their minor cultural tastes outside the mainstream mediascape. Hallyu fan culture in Chile shows how transnational cultural flows explore minor or alternative cultural tastes—especially among particular groups of people such as young women. In this regard, it is important to examine how Hallyu evolves as subcultural practices, while connecting its local (and global) fans.

In our study, most fans considered themselves subcultural or minority media audience members, in that their cultural taste was largely different from that of a majority audience. Given their residential areas, most Hallyu fans in our study were not socioeconomically privileged youth and struggled with social and individual difficulties in their transition to adulthood. The young people's engagement with Hallyu may imply how subcultural youth negotiate contradictions and frustrations that they encounter in the process of growing up through pop cultural practices. As observed by previous studies, Hallyu in Latin America seemed to be a subculture of lower-middle-class or working-class youth (Carranza Ko et al. 2014; Min 2017). Josefina, the aforementioned fan, also stated: "Most of the girls [i.e., Korean pop culture fans] live in the peripheral zones surrounding the city and belong to lower middle class. What kind of people live on the outer edges of Santiago? Most of the women are single moms who yell at their kids every day—there are lots of problems."

The working class-oriented, subcultural nature of Hallyu fandom in Chile was also confirmed by Magdalena, a twenty-one-year-old interviewee, who identified herself as coming from a well-off family: "Honestly, I belong to a high class in Chilean society. My friends couldn't believe it when they found out that I liked K-pop. They asked me why I like K-pop. My dad just shakes his head whenever he sees the posters on the wall in my room. My friends consider me strange. There isn't anyone who likes K-pop around me."

However, Hallyu fan culture is not simply homological to working-class youth culture, as the Hallyu phenomenon is not triggered solely by its appeal to a particular group of young Chileans. The fans' interests in Korean popular culture seem to be ignited by its cultural relevance to their daily lives. In particular, the young people's desire to escape the precarious future is observed in the K-pop subculture. Young K-pop idols' efforts and struggles in their transition to adulthood throughout the long period of training are appealing to the young fans who cope with their own pains and problems in growing up. The shared feelings of pains, struggles, and self-realization during transition to adulthood are evident in the K-pop group BTS and its global fans, called ARMY (Newsis 2018).[9] Several interviewees described typical K-pop fans as teenagers who go through difficult times in their transition to adulthood. As Carlos, the aforementioned twenty-six-year-old fan, stated, K-pop can function as an imaginary tool with which young Chileans escape the precariousness of society:

K-pop is a form of escaping and I think other fans might feel the same. In Chile, education, especially public education is terrible, family violence is terrible, and so on. In sum, total precariousness dominates the society. Young people look for hideouts and K-pop provides one. Young people copy the style of K-pop idols to feel as if they were in a different world.

As Carranza Ko et al. (2014) found in their study of Latin American Hallyu fans, Korean pop culture seems to be a cultural channel through which "individuals escaped from the social reality in which they found themselves and transferred their status to a different geographic, economic, and cultural context" (Carranza Ko et al. 2014, 319).

Several fans described their fan practices as ways of coping with their personal "problems" or "pains" and seeking a new identity. For example, Violeta, a nineteen-year-old female fan noted: "K-pop has totally changed my social life. I always had problems with interpersonal relationships. Since I began to cover dance, I've made new friends who understand my hobby and share the same taste as me. K-pop has helped to open my mind."

This finding resonates with Zubernis and Larson's assertion (2011, 86) of the "therapeutic potential of fandom in facilitating identity development." Indeed, Hallyu fan subculture offers the young people a moment of, and sense of, growing up. Ivanna (a twenty-five-year-old fan) stated: "[If I met Super Junior] I would like to tell them 'Thank you' for giving me a sense of security. Super Junior released a new album whenever I encountered a turning point of my life . . . K-pop has helped me to de-stress at every stage of my life."

Hallyu is a cultural resource for the young people to cope with the precarious future and to negotiate their identity in the making. Josefina, the aforementioned fan, pointed out what K-pop contributed to the fans' identity formation through their sense of belonging to a subculture.

> When you are at the stage of forming your personality and identity, you might belong to a specific group to have your own identity, but different from others. I think that's why many teenage girls like K-pop. Reggaeton [i.e., a Spanish language music genre influenced by hip-hop, Latin American, and Caribbean music] is loved by everyone, so you don't need to like it.

As cultural studies scholars have pointed out, pop cultural texts and performance may have subversive and/or evasive effects (Fiske 1989). Chilean fans seemed to enjoy Korean popular culture, such as K-pop, Korean variety shows, and K-dramas, as a way of escaping from stressful daily lives or challenging the existing social order. Similarly, Hallyu fandom in Latin American has been considered as evasive cultural consumption (Carranza Ko et al. 2014) or a subversive cultural expression that also involves moments of young people's self-empowerment (B. Han 2017).

The young fans' subcultural identities may not necessarily mean that they seek to belong to one collective subculture. Rather, despite their dedication to K-pop, some interviewees were skeptical about K-pop fan clubs and their collective activities. For example, Miguel, a twenty-six-year-old fan, pre-ferred "to be an independent fan" because "K-pop fan clubs seem militaristic, and their behaviors are too extreme." Olivia, a nineteen-year-old fan, suc-cinctly described what Hallyu fan clubs were like in Chile:

> There are hundreds of fan clubs in Chile. Fan clubs compete and quarrel with each other. They don't share the concert information, which means there is no communication among them. I don't understand why they organize fan clubs. Fan clubs organize on-line and off-line meetings, idols' birthday parties, watch-ing music videos together, cover dance contests, and so on. They charge 2,500 to 3,000 pesos (US\$ 3–4, approx.) to participate in their activities.

For this reason, some Hallyu fans often suspected that official or big K-pop fan clubs, which sometimes held local Hallyu events in Santiago, were commercialized or undemocratically managed. Several fans reported that larger Hallyu fan clubs were in competition with each other, and attempted to manipulate cyberspace (e.g., by exaggerating their size or disguising the members' real identities). Thus, the young people interviewed preferred to stay in small, intimate Hallyu fan circles, rather than in systematically orga-nized nationwide Hallyu fan clubs. This microsubcultural gathering was also observed in K-pop groups' participation in the 2019–2020 anti-government protest. Some interviewees' skeptical view on organized fan clubs was partly derived from their subject positions—how they distinguished themselves from younger and "crazy" Hallyu fans. The interviewed fans, most of whom were relatively well-educated and seemingly older than the assumed core fan cohort of Hallyu, were critical about early-teen girl fans.[10] The fans' direct connection with K-pop idols and other close fans seemed more important than the reliance on large or official fan clubs. "I don't need to identify with any fan club. It's enough just enjoying it myself," stated Rafaela, a twenty-one-year-old fan. In this manner, fans tended to use K-pop as a means of expressing their desired identity and developing their micro-friendships.

The young Chilean fans' engagement with Hallyu implies that Hallyu transnationalism evolves through subcultures, which are relatively fluid and disjointed, and thus does not necessarily fit the classical definition of a subcul-ture as a site of collective expression of resistance against the dominant social order. In this regard, Hallyu fandom in Latin America is similar to what soci-ologists have referred to as "post-subculture" (Bennett and Kahn-Harris 2004).

SOCIAL MEDIASCAPE OF PARTICIPATION

The (post)subculture of Hallyu fandom has evolved along with digitally savvy and social media-assisted fan activities. Transnational flows of Hallyu, as an alternative to dominant global media, would not have been possible without the emerging social mediascape. Social media-based consumption also diminishes temporal lags and geographic distance in Latin American Hallyu. As has been discussed throughout our book, the recent phase of Hallyu (Hallyu 2.0) has extensively and intensively exploited social media as a way to ignite global fandom and participatory culture. The relatively advanced Internet infrastructure (as discussed in an earlier section) may have positively affected the emergence of K-pop fandom in Chile among young people who are equipped with digital technologies. Thus, not surprisingly, the terms related to K-pop have emerged frequent keywords among Chilean Internet users.

Given the limited availability of Hallyu content in mainstream Latin American media, it is not surprising that the Internet and social media have been important in Hallyu in this region. The extensive use of social media among Hallyu fans in Latin America is similar with what we found in previous chapter's case study of North American Hallyu. "A friend showed me a K-pop YouTube video"; this is the most common narrative of the interviewees' introductions to K-pop. Additionally, several fans were exposed to K-pop or other Hallyu content as "being accidentally on YouTube." Social media is an effective tool for seeking and sharing information. Juliana, a twenty-two-year-old K-pop fan, stated how her day began with the social mediascape of K-pop: "As soon as I wake up, I check Facebook and Twitter to know what has happened in Korea overnight. Then, I exchange information [about K-pop] with my friends." Spotify and YouTube were popular online platforms for viewing and listening to K-pop, while Twitter and Facebook were intensively used for being connected with other fans and K-pop worlds.

The social mediascape of Hallyu may not only offer a platform for efficient, almost real-time delivery of the content produced overseas into Latin America but also facilitates fans' sociality and participatory culture beyond geographic boundaries. As Hallyu in Chile was a new and niche cultural phenomenon, some fans sought to find other fans with whom they can share content, information, and feelings. As discussed previously, due to limited resources of Hallyu (such as direct Korean-Spanish translation), secondhand translation or retranslation is often inevitable. In this process of secondhand translation, social media platforms help Chilean fans collaboratively retranslate, and "react" to, Hallyu content.

Moreover, the use of a particular social media platform entails a new friendship circle (or a fan network) based on a same cultural taste and efforts for making sense of the foreign cultural texts, often bridging online and offline fans. For example, aforementioned Juliana was in continuous contact with Korean fans whom she met offline by using a particular Korea-based social media app rather than Facebook and Twitter: "K-pop has broadened my circle of friends. I can meet new friends from all over the world that share my hobby. I started KakaoTalk chatting with some Korean friends that I met at a fan meeting." Such use of Korean-made apps for accessing Hallyu content and being connected with stars and other fans illustrates how Hallyu is not simply a transnational flow of content but also a flow of digital technology (see chapters 2 and 3).

The social mediascape of Hallyu among Latin American fans involves various forms of fan activities, which can be referred to as participatory production. As identified in Fiske's (1992) classical work on fan culture, media fans' activities are potentially productive, as fans reappropriate the meanings of the original text (semiotic productivity), share reappropriated meanings with other fans (enunciative productivity), and/or produce fan texts such as fan video (textual productivity). Although Fiske's tripartite schema itself has been criticized for the ideal-type based model's failure to explain the blurred boundaries between the different modes of productivity especially in the digital era (Hills 2013), Fiske's model is still relevant in the social mediascape of Hallyu, in which digital technology's technological affordances contribute to significantly enhancing fans' productive engagement with each other and their fan objects. Indeed, digital technology itself is an integral component of fans' productivity, which is different from mainstream media's official and institutional structure or media production. The social mediascape of Hallyu is a subcultural space in which young people equipped with digital media literacy distinguish themselves from older, mainstream audiences reliant on traditional broadcast media. Alejandra, a twenty-two-year-old fan, noted: "[Since I became a K-pop fan] I developed my Internet searching skills. . . . Today, younger generations were born with the Internet. Babies even listen to music on YouTube. The Internet makes younger generations naturally learn how to see the other worlds from a different perspective."

In understanding the social mediascape of Hallyu in Latin America, it is noteworthy that the fandom has revolved around the particular genre of K-pop, which is effectively integrated with digital technology and social media. K-pop is heavily reliant on social media for its global dissemination (by detouring the mainstream mediascape), but social media's role is not only restricted to content delivery but also integrated with other activities—various forms of appropriating, and participating in, Hallyu. Moreover, media convergence facilitates K-pop's connection with different cultural genres, such as variety shows and TV dramas, in which K-pop idols and their narratives of growing up are used as a key theme of storytelling. Social media and idol culture appear to feed each other and accelerate digital convergence of Hallyu (Jin and Yoon 2016a). K-pop idols as iconic characters and storytellers of Hallyu do not remain as singer/performance but are integrated into various Hallyu genres. Social media platforms allowing transmedia circulation and variation of storytelling substantially reinforce the one-source/multiuse process of idols.

The fans' participation in Hallyu is not limited to the online space, as it often appears in offline space as well. As shown in the previous chapter, the social mediascape is not detached from offline sociality of fans. GAM Cultural Center is one of the most popular places among K-pop fans. Since the October uprising in 2019, K-pop rallies and cover dances appear to be observed more widely across Santiago. In December 2019 Reuters reported, "On Friday, after Santiago residents were called to a 'K-Pop rally' in the city's central Plaza Italia, thousands of people gathered to bang pots and pans and chant anti-government slogans, with a massive deployment of police who moved in to disperse them with water canons and tear gas" (Laing 2019, para 5).

The young Chileans in their late teens and early twenties exercise and play K-pop dances, along with popular K-pop songs of idol groups such as BTS, TWICE, and Super Junior. "I began to listen to SHINee. As soon as I listened to the music, I just wanted to dance," stated Carolina, a twenty-year-old fan. For the young Latin American fans, K-pop was not simply music but performance. For the fans who were interviewed, K-pop was primarily a new breed of happy, dance music. Most young fans not only listened to music but also were "doing" K-pop. This performative dimension of Hallyu appears to enable the young people to "come out" as fans of a subculture on the margin. Maximiliano, a twenty-one-year-old fan, stated: "My friends who cover dance with me—they like me. I am originally from Peru, but I've been living in Chile for more than 10 years. It was impossible for me to make friends in Chile. The cultures in Chile and Peru are very different."

By "doing," the young Chileans, who would otherwise be marginalized, seemed to feel empowered. "K-pop has developed my capacity for expression. I listen to music, dance, and try to find a way to express myself," noted Bianca, a twenty-year-old fan. As recent studies have revealed, the social mediascape of K-pop appears to provide "affinity spaces" among Latin American K-pop fans who "participate in Korean sensibilities based on their personal engagement level with K-pop" (Min et al. 2019, 613). In particular, J. Choi (2014) emphasizes the role of digital technology, such as streaming sites and social media, in emerging transnational intimacy between K-pop and its overseas fans. The young Hallyu fans in Santiago affectively invested themselves in doing K-pop, whereby they seemed to gain "control over their affective life, which further enables them to invest in new forms of meanings, pleasure and identity" (Grossberg 1992, 65).

As discussed in this section, Hallyu might transform the way in which transnational popular culture is disseminated and consumed; digital flows of content, associated with constant senses and practices of participation in social mediascape, allow global audiences to appropriate Hallyu as relatable cultural resources. Hallyu might be one of the first cultural trends that effectively illustrates how transnational social media is integrated with corporeal local space of youth culture.

CONCLUSION

This chapter examined how Hallyu is integrated into young Latin American's everyday lives and discussed the development and contested meanings of Latin American Hallyu with the emphasis on Chile. The young people engaged with Hallyu as an alternative cultural resource through which they seek escape from realities or negotiate the realities. For some young people, Hallyu seemed to be signified as a new breed of their Asian pop cultural repertoire, by which mainstream cultural tastes are questioned, detoured, and/or challenged. However, young Chileans' consumption of Hallyu as Asian content may involve a risk of escapism and probable reproduction of Orientalism. Nevertheless, the process of fan translation from below and ongoing "doing" of Hallyu may allow the young people to feel empowered and to explore their cultural identities.

In the translation and consumption of Hallyu, social media's role was significant. The social mediascape allows young people—those who are relatively underprivileged and subcultural, yet equipped with digital technologies—to be connected to the world by simultaneous detouring of the official cultural sectors and the hegemonic West. In particular, social media-driven K-pop fandom is an evident example of how cultural circulation and consumption can take place outside official or institutional gatekeeping. Furthermore, K-pop's networked fan space in Latin America suggests how culture is translated through the West (in the form of secondhand translation) *and* without the West (detouring or being apart from American reception points).

Hallyu is a cultural resource, which may appeal to some Latin youth who cope with multiple societal contradictions partly due to complex temporalities—such as conflicting coexistence of indigenous culture and rapid neoliberalization (see García Canclini 1995). Hallyu content itself seems to be considered by young Chileans as an (ironic) combination of different genres and temporalities. Among different Hallyu genres, K-pop was the most popular among the interviewees because the genre was considered as a cutting-edge and hypermodern text through which they can "do" and imagine new cultural identities. K-pop fandom seems to constitute the most conspicuous, and also spectacular, audience culture of Hallyu in Chile.

In comparison, other cultural genres of Hallyu—K-dramas and variety shows—are not particularly popular even among Hallyu fans as they might not represent hypermodernity but rather remain somewhat old-fashioned or difficult to translate. For many Hallyu fans, Korean narrative genres were not considered to be closely relatable to their daily lives, as they were "exaggerated," "old-fashioned," or "just funny," while "American dramas are more realistic." Josefina, the aforementioned twenty-five-year old interviewee, pointed out the unrealistic aspects of Korean dramas: "Korean dramas show some reality, such as class struggles, but in unrealistic ways. Even the kiss is fake. In Korean TV dramas, even poor characters have a high-tech cell phone. That makes me laugh a lot."[11] Several interviewees considered Korean dramas as kind of Cinderella stories, being "similar to telenovelas." Moreover, the interviewees pointed out that characters of K-dramas seem to be "emotionally loaded" (similar with telenovelas). In comparison with Korean dramas, K-pop seems to have lower cultural barriers, as it does not require a high level of contextual information, but rather allows the viewers to enjoy choreographic images and rhythm, even without knowing the lyrics and their meanings. By consuming different genres across Hallyu—K-pop, K-dramas, Korean films, and Korean variety shows—young Latin Americans might experience different styles, time zones, and imaginations.

Latin American youth engage in the social mediascape of Hallyu through their participatory culture of secondhand translation. So far, Hallyu's impact on Latin American mainstream cultural markets is rather marginal, as the Hallyu content is not present extensively in mainstream media and public space. However, this does not necessarily mean that Hallyu is detached from mainstream Latin American media and culture. B. Han (2017, 2265) found that K-pop's "transnational subculture on the fringes of Latin American mass culture reluctantly yet slowly gets accommodated into mainstream culture." At this point, it is uncertain how the public reluctance about Hallyu and fans' enthusiasm will reconcile and thus enhance the visibility and intensity of Hallyu as a transnational cultural flow. However, young Chileans' participatory translation of Hallyu reveals how Korean popular culture provides cultural resources for alternative modernity and identity formation.

NOTES

1. Cover dance (or dance cover) is a term that refers to imitation of an original artist's dance choreography. The practice of cover dance has constituted a key component of K-pop fan culture. Fans' cover dances are often video recorded and uploaded on YouTube (Billboard 2011)

2. This number may be compared to that of the globally popular Canadian pop star Justin Bieber's Chile fan club Facebook followers (115,786 as of October 30, 2018) (see https://www.facebook.com/BangtanChile).

3. This female predominance was also evident in Chilean fans. We encountered far more female K-pop fans than men in K-pop cover dancing venues in Santiago during our field study. We also observed more female fans who gathered during the anti-government protests of 2019 and 2020.

4. Considering its sensitive nature, socioeconomic status (SES) questions were not directly asked in interviews; however, the interviewees were asked to indicate their residential areas. Santiago's residential areas tend to be segregated by social class (Seguel and Galilea 2016). In particular, four northeastern *comunas* (neighborhoods) in Santiago are known for upper-middle-class areas due to the residents' high levels of family income and education, clearly distinguished from those in other neighborhoods. Among our interview participants, only one person lived in the area of the four northeastern *comunas*. This demographic composition seems to confirm Min's (2017) observation that K-pop is not particularly known among upper-middle or upper classes in Latin America.

5. Similar to K-pop, Latin pop music has become rapidly popular on a global scale. With the record-breaking popularity of Luis Fonsi, whose *Despacito* music video has been the most viewed video on YouTube (as of March 2020), Latin American pop music has been described as "the most striking example of the 'local becoming global' phenomenon" (IFPI 2018, 23). This Spanish language pop song from the Puerto Rican artist topped the charts in forty-seven countries. Given Luis Fonsi's breakthrough is largely reliant on social media, the phenomenon may be comparable with several K-pop groups' YouTube-driven penetration into global markets. However, while Luis Fonsi is a local artist and his music was recorded in a local language (Spanish), the viral *Despacito* music and video were produced and released by the global giant Universal Music as a part of the company's year-long preparation and plan for global market penetration (IFPI 2018). In comparison, K-pop superstars such as BTS are produced by local (Korean) companies and have gone viral via social media and grassroots fans. Moreover, while Latin pop music's audience base includes a larger number of Hispanophones, K-pop's overseas audience base is primarily non-Korean speakers.

6. Regatieri (2017, 319) introduces a story of a Brazilian young woman to whom she taught Korean. The young women fantasized about Korean *oppa* (i.e., the term literally meaning an older brother but often used to refer to a male star by his female fans) as follows. "After she learned I had spent some time living in Seoul and then moved back to São Paulo, a young female K-pop fan I met at my Korean language class said: 'But why did you come back? If I went to Seoul, I would find myself an *oppa* before even leaving the airport and would never come back.' In this statement, the arrival at the imaginary Korean society goes hand in hand with meeting the idealized *oppa*."

7. Otaku often means Japanese pop culture fans—anime/manga fans in particular, who form a unique subculture dedicated to their fan objects. The Japanese term otaku can be best translated as "nerd" or "geek."

8. While the Gothic group typically means Gothic rock music fan groups, the term is also used to refer to the very enthusiastic fan group of Japanese pop culture in Chile.

9. As exemplified by numerous coming-of-age films, shows, and lyrics, the narrative of growing up is a common theme in popular culture. However, the growing-up narrative seems to be particularly well applied to Hallyu idols, such as BTS, who have dramatically risen up in the global mediascape. Also, this narrative seems appealing to Korean and overseas young people who feel marginalized by their mainstream peer culture. While the growing-up narrative is explored by the fans, stories of growing up are facilitated by the industries, as well. Indeed, Bang Si-Hyuk, the producer and record executive of BTS, pointed out that "growing up" is a key theme and selling point of the group (Newsis 2018).

10. The interview participants tended to distinguish themselves from younger fans who might be a core demographic of K-pop fandom. Josefina described K-pop fans she typically witnessed at K-pop concerts. "Most of the audience was teenage girls, around 12, 13 and 14 years old. I even saw a nine-year-old girl. The girls were yelling, crying and stamping their feet. It was total chaos!"

11. For this interviewee who enjoyed watching Korean dramas, the way actors kiss in K-drama did not seem "real," as did poor characters' use of a high-tech cell phone. This response to K-drama offers an important point about how Hallyu is interpreted and received among its Latin American fan audiences. For several interviewees who were not particularly familiar with Korean culture before, it might be difficult to understand the context of K-dramas. For example, twenty-four-year-old interviewee Pía stated, "American dramas are much easier for me to understand." Moreover, a few interviewees pointed out poor translations as one of the restrictions that interrupts their interests in K-dramas.

Chapter 6

Hallyu as a Total Work of Art in Europe I

INTRODUCTION

Hallyu has gradually been noticed among young people in European cities in the late 2010s and the early 2020s. While its first wave in the 2000s might not have been evident in Europe, its new wave through digital media platforms has undeniably emerged in European youth culture scenes since the 2010s. From Western European countries, including France, the United Kingdom, and Germany, to Eastern European countries, such as Hungary, Yugoslavia, and the Czech Republic, groups of Europeans—young people in particular—enjoy Korean culture like dramas, variety shows, video games, and K-pop. Due to the growth of Hallyu, an increasing number of Europeans learn Korean to enjoy Korean culture and to study Korean politics and society (K. Oh 2011a, 2011b).[1]

Europe is a relative latecomer in the global flow of Hallyu. According to a survey, conducted by the Korea Trade-Investment Promotion Agency (KOTRA 2016), European countries have been identified as locations that show a relatively recent or mediocre development in the global diffusion of Hallyu.[2] Therefore, it would be interesting to question why Hallyu arrived in Europe relatively late and how this wave may have been received in this region. Moreover, how might this wave be different from its counterpart in North America and Latin America?

To answer these questions, this chapter focuses on German Hallyu fan audiences—those who are primarily young, university students. Among European countries, Germany would offer a particularly interesting case for several reasons. Most of all, German cities, such as Berlin and Frankfurt, are known for their vibrant and hybrid youth cultures (e.g., Bennett 1999; Templeton 2006), and thus, German case studies of Hallyu, alongside Spanish case studies in chapter 7, may vividly reveal how a new transnational cultural flow is integrated into European youth culture. Moreover, as American pop culture's influences have been significant in German youth culture especially since World War II (Fluck 2004), Hallyu in Germany may show how the pop culture of a distant, East Asian origin is consumed in relation to the dominant American popular cultural repertoire. In particular, it would be intriguing to explore how Korea, a latercomer in media industries, which has long admired Germany's rapid postwar industrialization and reunification, has recently appealed to young consumers in Germany.[3] Given the lack of existing studies of European audiences of Hallyu, an in-depth analysis of the German context will provide insights to discover what lies beneath the Hallyu phenomenon in Europe.

By closely examining the German landscape of Hallyu, followed by the Spain landscape in chapter 7, we can better understand how Hallyu will further evolve in Europe. With recent growth in immigration, Germany has increasingly become a multiethnic society; approximately 23 percent of the national population has an immigration background as of 2016 (Statistisches Bundesamt 2018). Thus, the case study of Hallyu in Germany would help to anticipate how Korean pop culture would be diffused across different ethnicities and nationalities in Europe. The German young people who participated in interviews for this chapter had various cultural and ethnic backgrounds. Even compared with the interview participants in chapter 4 (North America) and chapter 5 (Latin America), German Hallyu fans recruited and interviewed for this chapter studies were relatively ethnically diverse, as explained in chapter 1.

Drawing on field studies conducted in German cities, here we will discuss how the fans in Germany engage with Hallyu in their everyday lives and how K-pop is signified in German society and among the fans, in relation to other forms of Asian pop culture and fandom. Who are the German Hallyu fans? As Hallyu in Germany (and Europe in general) is a recent and nascent cultural trend, it is difficult to clearly identify the demographic of Hallyu fans in Germany. Drawing on online and offline fan groups and their activities, Fuhr (2014) has provided a rough estimate of the number of German K-pop fans—5,000 K-pop fans, including 2,000 highly dedicated fans. According to this estimation, the interview participants in this chapter include both "active" fans and (less-dedicated) audiences. Interestingly, the German fans who participated in our study were much more multiethnic than North American and Lain American fans; in particular, ethnic minorities constituted more than half of the interview participants. During the interviews, the fans often noted that ethnic minority youth (such as Turkish Germans) constituted dedicated K-pop fan groups in Germany. Interviewees' ethnic background was indicated, when relevant.

UNDERSTANDING HALLYU IN EUROPE

The growing popularity of Korean pop music, films, and dramas in European countries, including Germany, France, and the United Kingdom, shows that Hallyu is making its way to Europe. While small niche audiences for Korean media and pop culture existed in a few European countries in the 2000s, it is in the 2010s that Europeans started to be exposed to various forms of Korean popular culture, from dramas to K-pop, and to animation (Korea Foundation 2017b, 2019). In particular, K-pop has emerged as the most significant cultural content representing the new phase of Hallyu in Europe. BTS's 2020 album *Map of the Soul: 7* massively hit several European countries' music charts, including the United Kingdom, France, Germany, Ireland, and Belgium (J. K. 2020). Given that the United Kingdom, France, and Germany's music markets constitute three of the five world largest national markets (IFPI 2018), K-pop's increasing penetration into the Western European markets is a sign of growing Hallyu in this region.

In Germany, K-pop group 2NE1's song *I Am the Best* ranked top of the famous VIVA Online music charts in 2011. Several other K-pop groups, such as MBLAQ, BEAST, 2PM, Super Junior-M, and Big Bang, also made their way into the top 100 on the same charts. VIVA News reported that K-pop, a new force to be reckoned with in the mainstream music industry, has moved beyond Asia and into Europe (*Chosun Ilbo* 2011). K-pop concerts have also been popular in Germany since 2011, despite the lack of mainstream media attention. Tickets for BTS's 2018 Berlin concert, held at one of Germany's largest arenas, were sold out only in record-breaking nine minutes (Y. Lee 2018a). In response to the rising popularity of K-pop, a Berlin branch of Germany's nationwide music retailer Saturn launched a K-pop section in its branch in 2018 (Y. Lee 2018b). The BTS new album, *Map of the Soul: 7*, has ranked No. 1 on the Offizielle Deutsche Charts, in the week of February 28, which made the group the first Asian pop group to reach No. 1 (J. K. 2020).

Meanwhile, France is known for its vibrant fan base across different Korean pop culture genres (Korea Foundation 2017b; S. K. Hong 2013). Hallyu fandom in France has grown solidly and comprises fans of Korean films, TV dramas, novels, video games, webtoons, and more recently K-pop, as evidenced by highly organized fan clubs such as *Korean Connection* and its regular events on Korean pop culture (S. Sohn 2012; S. K. Hong 2013). K-dramas have also been popular in France, and thus, major TV channels, such as TF1, have aired several K-dramas including *My Love from the Star* and *Dream High* (Ji 2016). In response to the growing visibility of Hallyu fandom in France, several studies have explored how French Hallyu fans are organized and engage with different K-pop genres (Cha and Kim 2011; S. Sohn 2012; S. K. Hong 2013). In particular, France is known for relatively well-organized K-pop fan groups (the estimated number = 34 as of 2017) (Korea Foundation 2017b), as shown in the hundreds of K-pop fans who organized a street rally and flash mob held in May 2011 after ticket sold-out for "SM Town Live World Tour in Paris" in Le Zenith de Paris; the fans asked the organizer (SM Entertainment) to hold an additional concert.

The United Kingdom has also been known for an emerging Hallyu fan base, as the number of K-pop and Hallyu events has visibly increased since 2011 when two K-pop concerts were held; there were three concerts in 2013 and four concerts in 2014 (Um 2014). The Korean newspaper *DongA Ilbo*'s big data analysis reveals that the United Kingdom is the most vibrant European country in terms of Hallyu-related data search online (*DongA Ilbo* 2012). Major news media have also consistently reported and reviewed K-pop as a recognized music genre since early 2011. For example, the British newspaper *The Guardian* has regularly covered K-pop-related news since 2012 when *Gangnam Style* hit the country. While British Hallyu scenes are driven by young people of diverse backgrounds (S. Yoon 2013, 2014), the rising Hallyu phenomenon is, to some extent, facilitated by Korean governments and conglomerates that have continuously sponsored and facilitated the infrastructure of K-pop fandom; for example, the Korean Cultural Centre (KCC) in London has hosted the K-pop Academy, a twelve-week free-of-charge education program for British K-pop fans (Um 2014).[4]

Of course, whereas Western European metropolitan cities, such as Paris, Berlin, and London, have often been reported as major sites of European Hallyu in news media, Hallyu has also emerged in urban locations in Eastern Europe. Recent studies conducted in a few other countries have reported European reception of Hallyu—Austria (Sung 2013, 2014), Bulgaria (Song and Nahm 2016), the Czech Republic (Mazaná 2014), Romania (Marinescu and Balica 2013), and Hungary (S. Yoon 2014). These studies have explored several common characteristics of Hallyu in Europe; Hallyu fandoms revolve around a particular genre (K-pop) and demographic (young female fans of various ethnic backgrounds) and heavily use digital media platforms (YouTube in particular).

Moreover, despite its relatively late arrival and small size, K-pop fan groups in several countries, such as Romania (S. Yoon 2014), are highly organized and solid.[5] Interestingly, studies of European Hallyu show the fan audiences' heterogeneity and flexibility, which might be comparable with the importance of social class in Latin American Hallyu fandom (see chapter 5). Drawing on her French case study, S. K. Hong (2013) suggests that European flows of Korean pop culture are driven by cultural "omnivores" who consume different types of cultural content. Thus, homological connections between cultural capital (such as social class, age, and gender) and cultural texts, which have been supported in subcultural pop culture studies (Clarke 1976), may no longer be valid for explaining European Hallyu fandom. Similarly, in her study of British K-pop fans, S. Yoon (2013) argues that K-pop fans do not necessarily form a resistant youth culture, but rather they engage with the reproduction or reimagination of Westernized styles by consuming Hallyu.

Given the existing studies and media reports, Hallyu seems to have arrived in Europe later than North America and Latin America. Despite the highly praised global spreadability of Hallyu via social media (Jin and Yoon 2016a), Hallyu has not penetrated Europe until recently. In other words, as elsewhere, offline hurdles in the diffusion of Korean pop culture in Europe may be overcome through social media, into which the new phase of Hallyu has increasingly been integrated. However, why is social media-driven Hallyu not spreadable equally across different countries? For a better understanding of the ebbs and flows of Hallyu in Europe, it is necessary to discuss what forces have shaped Hallyu and its fandom in Europe and how fans have negotiated the structural forces.

To examine fan audiences of emerging Hallyu in Europe, field studies were conducted in three urban areas of Germany. While being aware that Europe is not a single entity, we selected national contexts, through which we can examine an emerging cultural trend of Hallyu. For a better comparison with other regions, we chose Germany and Spain (in chapter 7). By examining Germany, we intended to make an effective comparison with the United States, Canada, and Chile. In chapter 7, we chose Spain, another European location, to compare Latin American and European countries that share the same language—Spanish.

CONSUMING A *GESAMTKUNSTWERK*

In Germany, Hallyu is a new breed of youth culture, which can be contrasted with the mainstream German or American cultural forms, and is often consumed in relation to the existing Asian pop cultural repertoire. The uniqueness of Hallyu seems to be its kaleidoscopic and diverse cultural forms and content. Several interviewees referred to it as a *Gesamtkunstwerk* ("total work of art") that is composed of songs, dance, styles, people (idols and fans), narratives, and technologies. The young people engaged with Hallyu primarily in two different yet interwoven processes of meaning making. On the one hand, they consumed particular values and styles of Korean popular culture, which they could not find in the mainstream pop culture genres (e.g., German and American popular music); on the other hand, they consumed cosmopolitan styles associated with particular genres of Hallyu, such as K-pop.

Of the various Hallyu genres, K-pop was the most popular among the fans. However, many interviewees were not interested exclusively in K-pop, as they often navigated different genres (such as variety shows featuring K-pop idols) to explore Hallyu. For the German fans, Hallyu was a *Gesamtkunstwerk* or "universe," comprised of characters (idols), play (performance), narratives (idols telling their stories on variety or TV shows), and values (such as the Confucian norms). While K-pop idols and their performances that are projected on social media initially attracted the young people, social media platforms and networked fan cultures allowed them to explore the universe in which their favorite idols exist. This universe comprises not only music videos but also variety shows, TV dramas, films, video casting, and even TV commercials; thus, again, Hallyu is consumed as transmedia storytelling across platforms and genres. Similar to North and Latin American fans, German fans were introduced to Korean popular culture via social media platforms and peer networks. Moreover, the experience of transnational mobility (such as gap-year travel among young people) affected the transnational cultural flow of Hallyu, as shown in several interviewees' cases.[6] For example, Annika, a twenty-three-year-old fan in Tübingen, was exposed to Hallyu during her stay in Latin America.

> It was 2010. I lived in Ecuador, working as a volunteer. . . . One of my Ecuadorian friends told me that she liked K-pop because she felt as if she could escape to Korea when she listened to it. My experience in Ecuador was sort of strange. Many local people were watching the Korean drama *Boys Over Flowers*. I wanted to know the reason.

As this interviewee revealed, German Hallyu fandom might be influenced by other regions in which this new cultural trend emerged earlier, such as North and Latin America. Thus, in some cases, Hallyu seemed to come from somewhere other than Korea—that is, through fan sites in other countries. This interviewee's experience shows the possible traces of "secondhand translation" or even "thirdhand translation" (from Korea to the United States, from the United States to Latin America, and from Latin America to Europe).

Due to geographic and cultural distance between Korea and Europe, Hallyu in Europe is inevitably highly reliant on mediated experiences. German fans' interests in Hallyu were often ignited by their mediated experiences. While initial exposure to K-pop was triggered by online and/or offline experiences, the young people were "hooked" by not only the music of the genre but also its style, look, and atmosphere. Ben, a twenty-six-year-old fan in Berlin, recalled how his dedication to K-pop began with "a photo of a Korean girl":

> In 2014, I found a photo of a Korean girl on a funny website one day. I didn't know who she was, and afterward, I got to know that she was Jun Hyo-seong, a member of the girl group Secret. I was not interested in their music, but it was a sort of different music for me at that time. I listened to songs in Korean for

the first time. Listening to her song, I suddenly picked up some English words, and I was hooked.

This account illustrates succinctly how visual components (e.g., idols' look), hybrid content (e.g., the incorporation of English into the lyrics), and music are combined in K-pop and become appealing factors for overseas audiences. For the German fans, K-pop was not simply a musical genre; it was also a central sector of Hallyu as a *Gesamtkunstwerk*. "Korean groups change their musical styles every time. Fans are not only fans of the music. German fans love K-pop not only because of the music but also because of [the idols'] recognizable style," stated Ben. According to him, K-pop was compared to German pop music, which is "quite exposed to American pop music" yet lacks diversity. He also lamented, "There is no pop music in Germany. Germans produce only rap and rock music." In his view, the diverse forms of music, performance, and narratives in K-pop were particularly appealing for German Hallyu fans.

Hallyu as a *Gesamtkunstwerk* does not simply mean variety in styles and genres but also includes a universe that is represented by particular values. As the interviews progressed, it became evident that the young people were attracted by the values represented by Hallyu content, which are not found in the mainstream pop culture. For example, as Sophie, a nineteen-year-old fan who pursued Asian Studies at a university, stated, "K-pop doesn't talk about sex and violence like American pop." The young people's accounts of the innocence inscribed in the K-pop narratives may resonate with the existing claims about Hallyu's Confucian ethos, in which collectivity, respect for elders, and abstinence from individual sexuality are encouraged (Kim and Kim 2015). The K-pop idol groups' collective and collaborative performances also appealed to fans, as these are rarely found in current German or American pop music styles. As Ben, the aforementioned university student in Berlin, noted, "There is no boy-group or girl-group culture in Germany. We don't have so-called groups. American music doesn't have groups, either. One uniqueness of K-pop is these groups." According to Lina, a twenty-year-old student of Chinese-Spanish heritage, "One day, my Korean friend showed me a music video of Girls' Generation. I liked it. It was totally different from other pop music. I have never seen such a well-organized pop music group that consisted of so many members." The K-pop fans were intrigued by the collectivism and innocence of K-pop idols, which were contrasted sharply with the norm of the Western pop culture industry's star system, which is based on individual stars' originality, creativity, and attractiveness (Kim and Kim 2015).

The alleged Confucian ethos in K-pop, which seems to differ from the ethos of the American pop music, appeared to be the genre's most appealing factor, especially among ethnic minorities. Charlotte, a twenty-one-year-old Ukrainian-born German woman, noted, "For me, K-pop is the opposite of the American pop music style. I really hate the sexism and violence of American music." According to the interviewees, while German and American pop culture content often portrays individualized lifestyles, K-pop delivers a distinguishing ethos that includes a collective and group-oriented sense of growing up, which is often accompanied by the avoidance of explicit sex and violence codes. As reflected in K-pop idols' collective performance, their acts are perceived by Western fans as soft, happy, and a safe mode of globalization (K. Yoon 2018).

For the young Germans, another appealing aspect of K-pop was its sense of pop-cosmopolitanism (Jenkins 2006b), which enabled the young people to imagine possible lives and identities by engaging with cultural texts that differed from those originating in their own culture. Owing to the high level of genre mixing and the involvement of multinational composers, K-pop has been known for its nonnational or cosmopolitan sound. The interviewees did not clearly identify Koreanness or authentic feelings but, rather, considered this music as a multigenre or hybrid package. This response is not surprising, given the K-pop industry's efforts to "glocalize" its content (see S. M. Lee 2016), as shown in the various cultural backgrounds of the producers and composers of popular K-pop songs. For example, 60 percent of the K-pop songs performed at concerts in London and Paris in 2011 and 2012 were written by composers from America, Sweden, Denmark, Britain, Norway, and other countries outside of Korea (S. Yoon 2013, 142–43).

CONSUMING HYBRIDITY

The pop-cosmopolitanism of K-pop among German fans implies that Hallyu content and style may increasingly supplement, if not replace, the dominant American music, at least in the niche segments of young audiences. For German fans, Hallyu is a cultural trend that cannot be imagined without its American popular cultural influences. However, the visibility of these influences in Hallyu does not mean that Korean content is simply an imitation of its American counterpart. The German fans recognized the hybrid potential of Hallyu, in which alternative cultural meanings emerge. For the Hallyu fans, Korean pop music and dramas in particular were considered to be hybrid resources with which they could bypass or negotiate American pop cultural influences.

During the post–World War II period, American pop culture has been a source of fear due to its hegemonic power; however, it has facilitated the growth of hybrid forms of pop culture that challenge the traditional cultural order and hierarchy of German society (Fluck 2004). In his book *BRAVO Amerika* (1992), German critic Kaspar Maase argued that American pop culture may result in an influx of particular attitudes: (1) the "materialistic" and flexible approach that undermines the "idealistic approach"-oriented German society; (2) equal communication that diminishes the symbolic distance between groups in different power relations; and (3) the new, more relaxed, gender conception that dismantles or replaces the dominant norms of masculinity and femininity (quoted in Fluck 2004, 21). Despite ongoing social concerns about the Americanization of Europe in the neoliberal globalization era, American pop music has significantly influenced the transformation of German youth culture. For example, Richard and Kruger (1998) claimed that the America-influenced rave dance culture has allowed more young women to participate in dance scenes. According to Richard and Kruger's (1998, 165) overview of German youth culture in the 1980s and 1990s, the German pop music scene was "slow to organise and recognise" the significance of new pop music genres, such as raves.

Several of the young interviewees characterized German popular culture by its lack of diversity and openness; however, this view does not necessarily mean that there is celebratory acceptance of American popular culture as a liberatory force. The German Hallyu fans were not particularly fond of American pop culture, which was considered to be no different from the conventional and mainstream cultural form.

The hybrid aspect of Hallyu is often identified in K-pop, among other Hallyu genres. Due to its highly hybrid nature and effective combination of visual and choreographic components, K-pop was seen by interviewees as more diverse than German or American music. However, for the fans, K-pop's hybridity was not a random consequence of mixing different cultural influences but, rather, an outcome of a well-designed production line and highly trained idols who embody the design; that is, the hybridity of K-pop seems to be perceived as manufactured. As Ben, the aforementioned fan in Berlin, described, "K-pop has a different approach to music. K-pop is very systemized. Each member of the group has a specific function." Several interviewees considered the perfectionist efforts often shown by K-pop idols as manufactured, if not manipulated, personalities embodying cultural hybridity.

Lina, the aforementioned twenty-year-old fan, defined K-pop as a pop culture of perfectionism: "American pop music seeks naturality. K-pop seeks perfection." Some critics highlight that K-pop's production system, which seeks perfectionism, reproduces manufactured music products and idols and, thus, does not necessarily offer its audiences liberatory or empowering moments (Epstein and Turnbull 2014). Indeed, while its perfectionism is appealing, several fans expressed their concerns about this "forced" or "manufactured" perfectionism. They were well aware of how K-pop agencies train and control their trainees and idols. Lina lamented that her enthusiasm for K-pop recently decreased when she discovered how the industry functioned: "I almost stopped listening to K-pop since I got to know about the agencies. The idols are under too much pressure. K-pop lacks naturality." K-pop idols and trainees are reportedly under enormous pressure to deliver perfect performances and deal with intense ongoing competition, as evidenced by the tragic suicide of Jonghyun (1990–2017), a member of the five-member idol group SHINee. Referring to this incident, Johanna, a twenty-year-old fan and student with a Greek-German heritage, criticized the perfectionism forced by K-pop agencies.

> The idols are under pressure. For example, one of the SHINee members committed suicide recently. Fans will not judge idols because they are overweight. I would say the imperfection of perfection. They do not need to seek perfection to that extent. When BTS realizes that they cannot go further, one of the members may commit suicide, I think. I like K-pop only because of the music.

This criticism implies that K-pop fans are aware of the commodifying forces that drive the industry. The fans intervene and reimagine the manufactured hybridity of K-pop, and in so doing, they might engage with a new dimension of Hallyu—that is, its user-generated, bottom-up transnationalism, which reflexively questions the media industry's commodifying force on the one hand and attempts to challenge the conventional mainstream popular cultural forms (e.g., German and American pop music) on the other.

K-pop is not the only genre that engages with the hybridity of Hallyu. The German fans' reception of Korean dramas—another popular Hallyu genre that is often embraced along with K-pop—reveals a different way of consuming Hallyu and its hybridity. Similar to Latin American fans of K-dramas, several German fans described K-dramas as a form of pure fantasy that is full of clichés.[7] Johanna, the aforementioned twenty-year-old long-term Hallyu fan, described why the unreality of K-dramas attracted her: "I am a Korean drama fan. Since I developed an interest in Korean culture when I was nine, I've been watching Korean dramas. Korean dramas are typically cliché. Korean dramas are so unreal. German dramas are too related to reality and have so many episodes. I want to relate to unreality." This account resonates with the Chilean fans' comments on Korean dramas. The K-drama as cultural content full of clichés might not necessarily be relatable to overseas (mainstream) viewers. However, the hybrid texts that are composed of fantasies and clichés allow young people who are struggling with coming of age to imaginarily escape from reality. Moreover, while enjoying the excessive clichés in K-dramas, the fans also explore their emotional attachments with the characters and storytelling. Even if for overseas viewers, the characters and content of K-dramas might appear unrealistic on the surface, the young fans seem to find the texts relevant to their daily lives. According to Charlotte, the aforementioned Ukrainian-born German fan,

> I had lots of family problems, and K-pop helped me to escape from those problems. I could forget the problems while watching K-pop music videos and K-dramas. K-dramas opened my eyes and widened my perspectives. I thought that my parents didn't love me. One day, I watched the drama *Reply 1988*. I realized that everybody had problems and that my parents loved me. K-pop and K-drama always motivate me. For example, BTS motivates me to do something. I decided to pursue Korean Studies because of K-pop.

Some media researchers have suggested that transnational cultural texts are consumed actively by local audiences in relation to their particular everyday contexts (e.g., Liebes and Katz 1993).

The German Hallyu fans engage with K-pop and other Korean pop culture genres and, in doing so, may negotiate and play with the manufactured hybridity of Hallyu, which is exemplified in the perfect appearance and choreography of K-pop idols and the excessive bricolage of clichés in K-dramas.

CONSUMING ASIA

As Hallyu is a new cultural form and its place of origin is unfamiliar to Europeans, this cultural trend has had to find its place in the existing cultural schema of German society. Similar to any other new, foreign cultural forms, Hallyu has been signified, filtered, and negotiated by different audiences—for example, mainstream audiences and fans. Not surprisingly, mainstream audiences seem to consume Hallyu in the same way in which Asian (or non-Western) content has been consumed in Germany. In the modern era, Europe has sought its cultural identity by distinguishing it from America as the hegemonic opponent on the one hand and from the non-Western world on the other (S. K. Hong 2013). Popular German media may not be an exception with regard to its reproduction of these two imagined opponents of Europe (Fluck 2004). Korean pop culture has been integrated into the niche market of East Asian culture in the German mediascape.

In comparison, the German Hallyu fans consumed Korean pop culture in the niche market that had been explored for other East Asian cultural products, such as Japanese anime. Similar to the Chilean fans, some German fans were introduced to K-pop through or in relation to their previous interest in Japanese pop culture—anime and manga in particular. Accessing Hallyu in relation to Japanese cultural content was common, especially among longtime K-pop fans. This exposure to Hallyu in the context of consuming Japanese content may not be surprising, given that K-pop was almost invisible, even among young people, in Germany before the *Gangnam Style* phenomenon. Several fans recalled that their interests in anime led them to K-pop. Mari, a twenty-five-year-old fan of Vietnamese descent in Berlin, noted, "I liked Japanese culture a lot before I liked K-pop. I got to know K-pop through Japanese anime. The title song was sung by a Japanese band that collaborated with G-Dragon. It was 2008." Similarly, Emilia, a nineteen-year-old fan of Russian and Ukrainian descent, recalled, "I was searching for Japanese music because I liked Japanese manga and anime. I accidentally watched K-pop music videos on YouTube. They were Big Bang and 2NE1. K-pop was so catchy." According to a few interviewees, the fans of manga, anime, and K-pop tend to get along and collaborate. Anna, a nineteen-year-old member of a K-pop cover dance team, noted, "I got to know them [my K-pop friends] when I was 12 years old. I grew up with them. I met my best friends through K-pop. People who like Japanese manga and anime, as well as K-pop, gather in the park sometimes."

Johanna, the aforementioned twenty-year-old fan, assumed that Japanese music influenced the early K-pop songs: "[The first K-pop songs I listened to] were like Japanese pop music. The group was Orange Caramel, and it had a very Japanese style." Because Japanese anime penetrated the German youth culture a decade earlier than Hallyu, a few interviewees grew up watching popular Japanese animation, such as *Pokémon*. Due to its arrival in German youth culture prior to Hallyu, Japanese pop culture might have contributed to an emerging fan base that is more accepting of other Asian pop cultural content and styles such as those of Hallyu.

The role of Japanese pop culture in Hallyu's arrival in Europe has been examined in several recent studies. In his German case study, Fuhr (2014, 185) stated that "the consumption of Japanese pop goods in the past provided the fertile ground for today's K-pop fandom." This tendency may not be generalizable to all the Hallyu fans who were interviewed in Germany. However, many interviewees confirmed that Japanese pop culture fandom in Germany functioned as a path to Hallyu and K-pop. Exposure to K-pop through Japanese pop culture has been observed in other European countries, including in France (S. K. Hong 2013) and Eastern Europe (S. Yoon 2014). Moreover, some fans in other countries who are addressed in this book pointed out that Japanese pop culture fan bases played a role in paving the way for the rise of K-pop fandom. Interestingly, some K-pop fans were adopting fan activities that were often observed among Japanese pop culture fans (such as costume play) (see Um 2014). Moreover, those fans who were first exposed to Japanese pop culture gradually transitioned and tried to distinguish Korean pop culture from Japanese or any other East Asian pop culture genres. Luisa, a twenty-year-old fan of German-Arabic descent, who used to be an "otaku" according to her own description, stated the following:

I also met many friends through the otaku meeting in Berlin. The otaku meeting is a monthly meeting. The members like Japanese manga and anime as well as K-pop. I also like Japanese manga and anime. I liked them before I got to know K-pop. We talked about Japanese manga and anime and newly released K-pop songs when we met. But I don't go to the otaku meeting anymore. It's too much for me.

Due to several unique characteristics of K-pop, such as its nature as "a total work of art" and the close idol—fan relationship, several dedicated fans distinguished themselves from other types of fans. Such efforts to distinguish themselves from other subculture members are observed among many other subcultural youth; pop music fan cultures are distinguished from each other not only by the music genre they consume but also by particular cultural codes that are learned from fan activities and interactions with other fans within the subculture (Laughey 2006).

To better understand how German fans arrived at Hallyu via Japanese pop culture fandom among German youth, it may be necessary to examine how Asian pop culture has been signified in German society. Similar to the public perception of Hallyu in Latin America, Asian pop culture in Germany has been stereotyped and has remained primarily in niche media markets. Even the Japanese anime genre, which has already been regularly aired on mainstream German TV channels, has not necessarily acquired symbolic capital as a trendy cultural phenomenon. Moreover, some older audience members may still disapprove of Japanese pop culture, although it has been incorporated into German youth culture for a while. Emma, a nineteen-year-old fan in Tübingen, recalled how her interest in anime worried her mother: "My mom thought that something was wrong with me. Every Friday evening, I watched anime on TV. I got into it. My mom took me to a psychologist. But the doctor said I was OK. I could never share my interest with anybody at school." This type of parental concern was not exceptional; many interviewees often encountered worrisome responses to their interests in Korean or Japanese pop culture. Such stereotyping has resulted in negative perception of Asian pop culture fans in general and K-pop fans in particular in German society.

Ignorance of and prejudice against Korean culture in German society were often pointed out in the fans' accounts. Johanna, the aforementioned Greek-German fan who majored in Korean Studies, noted, "Most people confuse 'Korean' with 'Koran.' People think that I study the Koran. After they get to know I study Korean, people wonder why I like Korean culture and pursue Korean Studies at the university." Aforementioned fan Emilia pointed out people's prejudice: "People have prejudice. When they listen to K-pop without knowing that the song is K-pop, they like the song. But after they know that the song is K-pop, they say the song is weird." Thus, some fans do not reveal their penchant for K-pop: "[I] don't tell people that I like K-pop. But their judgment doesn't affect my taste" (Moritz, a twenty-year-old man of Nicaraguan-German heritage).

According to the interviewees, one of the common stereotypes of K-pop and its idols was the feminization of male idols. "My parents told me that I am crazy. They said that K-pop male idols look like girls," noted Luisa, the aforementioned fan of German-Arabic descent. "They say the idols are gay, they are Chinese, you only love Asian people, etcetera," lamented Melissa, a sixteen-year-old fan in Berlin. The peers of several interviewees often associated them with gayness because of the latter's dedication to K-pop idols. Ben, the aforementioned fan in Berlin, stated, "In Germany, male [K-pop] fans are considered gay." The public perception of male K-pop idols and their fans may resonate with the long-standing emasculation or feminization of Asian men in Western media (Ling 1997; S. Jung 2011). S. Jung (2011) argues that K-pop idol boy bands' masculinity is decoded and consumed by overseas audiences in versatile ways; in particular, K-pop idols who perform choreographed dance moves and wear makeup symbolize the soft mode of masculinity, which is relatively scarce in the dominant Western media.

While this "versatile masculinity" (S. Jung 2011) is often considered a "cool" aspect of Hallyu among its fans, mainstream audiences seem to associate this attribute with gayness or a lack of masculinity. The legacy of this racialization and feminization of the Asian body can be traced back to the early colonial period (Said 1978). The stereotyping of Korean idols and K-pop, which was also observed in Latin America, appears even more pervasive in German society. Owing to the pervasive negative stereotypes of K-pop, "liking K-pop can never be considered 'cool,'" lamented Rebecca, a twenty-year-old fan in Frankfurt. Katja, twenty-one-year-old fan in Frankfurt noted, "I dared to come out to my family by telling them that I like K-pop, and they were shocked." The pervasive Orientalist discourse about Hallyu may partly explain why some ethnic minorities (such as Turkish Germans), who might struggle with the dominant racial order, constitute the most dedicated K-pop fan base.

INDIVIDUALIZED FAN CULTURE

Being a fan means developing a particular relationship with not only fan objects (e.g., stars, texts, and merchandise) but also other fans (Duffett 2013; Sandvoss 2005). These relationships enabled the fans to cope with their transition to adulthood. For some, their cultural taste for Korean popular culture provided a moment in which they realized their difference. As Kathryn, a twenty-year-old woman in Berlin, noted, "After I knew K-pop, I became an individual. I feel I am different from others, and my friends consider me as being different." This experience of "becoming an individual" through K-pop indicates the role of pop culture in young fans' identity formation. By choosing to engage in a different cultural taste, the young fans differentiated themselves from others who may be habitually exposed to the dominant cultural tastes and, thus, conform to the existing social order. These young German fans' accounts reveal how the alleged Confucian ethos of K-pop, which is often represented by an emphasis on norms such as collective harmony and work ethics (Kim and Kim 2015), may not necessarily be accepted by overseas audiences but, rather, may be reappropriated for diverse processes of meaning making. The Hallyu fans who were interviewed seemed to appropriate Korean pop cultural forms to distinguish themselves from others and potentially seek alternative ways of transitioning and growing up.

In the process of engaging with K-pop, some fans sought other Hallyu fans or Japanese pop culture fans with whom they could share their cultural tastes and interests. However, there was diversity in their fan activities and preferences, as several fans preferred to enjoy Hallyu individually rather than making any visible efforts to seek out other fans. In comparison, other fans were eager to identify and join fan events and gatherings. For example, while most interviewees agreed that dance was a key component of the global K-pop culture, many did not participate in cover dance scenes. Some fans seemed introverted and quietly dedicated to Korean popular culture and idols. They noted that a lack of interest in doing cover dances might be one of the characteristics that German K-pop fans share. The aforementioned Kathryn stated humorously that "German fans do not cover-dance. Germans are known to be bad dancers." The interview participants, most of whom were university students in their twenties, seemed to distinguish themselves from teenage fans who excessively "follow" the idols on social media, do cover dances, and identify themselves exclusively as K-pop fans. For example, nineteen-year-old Sophie noted, "I just enjoy the music. I'm not interested in the people who organize it. I don't care what the idols do every day. Fan club activity is not a [part of the] German culture. It's enough for me to share my interest with a small group of friends." Similarly, twenty-one-year-old Charlotte stated:

> I see myself as a part of the fandom, but I don't interact with other fans. Most of the fans are younger than me. They think they know everything about Korea. I don't want to connect with them. Liking K-pop is a personal thing to me. I met friends through K-pop. I don't need to share my hobby with everybody.

Moreover, according to the interviewees, few German fan groups were available online or offline. The fans tended to note that "there are not many offline fan meetings in Germany" (Kathryn), which partly explained why

K-pop and Japanese pop culture fans had to meet and/or share their resources (as discussed in the earlier section). According to a recent report, only six Hallyu-related fan groups are active in Germany, which can be contrasted with thirty-four in France (Korea Foundation 2017b). The fans' accounts of the lack of Hallyu fan groups in Germany echo Fuhr's (2014, 144) observation of K-pop fan groups in Germany—as those who are "mostly loosely organized, widely dispersed and decentralized, relatively isolated, and often engaged in very mixed Korea-related activities that go beyond mere K-pop music consumption (i.e., cooking Korean food, watching K-drama, playing games)."

The "loosely organized" Hallyu fandom in Germany implies that media fans are becoming so diverse that they can no longer be easily captured by the concept of subculture. The concept of youth subculture draws on the imagined homological relationship between a cultural form and a particular form of identity (in terms of social markers, such as class, gender, and ethnicity), and it defines subcultural styles as collective symbolic resistance exerted by underprivileged groups of young people (Williams 2011). However, given the increasingly diverse and fragmented nature of late modern society and transnational cultural practices, a group of scholars has proposed the concept of "post-subculture" to confirm that "the once-accepted distinction between 'sub' and 'dominant' culture can no longer be said to hold true" (Chaney 2004, 47). This post-subcultural tendency is not unique to German Hallyu fans, as discussed in the previous chapter on Chilean fans. In comparison with the Chilean fans, the German fans seem to illustrate a relatively individualized mode of cultural consumption.

The young German fans seemed to move beyond subcultural identity and toward the identity of culturally omnivorous networked individuals. This tendency was also shown by North and Latin American fans. The tendency of post-subcultural fandom is observed in fan identity/membership and the use of media for networked individualism. Most of all, the young people's fan identities were by and large individualized. As Kathryn, the aforementioned twenty-year-old fan in Berlin, noted, "German fans are private and individual." German fans appeared to embody the process of individualization, through which young people cope with emerging uncertainty and cultural fragmentation along with imperative personal choices in late modernity (Beck and Beck-Gernsheim 2002). Regardless of their level of dedication to Hallyu and K-pop, many interviewees were "cultural omnivores" (S. K. Hong 2013), who seek and consume different cultural genres. For them, exclusive boundaries between Hallyu and other cultural genres did not seem to necessarily exist. Of course, as Hallyu was generally considered a "total work of art," they seemed to spend an increasing amount of time navigating the virtual world of Hallyu via social media, through which they were able to enjoy different forms of music, narratives, performance, and technologies. Hallyu was a cultural trend that enabled the fans to reflexively choose, engage, and translate.

The individualized consumption of K-pop does not mean that there are no fan interactions. On the contrary, individual fans were involved in various (primarily virtual) networks. Internet-connected smartphones enable some young people, who would otherwise have limited access to cultural resources, to easily access, use, and recreate cultural texts. In particular, social media's integration into the digital mediascape has been a key factor that facilitates networked individualism—that is, networks of individuals, which provide a virtual or real support system and a sense of belonging (Rainie and Wellman 2012). According to twenty-year-old fan Johanna, "K-pop generates a community concept . . . I mean, fandom. Fans don't feel judged by other people when they share their fandom among fans, whether you participate in fandom activity or not. Fans communicate through the Internet."

In addition to the emerging post-subcultural identity, Germany's technological environments may be a factor that accelerated the young people's individualized engagement with Hallyu. Germany has been known for its highly advanced technological infrastructure. In particular, 99 percent of German youth aged eighteen to thirty-four use the Internet, while 92 percent of the youth own a smartphone as of 2015; these rates are significantly higher than those in many other countries (e.g., Chile: 96 percent and 86 percent, respectively) (Poushter 2016). However, the high Internet/smartphone penetration rates do not guarantee the vibrancy of the social mediascape of Hallyu. German youth's social media use is not as pervasive as it is among the youth in some other European and non-European countries. As of 2018, 74 percent of German youth aged eighteen to thirty-four used social media, which is significantly lower than the rates in other Hallyu-receiving countries (Chile: 88 percent, China: 90 percent, United States: 86 percent) (Poushter et al. 2018). It has been suggested that American-oriented social media platforms may not be entirely appealing in the German context, owing to cultural differences, such as language and how human relations are defined (Kraemer 2014).

Moreover, German-specific regulation/gatekeeping on social media may influence the individualization of the social media landscape of German Hallyu fans. Owing to the legal dispute between YouTube and the German copyright holders' association, which is known by the German acronym GEMA, Germans were often blocked from popular music videos and encountered a small red TV icon indicating that the content was unavailable whenever they attempted to access popular music videos on YouTube. Due to the seven-year dispute (2009–2016), German pop music consumers had difficulty enjoying music through the globally dominant free-of-charge platform. According to a study reported in the German newspaper *Süddeutsche Zeitung*, 61.5 percent of the 1,000 most popular YouTube clips were blocked in Germany as of 2013, which was sharply contrasted with 0.9 percent in the United States and 1 percent in Switzerland; indeed, many popular videos, such as the K-pop mega hit *Gangnam Style* and Justin Bieber's videos, were unavailable on YouTube in Germany (Expatica 2013; see also Stade 2014).

This limited accessibility might be one reason that Hallyu arrived in Germany only recently. However, the impact of the dispute on Hallyu in Germany may be open to further debate. Fuhr (2014, 143) estimates that the YouTube dispute had "little impact on the German reception of K-pop" because K-pop fans have explored "ways to circumvent this technical boundary and to access the videos either by using unblocking-software tools or by visiting alternative video platforms, such as Metacafe.com and Vimeo.com." Indeed, the *Gangnam Style* video was nevertheless popular in Germany because of its frequent mainstream media coverage—via news media and radio shows, for example—along with the fact that it was repeatedly played at nightclubs and bars; thus, Hallyu arrived in Germany even without the extensive use of YouTube (Fuhr 2014).

As the YouTube dispute did not block all K-pop content, and media-savvy young people knew how to eventually access the videos, the dispute might not be considerably detrimental to the rise of Hallyu. The interviewees recalled that their access and enjoyment were not interrupted severely by the unavailability of K-pop YouTube video clips, as they increasingly figured out how to circumvent the legal boundaries. Rather than simply preventing the German fans' access to K-pop, the YouTube dispute paradoxically allowed them to develop particular strategies for accessing the videos. As shown in twenty-year-old Isabel's account, several fans were introduced to cover songs (which were apparently unblocked on YouTube and were, thus, available even during the dispute period) and then explored the original songs through alternative streaming sites or YouTube (if available):

> I found a cover song on YouTube. The guy was Korean-American. He and his friends covered "Bad Boy" by Big Bang, and I couldn't stop listening to it. It was 2014 or 2015. Then, I wanted to listen to the original song. I listened to it and fell in love with it. Big Bang's blue hair caught my attention. I searched through other songs that appeared on the suggestion list on YouTube.

According to this fan's account, while on YouTube in 2014 or 2015, she came across a cover of a popular K-pop song that had originally been released in 2012. This two- to three-year time lag might have been partly affected by the YouTube dispute. However, interestingly, she was exposed to the song through a fan-made cover. While YouTube has been a default platform for

K-pop, especially among its overseas fans, the ways in which they use the platform can be influenced by several external factors, such as corporate gatekeeping. Moreover, the fans' practices when it comes to circumventing YouTube might, to some extent, affect the ways in which they interact with cultural content and other fans. The fans did not unanimously engage with YouTube but explored other routes, and they adopted individualized ways of understanding and appropriating the regulated cultural content.

Overall, the young Germans engaged with digitally mediated networked individualism. While the young people individually navigated and consumed the transnational cultural form of Hallyu, they did not abandon the sense of community. Rather, a loosely organized community, which anyone can participate in and relate to, was sought. As Fabienne, a nineteen-year-old fan of Lebanese heritage, noted, "It doesn't matter which fandom you are in; everybody shares the same love of K-pop."

CONCLUSION

Hallyu arrived in some parts of Europe, including Germany, later than in its other major global fan sites, such as the United States and Latin America. While the German fan base may be relatively small, it is growing and reveals a unique cultural landscape. Its geographic and cultural distance from Korea may have delayed the arrival of the waves in Germany. As Latin American fans sometimes retranslate English versions of Hallyu, German fans appeared to initially access it through the process of "secondhand translation." However, as far as our interview participants are concerned, compared with Chilean fans, German fans were much better equipped with English language literacy and the financial resources to make transnational moves to enjoy K-pop live at concerts in Korea or elsewhere. Thus, the German fans could individually access and retranslate English translations of Korean pop culture materials without waiting for German fansubbing.

Young Germans engage with Hallyu by negotiating structural forces—that is, pervasive stereotyping and technological regulation that have influenced the evolution of Hallyu in Germany. In negotiating the structural forces, the fans explored their own strategies. They challenged the pervasive stereotyping of K-pop and its fans while opening up the meanings of Hallyu and being Hallyu fans. By rejecting and criticizing the fixed meanings of Hallyu as a cultural form of the Asian other, which might be drawn from the Orientalist desires of German society, the young people reflexively engaged with diverse facets of Hallyu. Moreover, the difficulty of accessing YouTube videos allowed the fans to explore alternative social media/streaming services and to familiarize themselves with different forms of cover music and dance.

Hallyu fans' activities and identities are diverse and, thus, cannot simply be reduced to a homogeneous subculture. Instead of following a uniform identity as Hallyu fans, the young German interviewees explored individualized fan activities through networked digital technologies and their individual capabilities to navigate the transmedia storytelling of Hallyu. While being deeply immersed in different media forms of Hallyu, the young fans chose and negotiated which aspects of Hallyu to engage with. That is, the German fans considered Hallyu and K-pop to be a *Gesamtkunstwerk* and, thus, found diverse dimensions that can be related to their everyday lives. As Hallyu was a new cultural form, it tended to be integrated into the existing cultural niche of East Asian pop culture. Thus, some fans consumed K-pop in relation to Japanese pop culture, and K-pop and anime fans even shared resources. The ways in which the fans engaged with Hallyu were diverse; some enjoyed personal engagement with K-pop without much affiliation with any types of fan groups, while others were dedicated to cover dancing and clubbing to perform K-pop and to connect with other fans. The diversity within the Hallyu fandom implies the process of the individualization of German youth culture, especially in comparison to its Chilean counterpart. The diverse fan practices and identities, which are accompanied by an increasing tendency toward individualization, also imply that young people in Germany seek an alternative mode of pop culture that contrast with the hegemonic global (American) and national (German) cultures.

NOTES

1. On the surface, underdeveloped Korean communities in Europe (when compared to those in North America in particular) may be an influential factor that might have delayed the deep integration of Hallyu into Europe. Except for Germany and the United Kingdom, where approximately 40,000 Koreans (including students) reside as of 2017, most other European countries have small Koran populations (under 10,000), and thus, Korean ethnic economy and culture remain underdeveloped in Europe (K-Stat 2018). In addition, Europe's geographic, cultural, and economic distance from Korea is a factor that might have decelerated Hallyu in the region. For example, Korea's economic and cultural exchanges with European countries were not as vibrant as its exchanges with Asia-Pacific countries. As of 2018, no European countries are among Korea's top ten international trade partners, which are primarily Asian countries except for the United States (the second) and Mexico (the tenth) (K-Stat 2018).

2. According to the survey (KOTRA 2016), in which sample countries are identified by their level of Hallyu content consumption, European countries are positioned in the phase of "mediocre-popularity and development." In comparison, Latin American countries are identified as being in either a mediocre- or high-popularity phase.

3. Germany has also been known for its influence on Korean modernity. The Korea–German relationship has a long history back to the early twentieth century. During the colonial period, German culture, albeit indirectly, was introduced to Korea through Japanese colonizers and influenced the shaping of Korean modernity (Chun 2018). For a comprehensive discussion of the Korea–German relationship in cultural domains throughout the twentieth century, see Cho and Roberts (2018).

4. As also discussed in chapter 7, this Korean government-supported Hallyu event has been one of the most popular Hallyu events targeting young people, and has been held in several European countries, such as Germany, the United Kingdom, France, Spain, and Belgium, since the early 2010s.

5. S. Yoon (2014) finds that Eastern European Hallyu fan bases are highly organized; especially in Romania, where Hallyu fan clubs are eager to be recognized as nongovernmental organizations (NGOs) by the government and thus to acquire public funding, Hallyu fans tend to be effectively organized.

6. Interestingly, compared to the fans who were interviewed in North and Latin America, the German fans had more overseas experiences, including transnational migration. Five interviewees had been to Korea for Hallyu-related activities, in sharp contrast with the Chilean fans, none of whom had been to Korea.

7. Compared with K-pop, K-dramas are not enjoyed by all the Hallyu fans. Several interviewees were not interested in K-dramas or even disliked the genre, although they were enthusiastic about K-pop. According to those who have a relatively weak interest in K-dramas, the genre was too repetitive and old fashioned in terms of gender stereotypes. For example, Moritz, a twenty-year-old man of Nicaraguan-German heritage, stated, "I watched K-dramas before, but I do not watch them anymore. All the dramas have the same topic. I got tired of the love story between a stupid pretty girl and cute guys."

Chapter 7

Consuming the Contraflow
of K-pop in Europe II

INTRODUCTION

Hallyu has gradually been noticed in Europe since the late 2010s. While the United Kingdom and France are two major countries, several countries, both Western European countries, like Germany and Spain, and Eastern European countries, including Hungary and the Czech Republic, have showed their great interests in Korean popular culture and digital technologies, as briefly discussed in chapter 6. Among these, Spain offers a unique standpoint, as Spanish fans' engagement with K-pop, and the Korean Wave in general, offers an interesting empirical example that enables a better understanding of Hallyu as transnational "contra" cultural flows "originating from the erstwhile peripheries of global media industries" (Thussu 2006, 10). In other words, Spain is a useful example to illustrate how Hallyu spreads beyond zones of geocultural proximity and also be a reception point comparable with many Latin American countries in which Spanish is an offical language. Spain also provides a case that is comparable with its Western European counterpart Germany.

As Vanessa, a nineteen-year-old student in Madrid, Spain, explained during our interview, many teens and early twenties have recently paid attention to the Korean Wave. As a relatively new fan of Korean pop music, she imagines herself to be a future K-pop idol or to at least be able to perform as well as the idols do. She knew little about Korea and its culture; however, she became captivated while listening to a song by EXO, a popular K-pop idol group (2012–present). Vanessa recalled: "One day, I accidentally came across K-pop on YouTube. I thought the K-pop idols sang and danced very well. Among K-pop groups, my favorite is EXO. I went to a couple of K-pop concerts [held in Spain], although they were quite expensive. These days, I go to the K-pop Academy four times a week to learn K-pop dance and stuff."[1]

Vanessa's initiation as a K-pop fan is not exceptional; it was common among Spanish K-pop fans who were interviewed for this chapter in 2018. Many Spanish fans were introduced to K-pop through accidental online encounters, after which they participated physically in K-pop concerts or events. Vanessa and other fans became dedicated to Korean popular culture, which their peers sometimes considered as a *Chinos* (Chinese) commodity (see chapter 5). In so doing, these fans distinguished themselves from others. While seeking a unique self- or group identity through identification with fan objects is common to most types of media fandom (Sandvoss 2005), consuming K-pop in a particular context, such as Spain, in which Asians and their cultures have been homogeneously stereotyped, further complicates the meanings of fan activities.

In particular, as an emerging overseas fan base of the Korean Wave, Spain can be compared with older intra-Asian reception points, on the one hand, and other newer fan bases in the West, on the other.[2] Spanish Hallyu fans may illustrate how this cultural trend is signified and consumed in a context that is geoculturally distant from the place of origin and demonstrate that the wave arrived relatively late. In light of Hallyu's recent arrival and rapid emergence in Spain, it is timely to explore how this transnational cultural flow is negotiated by its early adopters in this different geocultural context. In their analysis of Hallyu fandom in Israel and Palestine, Otmazgin and Lyan examined the roles of early adopters who "are ready to 'take the risk' and be the first consumers of a new cultural genre" (2014, 34). This chapter closely examines how Spanish fans engage with Korean cultural content as a new cultural form. It especially questions how the geocultural difference and distance signified by Hallyu are consumed in the Spanish context, in which Asian cultural forms have been othered and marginalized.

CONTRAFLOW OF HALLYU IN THE WEST

When Korean popular culture emerged primarily in Asian countries leading up to the mid-2000s, the intra-Asian flows of K-dramas and K-pop were examined in terms of cultural proximity (see Straubhaar 1991) emphasizing the content's geolinguistic and cultural similarities with those of its intra-Asian audiences.[3] In comparison with Hallyu in the intra-Asian context, more recent flows of Korean popular culture—K-pop in particular—have been considered by media researchers as an example of the "contraflow" (Thussu 2006) of cultural forms from a non-Western country to Western societies (Jin 2016). Hallyu as a contraflow in Spain raises the question of how and why distant and different cultural content is consumed in countries that do not have geocultural proximity to Korea. However, few academic studies of Hallyu in Spain exist; the exceptions include a few student theses (e.g., Olmedo Señor 2018) and an online survey-based study conducted by Madrid-Morales and Lovric (2015). In this regard, it would be helpful to review how Hallyu has been examined as a contraflow in the Western context.

Several empirical studies examining Hallyu outside Asia as a contraflow have revealed cultural barriers to the Western consumption of Korean popular culture. According to these studies, cultural barriers and distance entail the othering of Korean popular culture as the distant and racialized variant of its Western counterpart. Even the recent rise of K-pop on a global scale may not be free of the racialization of non-Western cultural forms (D. Oh 2017b; E.-Y. Jung 2013; G. Kim 2017; Glynn and Kim 2013; K. Yoon 2019). As illustrated in these studies, the othering of Hallyu (especially K-pop) outside Asia is observed (a) when Korean popular cultural forms are represented in the Western mainstream media and (b) when overseas audiences interpret and engage with Korean popular culture.

Most of all, as evidenced by the U.S. media's coverage of K-pop idol groups, at least until the mid-2010s, Western mainstream media have racially stereotyped Hallyu stars, content, and fans (E.-Y. Jung 2013; G. Kim 2017). According to E.-Y. Jung's (2013) analysis, the K-pop girl groups, such as Wonder Girls and Girls' Generation, were explicitly racialized as sexy and vulnerable Asian women in their media representation in the United States. Jung found that these representations of the K-pop groups conformed to the American audience's racial imaginations, in which Asians are stereotyped as "the perpetual foreigners in the U.S. who 'can't speak English'" (E.-Y. Jung 2013, 116). Interestingly, not only the U.S. media but also K-pop corporations reproduced the stereotypical representation of K-pop for Western markets. G. Kim's (2017) study of K-pop's U.S. market penetration with reference to the representation of Girls' Generation in the U.S. media also addressed how the K-pop industry reproduced and conformed to Western mainstream media's stereotypes of Asian culture. G. Kim (2017, 2379) argued that K-pop is "the product of a systematic value structure that has conditioned Korean society to consider anything American as the most desirable ideal." K-pop's cultural and industrial practices in the recent phase of Hallyu are not free of the Western discourse of the Orient; this can be considered an example of Orientalism (Said 1978). That is, the Western media's representation of Korean popular cultural texts may reproduce lingering Western fantasies through which non-Western cultural forms' exotic differences are consumed and reinforced.

Second, it has been found that Western audiences consume Hallyu as the cultural form of the other. Several studies have explored how Western audiences consume Hallyu as a set of non-Western cultural texts (D. Oh 2017b;

K. Yoon 2019; Mazaná 2014) and illustrate how Korean popular culture is racialized among mainstream audiences in non-Asian countries and partly among Hallyu fans in the region. While mainstream audience members in non-Asian countries are increasingly exposed to Korean popular culture, they tend to disapprove of this new cultural trend; thus, its fans are reportedly marginalized (Mazaná 2014; K. Yoon 2019). The racialization of Hallyu is even noticed among fans. A few studies conducted in North America have examined, at least in part if not entirely, the racialization of K-pop among Western (White) fans. D. Oh (2017b) studied White fans' reactions to K-pop music videos and investigated how the existing racial order and White privilege may be reproduced. He suggested that, compared to other racial groups, "White fans have relatively more power" to "fetishize K-pop or to be dismissive of it" (D. Oh 2017b, 2282). K. Yoon's (2019) ethnographic study also examined Western (White and other racial groups) fans' consumption of K-pop and its implications for the discussion of the racialization of Hallyu in the West; some White fans in his study considered K-pop as an item of "choice" that can be consumed conveniently, whereas fans of Asian heritage interpreted and enjoyed K-pop in relation to their own ethnic identities.

The racialization and marginalization of K-pop in non-Asian contexts have also been reported in a case study of Eastern Europe. In her study of mainstream audiences' response to Hallyu in the Czech Republic, Mazaná (2014) found racist attitudes, in the form of Korean male stars being largely disregarded and stereotyped and Hallyu fans being bullied in public. She concluded, "Racism is rooted in Czech society and the rising popularity of K-pop does not seem to have an impact on changing these attitudes" (Mazaná 2014, 56).

The aforementioned studies show how Hallyu may be othered by mainstream media and audiences in geocultural contexts that are distant from the wave's origin. However, they do not necessarily confirm that Hallyu is always and homogeneously othered. Rather, they acknowledge that different audience groups may engage with Hallyu based on their own perspectives (D. Oh 2017b; K. Yoon 2019) and that media representations of Hallyu are evolving as this cultural wave continues to spread widely. In particular, one group of studies illustrated that dedicated K-pop fans in non-Asian regions consume this cultural form as a signifier of the exotic and racialized other, yet appropriate it positively and as a tool of self-empowerment and the symbolic negotiation of their daily lives (Carranza Ko et al. 2014; B. Han 2017; Min 2017). In those studies, the fans fantasized about the kaleidoscopic world of K-pop as the exotic other of the familiar Western or national popular culture. In so doing, they imagined the "K" in "K-pop" as a signifier of difference and distance. In her study of French fandom of Korean popular culture, S. K. Hong (2013) found that Hallyu did not represent the Orient desired by the

West as the primitive other but, rather, was characterized by ambivalent Western desires as the hybrid, postmodern other. That is, the recurring Orientalist consumption of Hallyu as the other of the West is reinterpreted and questioned, at least in part, by the dedicated fans of this cultural trend.

These existing studies of Hallyu in non-Asian contexts—the Western context in particular—have only partially examined how Korean popular cultural forms are othered; thus, further empirical investigations and theorization of how the otherness of Hallyu is negotiated by overseas audiences are needed. While some critics have suggested that the increasing media coverage and exposure of Hallyu in the West may contribute to toppling Asian stereotypes and racism (S. Lim 2018), there is a lack of academic analysis of how Hallyu is received by its overseas fans in relation to the existing racialization and othering of non-Western culture. In light of the previously mentioned case studies that were conducted in North America, Latin America, and Europe, this chapter addresses Spanish fans' consumption of K-pop. Given that Spain is a new territory of K-pop fan bases, this chapter explores how fans as early adopters of an unknown cultural form are involved with or challenge the consumption of the other.

MEDIA REPRESENTATION OF HALLYU IN SPAIN

Until the mid- to late 2010s, Hallyu was almost invisible in Spain, with the exception of sporadic media attention to K-pop and the activities of a small number of grassroots fans. Reportedly, only six small Korean popular culture fan clubs were active in Spain in 2017, and some of them were not dedicated exclusively to Korean popular culture but, rather, engaged with Asian popular culture more generally (Korea Foundation 2017b). In 2018, when the fieldwork was conducted for this chapter, the Spanish fans confirmed the relatively late arrival of Hallyu in their country, which was also often noted in our interviews with German respondents. The Spanish interviewees pointed out that the Spanish-speaking Latin American countries might have adopted Hallyu earlier and that most of the earlier Spanish language subtitles of Korean dramas and K-pop music videos were, therefore, produced by Latin American rather than Spanish fans.

The Spanish media's representation of Hallyu can be examined by looking at how K-pop was addressed in major national newspapers. Until the late 2010s, the Hallyu discourse was nearly invisible in the Spanish media, with the exception of the short-term attention that was paid to the *Gangnam Style* video and K-pop in the early 2010s. The Spanish media reports on Korean popular cultural stars and texts have continued to be rather sporadic. Even during and since the *Gangnam Style* phenomenon (2012–2018), *El País*,

El Mundo, and *ABC*, three major Spanish broadsheet newspapers, covered K-pop fewer than five times annually, and it was excessively represented by Psy and *Gangnam Style*. The random and irregular coverage of K-pop in the major Spanish newspapers may imply that, until recently, Spain's mainstream audiences have not been exposed to Hallyu.

Until recent rise of BTS and a few other K-pop groups in the late 2010s and the early 2020s, the Spanish media have shown some interest in Korean popular culture. However, media coverage of Hallyu, especially by the aforementioned three newspapers, continues to be rather sporadic. With a few exceptional years (such as 2018), K-pop was addressed fewer than five times per year in each of the three Spanish newspapers between 2012 and 2018. Moreover, many of the articles focused on Psy or the *Gangnam Style* video. Over a third of all the articles published on K-pop in *El País* and *El Mundo* addressed Psy rather than any other K-pop musicians. With the exception of one, all the articles related to K-pop (n = 12) that were published in *El Mundo* between 2012 and 2014 covered Psy and/or *Gangnam Style*. During the seven-year period that was analyzed, no more than thirty-three articles in each newspaper addressed K-pop as their key theme: thirty-three in *El País*, thirty-three in *El Mundo*, and twenty-two in *ABC*. These numbers exclude several articles whose main content did not focus on K-pop despite the inclusion of the term.

Among the three newspapers, *El País* tended to publish relatively in-depth articles on K-pop, while *ABC*'s articles seemed to cover K-pop only briefly. *ABC*'s lack of K-pop news may be explained by the traditional and conservative nature of the newspaper. The news articles related to K-pop that were published in *El País* were articulate in content.[4] However, as noted above, news reporting on K-pop in all three newspapers is rather random and scarce; thus, it is difficult to identify any particular trends. A noticeable trend in recent years might be the visible increase in newspaper articles related to K-pop; approximately one-third of the articles written about K-pop during the period 2012–2018 were published in 2018, which is when international K-pop events occurred: the K-pop concert in Pyongyang that was attended by the North Korean leader Kim Jung Un; the 2018 PyeongChang Olympic Winter Games ceremony, where several K-pop groups performed; and BTS's speech at the United Nations headquarters. Most of the articles in the three newspapers focused on a few famous K-pop stars—Psy and BTS, in particular—and only occasionally addressed other idol groups and stars, such as Jonghyun, the member of SHINee who committed suicide in December 2017.

Overall, while there were occasional celebratory tones in the news coverage of K-pop, some articles included stereotypes that depicted it as a manufactured and commodified form of music. For example, an *El Mundo* article introducing K-pop shortly after the PyeongChang Olympics pointed out the "dark sides" of the music genre, such as its artificial beauty standards and companies' exploitation of its idols and idol trainees (Prieto 2018). Along with a photo of the K-pop girl group Six Bomb, whose members publicized their plastic surgery procedures, another article published in *El Mundo* introduced K-pop and Korea's media industries as the key sectors that reinforce the "culture of plastic surgery in Korea" (Arana 2017). In this report, K-pop groups' beauty standards were presented as an example of the pervasive Korean culture that emphasizes women's appearance and gender inequality.

Due to the overall scarcity of newspaper articles about K-pop, it is difficult to confirm that they systematically reproduce Orientalist tones. It may be fair to state only that K-pop and the Korean Wave remain underrepresented in the major Spanish newspapers. Additionally, the random and irregular coverage of K-pop in the major newspapers may imply that, until recently, Spain's mainstream audiences have had minimal exposure to K-pop and the Korean Wave.[5] Given the lack of mainstream media coverage of the Korean Wave, it is important to explore how the fans feel and think about this new cultural wave. The lived experiences of K-pop fans in Spain may show how the phenomenon is integrated into the Spanish context, in which Asian and, more specifically, Korean culture is stereotyped.

Despite its late arrival, the recent surge of Hallyu in Spain has been noticeable. We are able to observe dedicated fans and their knowledge about different forms of Hallyu content. Since 2019, several major K-pop concerts have been held in Spanish cities. In 2019, a handful of K-pop groups, including Blackpink and Monsta X, performed in Spain. In July 2019, Blackpink successfully held a stadium concert at the Palau Sant Jordi arena in Barcelona; it was the first K-pop group to have ever performed at this stadium, and 10,000 tickets were sold out quickly. Given the announced lineups of 2019–2020 K-pop concerts (Jay Park, GOT7, and Day 6, in addition to the aforementioned Blackpink and Monsta X), Madrid and Barcelona are apparently becoming regular destinations for K-pop groups on world tours.

The emergence of K-pop and its live and online music market in Spain, similar to other receiving locations, occurred as a result of this cultural form's integration into social media. In a recent investigative report, Pitch Tune, a K-pop promoter in Spain, identified social media as the main element influencing the emergence of Hallyu in the country: "The main factor has been, above all, social networks . . . Nowadays, with its immediacy, it is much easier to share, explore, discover what happens in the other part of the world even at the hands of own artists and their companies. It's much easier now to be an international fan than it was before" (Coca 2019).

In response to the social media buzz among K-pop fans, Spanish mainstream media have now begun to pay more detailed attention to this new cultural trend. Illustrating the increasing public attention to K-pop, the major

Spanish daily *ABC* described the enthusiasm and liveliness of the atmosphere at Blackpink's 2019 concert in Barcelona: "Everyone sang (in Korean) as if there was no tomorrow" (Morán 2019). Another daily newspaper, *El Periódico*, described Blackpink's performance as a revelation of "Hurricane K-pop" that "wants to dominate the world" (Freire 2019). Both BTS and Blackpink appeared on Spain's major music charts, such as Los 40 radio station's Top 40 in 2018 and 2019. According to the music-streaming service Spotify, as of 2019, Spain is ranked eighth among the top ten overseas K-pop-streaming markets outside Asia. Spotify-based streaming of K-pop in Spain increased 7.2 times between 2014 and 2018. While the number of K-pop fans has increased gradually since the early 2010s, there has been a noticeable emergence of larger K-pop markets in 2018 and 2019, when several new BTS songs hit the Spanish markets and rose as high as number three.

CONSUMING THE CHINOS

According to the interviewees, a common perception regarding Koreans and Korean culture in Spain can be summarized in association with the term Chinos. Reportedly, ethnic Asians, including Koreans, have been discriminated against and homogenously stereotyped as "Chinese" in public (Rosati 2018). This tendency, which is also widely observed in Latin America, resonates with what Kibria (2003) in her study of Asian Americans refers to as "the racialization of ethnicity," in which Asian Americans were often assumed to be members of "a generalized Asian community" and to have an Asian identity. The lack of a Korean cultural presence and the racialization of ethnicity in Spain—a situation similar with Chile in chapter 5—may be related in part to the small Korean ethnic community in the country. The Korean community in Spain is much smaller than in some other countries with major Hallyu fan bases, such as the United States, Canada, and Mexico; in 2017, only 4,520 ethnic Koreans resided in Spain (Ministry of Foreign Affairs 2017). In addition to the small population of ethnic Koreans, which may have led to a lack of representation of this ethnic group among the public, the recurring racialization of East Asians in Spain may have affected how Koreans and their culture are signified.

For the interviewees, other Spanish people's most common response to their interest in Korean popular culture was derogatory surprise, due to the pervasive association of Korean culture with the term Chinos. As discussed in chapter 5, the literal meaning of "Chinos" is "Chinese" in Spanish. It is not necessarily a term that is used neutrally to refer to a nationality or ethnicity; rather, it is frequently used to racialize Asians. In Spain, the term Chinos is often used to label and stereotype Asians, including Chinese, Korean,

Japanese, and Vietnamese people, and their cultures. In the discourse surrounding the term Chinos, Korea is reduced to a homogenous and essentialized entity of Asia, and prejudice against the Chinos is a common barrier that Spanish K-pop fans encounter. According to Diana, a twenty-seven-year-old young professional, "[When they noticed my interest in K-pop,] my friends said [in a derogatory tone], 'Ah, the Chinos! You like Chinos! How weird!'" Mariana, a thirty-three-year-old fan and tour guide in Madrid, lamented that her dedication to K-pop even caused conflicts with her family members: "I have had serious discussions with my family. My mom doesn't understand why I like the Chinos. She doesn't understand why I want to go to Korea. Now, she asks me, 'When are you going to Korea? Get out of this house.'"

Fans frequently pointed out stereotypical representations of Korean culture and K-pop in the public. Even among their peers, interest in K-pop was considered odd. Gabriela, a twenty-seven-year-old student, stated, "My friends consider me freaky." However, for younger K-pop fans, it seemed that such cultural stigma was gradually being diluted. Significantly, Leticia, a sixteen-year-old fan, commented on the gradual change in her peers' attitudes: "K-pop is a lot more widespread now, and liking K-pop doesn't look as bad as before. Previously, people asked me, 'Why do you listen to K-pop?' [in a derogatory tone]. Now, people ask me, 'What do the lyrics mean? It sounds different' [with a tone of interest]."

According to the fans' accounts, Hallyu in Spain seemed to be stereotyped as an item constituting the racial and cultural repertoire of Asia. The fans were critical of such stereotyping through which different Asian cultural forms were reduced to and associated with the term Chinos as a racialized signifier (Said 1978). The association of Korean popular culture with the term Chinos may reflect the dominant way in which Asian cultural forms are represented and consumed in Spain. That is, the imagination of Asia in Spanish popular media and public discourse has resembled what is referred to as Orientalism—the dominant discourse about non-Western societies, which was observed in the previous chapters; as a discursive system constructed in the West, Orientalism draws on an essentialist myth of the Orient as an inferior, primitive other (Said 1978).

APPROACHING K-POP THROUGH JAPANIMATION

Similar with fans in the previous chapters, Spanish fans of Hallyu acknowledged that Japanese popular culture was deeply incorporated into Spanish youth culture and thus more accepted than its Korean counterpart among young people. This tendency also appeared among Chilean fans, which was addressed in chapter 5. Compared to Japanese animation, K-pop seems to have been a marginal cultural taste in Spain until recently. A few fans noted that the public was more accepting of Japanese popular culture than K-pop. According to Bianca, a twenty-five-year-old fan, "Japanese manga and anime are not considered as weird as K-pop. However, when I tell people I like K-pop, they say, 'So, what is that?' [in a derogatory tone]." The relative acceptance of Japanese animation and its fans in Spain may be due to their decades-long presence. Several Japanese animations, such as *Dragon Ball*, were imported and released on a wide scale in the early 1990s; thus, it is not surprising that the interviewees grew up along with Japanese characters, such as *Pokémon*. Indeed, Spain is known for its early lead in the consumption of Japanese manga and anime in Europe (Malone 2010).

Some Spanish fans' initial encounters with and interests in K-pop were triggered by their earlier interest in Japanese popular culture. For example, Vanessa, the nineteen-year-old fan who was introduced at the beginning of this chapter, recalled, "I liked Japanese manga and anime before I liked K-pop." Several other fans also expressed their previous or ongoing interests in various Asian cultural forms in addition to K-pop. For them, Asian popular media content was a cultural repertoire comprising different genres, stars, and styles, which were, thus, sometimes consumed in relation to each other. Several interviewees had already been longtime fans of Asian popular culture. Bianca stated, "I always liked Asian culture, such as manga and anime."

Mariana noted how different Asian popular cultural forms can be potentially synergetic: "I liked Japanese manga and anime. I found out about Korean dramas through Japanese culture. I also liked Taiwanese manga and dramas. When I found out about Korean dramas, I was hooked. I looked for different versions of dramas that were based on manga. Then, I found K-pop." As this interviewee noted, K-pop is not necessarily a stand-alone cultural form but, rather, is potentially related to other Asian cultural texts. For some interviewees, K-pop represented a relatively recent form of Asian cultural content that may partly replace or supplement other Asian cultural content. This finding resonates with those of S. K. Hong's (2013) France-based study, in which the Hallyu fans' earlier interests in Japanese media led them to Korean TV shows and music videos inserted in Japanese content or recommended by fans of Japanese media.

The Spanish fans' consumption of K-pop as a new addition to their Asian cultural repertoire might resonate with the dominant perspective, in which Asian popular cultural forms are consumed as an imagined and different entity. As Estela, a twenty-year-old university student, noted, "I like K-pop songs because they sound entirely different from Spanish or American songs . . . I always liked Asian culture in general." Likewise, the interviewees tended to consume K-pop as a part of their Asian popular cultural repertoires. In several fans' narratives, K-pop and other Asian popular cultural forms were collectively and categorically distinguished from mainstream Spanish popular culture. K-pop idols were perceived as mysterious yet attractive stars who differed from the familiar Western personalities. For example, Amalia, a thirty-three-year-old photographer and dedicated fan of the K-pop boy band Big Bang, stated, "The four members of Big Bang have an absolutely different style of masculinity. It's *so* cool when male singers apply makeup." For several interviewees, K-pop idols are particularly attractive because they may represent what S. Jung (2011) defines as "soft masculinity," which involves attributes such as tenderness, charisma, purity, and politeness. A few fans described K-pop as more soulful than familiar popular music styles; for Gabriela, a twenty-seven-year-old student, the music of some K-pop artists, including her favorite girl group Mamamoo, is "different from American and Latin American pop music, which is always the same. For example, Mamamoo's songs have a soul. Even compared with other K-pop groups, Mamamoo is less artificial."

The Spanish fans' attraction to the difference signified in K-pop might resemble that of the French K-pop fans in S. K. Hong's study (2013), in which the genre's appeal among the female fans was driven by the male idols' images of enigmatic Asian modernity, which was distinguished from materialistic Western modernity. According to S. K. Hong (2013), this consumption pattern may be a new mode of Orientalism, as it still draws, at least in part, on the homogeneous grouping of Asian cultural content as a mysterious other. Similarly, in her study of Hallyu in the West, S. Jung (2011) noted that "Western audiences fetishize and desire the different and transgressive modern aspects" (138) represented in Korean popular culture.

Such Western desire for the distant other may also be observed in Spanish fans' preference for Korean-language songs over hybrid K-pop songs. Despite the increasing use of English and Spanish in K-pop lyrics, Korean-language K-pop was preferred by most Spanish fans. They did not generally welcome the hybrid of Korean and Spanish lyrics, observable in several recent K-pop songs, although a few fans were tolerant of these lyrics. Diana, the aforementioned twenty-seven-year-old fan, commented on the incorporation of Spanish lyrics into K-pop: "I think K-pop incorporates lyrics in Spanish because there are many Spanish-speaking fans. I think it's OK but weird." Adriana, a twenty-five-year-old fan, was also critical of this linguistic hybrid in K-pop, stating, "The lyrics in English or Spanish make me nervous. They sound strange to me. I don't even understand the K-pop lyrics written in Spanish." For Gabriella, the aforementioned fan a "real" K-pop group would have "no lyrics in English or Spanish" in its songs.

The Spanish fans consumed Korean popular culture as the enigmatic other, rather than as a cultural form that can be easily incorporated into and hybridized with the Spanish culture. The fans seemed to consume the distance and difference signified in Korean popular cultural content to distinguish themselves from their peers, who were widely exposed to mainstream Spanish or Western cultural forms.

REIMAGINING THE OTHER

While the Orientalist consumption of exotic otherness was observed among the Spanish fans who fantasized about Korean popular culture as an expansion of their Asian repertoires, this tendency seemed to be eroded by some fans' reflexive engagements with Hallyu. Thus, the fans' appropriation of the difference signified in Korean popular culture was not simply to fetishize the exotic and primitive otherness. The fans challenged, at least to a limited extent, the essentialized otherness constructed through the Orientalist discourse of Hallyu as a "Chinos" commodity. They attempted to avoid an essentialist definition of Korean popular culture while differentiating themselves from mainstream audiences, who primarily perceived Hallyu as the essentialized other. Korean popular culture, K-pop in particular, was an alternative cultural resource that enabled escape from and negotiation of the dominant social order, as shown among Latin American fans (Carranza Ko et al. 2014; see also chapter 5). In so doing, Spanish fans rethought their local contexts and sought personal growth through their engagement with Hallyu. Moreover, several interviewees consumed K-pop and Korean TV shows as a way to engage in intercultural learning while distinguishing themselves from those who fetishize Asian culture. The difference inscribed in Korean popular culture was not only essentialized but also utilized as a versatile resource. The fans engaged with Hallyu by challenging the stereotyping of Korean popular culture in several different ways.

To begin with, some interviewees questioned any attempts to reduce the diversity of K-pop to one or a few representative idols and their songs. For the fans, K-pop was not a homogeneous entity but, rather, evolved in diverse ways, depending on the characteristics of the idols and their fans. As Mamamoo fan Gabriela noted, there are different styles of K-pop, thus generating diverse fan–idol relationships and worlds. She also lamented that K-pop was often represented by a few major groups, such as BTS: "BTS? I don't like the groups with mega popularity. BTS doesn't touch my heart as much as Mamamoo." Francisca, a twenty-three-year-old fan, emphasized that K-pop extended far beyond a few internationally known groups, such as BTS. She seemed to believe that K-pop is standardized and is being rapidly incorporated into mainstream music markets; she, thus, was not simply in support of K-pop's global fame. She noted: "I am afraid that recent K-pop songs lost the personality. I liked BTS when they debuted. But now, all the BTS songs sound similar. I am getting tired of people talking about BTS all the time."

Most interviewees appreciated the diversity of K-pop, as they were skeptical about the Western media's coverage of K-pop as a homogeneous genre of Korean popular music. Whereas several empirical studies on K-pop have described Western K-pop fans as those who are dedicated to K-pop as a clearly demarcated genre and style (e.g., H. Jung 2017), some interviewees were skeptical of this categorization. The fans seemed to have their own K-pop universe. Camila, a nineteen-year-old fan in Madrid, stated succinctly, "Others never understand why I like K-pop. I just like it." The "it" does not necessarily mean K-pop in a collective sense; rather, it refers to particular K-pop idols and their music.

Second, the fans seemed to distance themselves from those who consumed exotic otherness through Korean popular culture. While consuming the difference signified in Hallyu, the Spanish fans challenged the superficial understanding of this cultural form as a new and different consumable. Several longtime fans seemed to have in-depth knowledge of the context of Korean popular culture, including the K-pop idol system. In other words, they were keenly aware of the intercultural context in which Korean popular culture is produced and circulated. For these fans, being a Hallyu fan meant understanding the intercultural context without being simply fascinated by the content or stars. Leticia, the aforementioned sixteen-year-old fan, critically distinguished herself from other "simpleminded" fans: "Those fans would like to visit Korea only because they want to meet their favorite idols. However, those fans do not know much about Korea." This respondent, who had been enthusiastic about K-pop for about three years, was learning the Korean language to enable her to better understand the context of K-pop and Korean society. Mariana, the abovementioned longtime, thirty-three-year-old fan, critically observed some Spanish fans who were hyperactive and "too expressive" online. According to her, they were novices rather than genuine fans: "Most of the SNS of [Hallyu] fan clubs show something 'kawaii (cute).' They are very otaku.[6] Those kinds of people are beginners." Mariana, who identified herself as a mature and "truly dedicated" fan, compared those novice Hallyu fans who were "excessively" attached to their fan objects with the stereotypes of Asian popular culture fans in Spain and elsewhere. For her, the novice fans may consume Korean popular culture as a set of materials from the imagined Orient. Similarly, several other interviewees appeared to distance themselves from those novice fans who, albeit positively, stereotyped Hallyu as the other of their own culture, through which the meaning of Korean popular culture was essentialized as a component of exotic Asian culture. Twenty-three-year-old Francisca contrasted younger and older fans: "New teenage fans like K-pop to be different from other young people because K-pop is different from American or Spanish pop songs. Fans in their twenties and older have an interest in learning the language and culture, not only limited to the enjoyment of the music." In this manner, the interviewees tended to critically endorse their favorite Korean stars to avoid being deemed simpleminded fans—that is, those who, in their view, excessively expressed their cultural tastes and irritated other fans.

Third, for the Spanish fans, difference signified in Hallyu appeared to offer a means of reengaging with the local context and imagining an alternative future. This engagement resonated with the way in which Chilean and German fans appropriated Korean popular culture.

For example, K-pop's universe appeared to be imagined as a virtual space that is sharply contrasted with their locale. By consuming K-pop, the fans projected themselves into a distant temporal and spatial setting. K-pop's geocultural distance (from Spain) functions as an imaginary space into which the Spanish fans project their futures and desires. The cultural differences and distance signified in Hallyu seemed to allow the Spanish fans (especially the young ones) to fantasize about possible lives. In particular, K-pop appeared to represent an alternative future, which they could not imagine in Spanish society. The difference implied in K-pop seemed to offer the fans an alternative resource that extends beyond what is absent from mainstream cultural content. Isidora, a Madrid-based forty-four-year-old fan who was the oldest among all research participants interviewed for this book, emphasized that K-pop is a youthful cultural item: "K-pop is popular for young people because young people always look for something different from what is normal. Young people also know how to access such stuff through the Internet." For Isidora, being a K-pop fan might be the symbolic pursuit of cultural taste beyond the conventional, thus distinguishing her from other middle-aged people. According to a few fans who were especially interested in the lyrics, K-pop "addresses delicate social issues," such as the social class conflicts, whereas "Spanish songs always talk about the same thing—love (Estela, the aforementioned university student)."

Consequently, the fans often considered K-pop an alternative to the conventional mainstream culture and social order. For the interviewees, Spain was often described as a conventional and inflexible society. By pointing out the closed and conservative nature of Spanish society in regard to its acceptance of other cultures, thirty-three-year-old Mariana lamented, "There is no future in Spain." In this manner, by consuming the distant cultural item, the Spanish fans symbolically escaped the restrictive forces that they faced in their everyday contexts. These findings can be compared with those of Latin American case studies of K-pop fans (Carranza Ko et al. 2014; B. Han 2017). The Spanish fans' engagements with Hallyu not only involved the consumption of the essentialized, backward-looking Orient but also the potential versatility of the new cultural form.

Fourth, the Spanish fans sought personal growth through their engagement with Hallyu—especially the K-pop idols' universe. In particular, the fans were inspired by K-pop idols' work ethic and shared a sense of growing up with the idols and other fans. The interviewees often expressed their gratitude to their K-pop idols, who "work so hard—much harder than singers in Spain or the USA" (Estela, the aforementioned university student). The K-pop idols' work ethic was highly regarded by overseas fans, who were motivated by the idols' pursuit of "perfect" choreographies. Consequently, despite the public stereotypes of Korean popular culture, the Spanish fans considered their K-pop idols as role models. Twenty-three-year-old Francisca stated, "(If I could meet my favorite K-pop idols), I would say 'Thank you.'" While consuming the youthful images of K-pop, individual fans appeared to be touched by their idols' performances, characters, and effort. In so doing, they seemed to participate in the K-pop idols' narrative of self-development (K. Yoon 2019). Several K-pop idols, who made their debuts in their teens and underwent lengthy and difficult training, have effectively developed their identities, drawing on storytelling about "growing up" (Y. Park 2017). This sense of growing up was enhanced by the fans' imaginary attachments to K-pop idols beyond racial, linguistic, and cultural borders. Social media postings and webcasts covering the everyday lives of K-pop idols contributed to enhancing the transcultural affinities between the idols and their overseas fans, who are geoculturally distant from each other: "K-pop idols or their agencies offer a great deal of information about them. I like that. I know that Monsta X eats bacon every morning (laughs). I feel closer to them" (Diana, a twenty-seven-year-old fan and documentarist). The fans' identification with and love of K-pop idols offered them motivation and fulfillment. "I feel happier since being immersed in this universe. K-pop has definitely made me happier," stated Gabriela, the aforementioned twenty-seven-year-old fan who began learning the Korean language to enable her to better understand the K-pop universe.

The Spanish fans avoided simply consuming the exotic otherness of Korean popular culture in several different ways, while challenging the association of Hallyu with the term Chinos. Instead, they engaged with Hallyu as a way of rethinking their local contexts, imagining an alternative future, seeking personal growth, and exploring intercultural understanding. They attempted not to fetishize Hallyu as a signifier of the Orient or "Chinos." By negotiating the pervasive stereotyping of Korean popular culture as the culture of the "Chinos," these fans might engage in intercultural learning.

CONCLUSION

This chapter has examined how the difference signified in Hallyu is consumed and negotiated. Until recently, Hallyu has remained underrepresented in Spain. The fans, especially those who constitute an older group, recalled the cultural stigma associated with K-pop and K-dramas. Indeed, Hallyu fans in Spain had to cope with pervasive prejudices about the "Chinos," in which Korean popular culture was essentialized as a cultural form of the unknown other. By expressing their cultural taste for K-pop and other Korean popular cultural forms, the fans were stereotyped by their peers and families as enthusiasts of "Chinos culture." While the symbolic values of Korean popular culture were not recognized in Spanish society, the fans dedicated themselves to the cultural form and its universe. Their interests in this cultural form were often triggered by their previous interests in other Asian popular cultural forms, which were often contrasted with mainstream Spanish culture. The fans who had already enjoyed consuming the cultural differences signified in Asian popular cultural forms became interested in Hallyu. This practice of consuming Hallyu as a new component of their Asian repertoire may be partly indicative of the Orientalist consumption of the exotic other.

In response to the dominant consumption of Korean popular culture, in which its exotic otherness as a component of an imagined Asian repertoire is conveniently consumed, the fans seemed to explore new ways of consuming the "Chinos." That is, they questioned the pervasive association of Hallyu with the term Chinos and appropriated Korean popular culture as a means to imagine alternative possible lives. They appropriated Hallyu as a cultural resource for rethinking their local contexts, seeking personal growth. This fan appropriation of Korean popular culture in Spain may be similar with what we found among Chilean and German fans; that is, Hallyu seemed to offer the overseas young people "an alternative space of global cultural imagination that is not rooted in between the West and the East" (Min et al. 2019, 615). As early adopters of the new cultural trend of Hallyu, the Spanish fans seemed unafraid of the different language and the geocultural distance signified in this set of cultural texts. Sixteen-year-old Leticia, the youngest interviewee, described succinctly how Korean popular culture offered its overseas fans the moments of transcending cultural distance by providing a new way of enjoying the music of a distant geocultural context. She stated, "The way people listen to music has changed. K-pop taught me that it doesn't matter what language the music is in or what style of music it is. One can still enjoy the music."

The consumption of difference is a particularly important issue in analyzing contra-cultural flows, such as K-pop in Spain. The fans constantly question the dominant construction of Korean popular culture, involving stereotyping, while appropriating and reinterpreting this new cultural form. The practices of othering Hallyu in Spain, such as racialization, may not disappear completely in the near future. However, the fans may reinterpret the cultural difference associated with Korean popular culture, and in so doing, the dominant construction of Hallyu may be challenged and revised. For example, the racial implications of Hallyu may not be eradicated but reformed and resignified. The consumption of non-Western contraflows may reveal how cultural differences, such as race, are contingent constructs and thus likely to be reconstructed (Pitcher 2014). The Spanish fans as a group of early adopters question and attempt to move away from the Orientalist consumption of Hallyu as the essentialized, non-Western other. As discussed in this chapter, consuming Korean popular culture involves the ongoing negotiation of otherness. The contra-cultural flow of Hallyu reveals how difference, such as race, in popular culture is consumed, imagined, and incorporated into our everyday lives.

NOTES

1. As introduced in chapter 6, the K-pop Academy is an education program organized by the Korean Cultural Center, an affiliate of the Korean Ministry of Culture, Sports, and Tourism. As of 2019, the event is held regularly at twenty-five locations worldwide, including Madrid. The one-month program offers lessons on K-pop dancing and singing, as well as Korean culture (Kim and Lee 2019).

2. While Spain is often categorized as the West in the framework of the West versus the Rest, the country was defined as being "an edge of Europe" (McSweeney and Hopkins 2017, 3) and even an "Oriental" space, due to several factors such as its historical relations to Islam; that is, the country colonized and objectified some non-Western territories especially in Latin America and their cultures, yet was Orientalized by other Western Europeans. Thus, McSweeney and Hopkins (2017) argue that Spain assumed a paradoxical, "double position," in which it has been both subject and object of the Orientalist gaze. However, despite Spain's ambivalent position in Europe, the country's public imagination of Asia has not differed substantially from other Western countries' othering of non-Western cultures (McSweeney and Hopkins 2017; Prado-Fonts 2018).

3. This cultural proximity did not necessarily relate to essentialized cultural norms, such as Confucianism, but included similar experiences with regard to modernization (Chua and Iwabuchi 2008; Iwabuchi 2002). Moreover, the way in which cultural proximity operates in Asia might be diverse, depending on several factors, such as genres and audience groups: Korean dramas tend to revolve around family norms, which might be shared among intra-Asian audiences, while K-pop has engaged with the trans-Asian urban youth culture (Chua 2012).

4. This can be explained by *El País*'s target audience and the global nature of its journalists and contributors. *El País* has published an English edition since 2001 and reaches a wide global audience. It is known as the most international Spain-based newspaper, as its English edition can be accessed via the websites of several international newspapers, such as the *International Herald Tribune*. Moreover, the readership of the Spanish edition is not limited to Spain but extends to a wide range of Latin American countries. The newspaper also includes news reporting and translated columns written by international journalists. The relatively frequent and detailed

coverage of K-pop in *El País* may, to some extent, target not only readers in Spain but also those in Latin America, where K-pop has rapidly gained popularity.

5. Given that the mainstream, broadsheet newspapers targeting general audiences may not often cover niche cultural tastes, such as K-pop, more popular news and media outlets, such as tabloid newspapers and TV talk show programs, may overtly reveal Orientalist perspectives on K-pop. For example, in an episode of the Spanish TV talk show *El Hormiguero*, aired on Antena 3 (a terrestrial Spanish channel) in July 2013, famous fashion designer Vicky Martín Berrocal discussed her experience at a fashion event in Hong Kong, where she met Siwon Choi, a member of the K-pop group Super Junior. Martín Berrocal and the show's host repeatedly referred to Siwon as "El Chino (a Chinese man)," comically describing how this "Chino" had attempted to flirt with her at the event. As discussed in Spanish K-pop fan forums later, this show seemed to make fun of the K-pop idol and to stereotype him as a Chinese man. This episode may not be an isolated episode but, rather, a typical example of the stereotyping of K-pop and Koreans in Spanish society.

6. In this quotation, the interviewee seemed to refer to the novice Hallyu fans as "otaku" to emphasize their obsession and excessiveness in fan activities. The term otaku also appeared in our interviews with Chilean and German fans, as discussed in chapters 5 and 6. In Chile, Germany, and Spain, the connotation of otaku did not seem very different. The term otaku often involved the meaning of negative, obsessive fan activities. However, some fans also acknowledged a particular role of otaku practices in youth culture. That is, while otaku tends to be regarded negatively because of his/her antisocial attitudes, some argues certain otaku subcultures can contribute to collective social actions (Sone 2014).

Chapter 8

Conclusion: Gained in Translation

INTRODUCTION

During the same week in September 2019, two different programs on the American Broadcasting Company (ABC), an American network channel, illustrated somewhat different perspectives on the rise of Korean popular culture. One program, *Good Morning America* (GMA), one of the major morning news shows in the United States, invited BTS to the show and designated September 26 "BTS Day" on GMA. The main GMA anchor introduced BTS as the largest boy band in the world. Meanwhile, on September 25, Kendis Gibson, a male anchor of another ABC program, *New World News Now*, showed his disrespect for BTS by saying that they were "a bunch of boy bands from Korea." Although the female anchor next to him stated that BTS's speech at the United Nations during the same week had been excellent, he continued to claim, "It's a boy band from Korea," finally stating, "They've got choreographed dance moves" in an apparent effort to reduce BTS to a manufactured boy band rather than creators/artists/role models. These unparalleled perspectives on Hallyu arguably reveal an existing gap between the fandom (in the case of GMA's coverage of BTS) and the public reception of Hallyu (in the case of *New World News Now*).

These anecdotes may explain the different attitudes in global audiences' and media's responses to Hallyu. Our observation and interviews, which were conducted in different locations outside of Asia between 2014 and 2020, reveal that overseas mainstream audiences, who are situated outside of the solid Hallyu fan base, have not yet been widely exposed to Korean digital and popular culture. While a few K-pop groups' remarkable global hit records have helped to direct public attention toward Hallyu in several countries, there may still be a significant discrepancy between enthusiastic fans and general audiences in regard to their awareness and reception of Korean culture. Nevertheless, while approaching the completion of this book in 2020, we have noticed the further dissemination of Korean popular culture in various locations, including those in which we conducted field studies. In interviews, newer Hallyu fans have noted that a wider range of people—that is, teens to sixties—are exposed to K-pop, K-dramas, and K-films. In this book, we focused on Hallyu fans, but we observed and/or heard about diverse audience groups who were not explicitly dedicated fans but nonetheless regularly accessed Korean popular cultural content via social media platforms or streaming services. This cultural wave that emerged from a non-Western country that had a small and insignificant media industry until the 1990s illustrates how cultural globalization is diversified. Based on our field studies and structural analyses, we argue that Hallyu has opened the door not only to Asian audiences but also to an extensive range of transnational audiences, exercising transnationalism at the macro and microlevels.

A MACRO- AND MICROLEVEL ANALYSIS
OF THE KOREAN WAVE

This book has examined how Hallyu has evolved as a transnational and digital wave. The structural analysis herein has explored how the interplay between Korean cultural industries, governments, and IT sectors paved the way for Hallyu. The book's audience studies section has addressed how overseas fans engage with different forms of Hallyu content and practice. On the one hand, we have conducted a macrolevel, structural analysis of the political economy and history behind the transnational rise of Korean popular culture by examining the development of Korea's cultural industries and policies, as well as its media infrastructure. On the other hand, drawing on in-depth interviews with overseas Hallyu fans in five different locations—the United States, Canada, Chile, Spain, and Germany in three continents—we have closely analyzed how these fans consume K-pop, K-dramas, and other Hallyu content. This structural analysis has illustrated that Hallyu is an ongoing process through which neoliberal capitalism is articulated with national, cultural and technological infrastructure.

Our historicization of Hallyu shows that this cultural trend did not emerge suddenly; rather, there were foundational moments, which are referred to in this book as the "seed phase of Hallyu." It is ironic that the term Hallyu began to be used and became popularized overseas, especially in 1997 and 1998, when Korea underwent a devastating economic crisis, which was followed by the International Monetary Fund's (IMF's) bailout and neoliberal restructuring. Moreover, it is intriguing that the media infrastructure for digital Hallyu was also established during the postcrisis era. The Korean cultural industries have expanded their transnational markets and enhanced the hybrid aspects of cultural content for overseas audiences during this postcrisis period. Despite the economic and social turmoil, the IMF crisis seemed to force the Korean government and media/entertainment industries to develop survival strategies—exportation of digital and popular culture products. Globally targeted cultural sectors that produce highly value-added content products have emerged since the financial crisis. The cultural industry benefits from government policies and from the efforts of the IT industry, which has diligently pursued global market penetration. Transnational market exploration and digital integration have been major strategies that Korea's cultural industries have used to respond to the rapid forces of global capitalism since the mid-1990s.

As our political economic analysis of Hallyu has revealed, the Korean cultural industries' responses and growth during the post-IMF period have, however, increased the commodification of culture: cultural content is incorporated into the highly systemized management and industrial system, and user experiences are extensively monetized (Hjorth 2011). Hallyu's extensive and intensive integration into the social media environment suggests that contraflows can benefit from or take advantage of new digital media platforms. However, as shown in failed attempts at global diffusion of the domestically popular Cyworld and its user culture, local digital platforms may encounter structural barriers in the global mediascape, in which global mega-players, such as Google (YouTube) and Facebook, maintain and increase their global domination.

Contemporary Hallyu (the "New Korean Wave") has increasingly witnessed the swift growth of Western platforms as major international distributors of Korean media content. The content and practices of Hallyu, such as K-pop music videos, fans' reaction videos, and idol–fan interactions on Twitter, have increasingly been incorporated into globally popular social media platforms owned by global media corporations (Fuchs 2014). This platform ecology implies that local cultural industries are not always able to control the dissemination of their popular culture (Fuchs 2014) as American-based digital platforms, such as Netflix, YouTube, and Facebook, take on a key role in the circulation of local popular culture. The digital wave of Hallyu does not simply project a participatory mediascape in which media users are empowered and become creative audiences. Despite the creative potential of grassroots media convergence and user-generated content/culture observed among transnational Hallyu fans, ongoing structural forces restrict the capabilities of Hallyu fans and audiences. Digital and social media help to explore users' socialities, which are exploited to generate profit. In this endless loop of "free labor" in the social mediascape, users often unknowingly produce attention, networks, data, and content (de Kosnik 2012; Fuchs 2014).

In addition to the structural conditions and forces of Hallyu, this book has examined how audiences make sense of and engage with Hallyu. Transnational Hallyu fans appropriate Korean popular culture as an alternative cultural resource that is distinguished from the mainstream media—national and/ or American media. Audiences in Europe and the Americas found this difference signified in Hallyu as a unique cultural resource. For the fans, Hallyu's geocultural distance seemed to be overcome by their emotional engagement with the universe of K-pop idols via social media. The cultural and linguistic distance and difference signified by Hallyu in overseas contexts ironically provided overseas fans with room for interpretation of and participation in this new cultural trend. The fans shared and accumulated their fan knowledge and user-created content, transcending the conventional gatekeeping carried out by media institutions. In response to the lack of official translations of the increasing Korean content, the fans participated in translating, interpreting, and sharing it via social media platforms. In this process, they relied extensively on commodified platforms, such as YouTube, which exploit fans' "free labor" (de Kosnik 2012).

Moreover, the fans' extensive use of YouTube and other social media platforms may sometimes violate copyrights and thus adversely affect digital media ecology to some extent. The Hallyu fandom reveals how the social media-driven participatory culture facilitates the translation and diffusion of foreign cultural forms and how contraflows allow for cultural circulation that may not necessarily be filtered and controlled by the global media center but move beyond the center/periphery binarism. That is, while the fans appropriate the major social media platforms, most of which are owned and maintained by American-based multinational corporations, they often question the American-dominated mediascape and the racialization of Hallyu, which are observed in the mainstream media in overseas countries.

Our audience studies show differences and similarities in the reception and negotiation of this new cultural trend of Hallyu. In the United States and Canada, where Hallyu emerged relatively early via the well-equipped social media infrastructure and the Asian diaspora (Yoon and Jin 2016), the interviewees vividly recalled and discussed how Hallyu has evolved, especially among young people. North American Hallyu fans might have taken advantage of the rapid rise of social media and accelerated the global circulation of K-pop, K-dramas, and other Hallyu genres. However, as evidenced by the Korean film *Parasite*'s recent winning of four Academy Awards, Hallyu in North America is not simply driven by social media; it also benefits from the conventional mainstream media. In the final phase of our field studies, we noticed that an increasing number of Hallyu fans were "coming out" and identifying themselves as enthusiasts of K-pop, K-drama, and/or other local cultural forms; this cultural wave in North America seems to be gradually incorporated into the youth culture scenes and the general public after the initial phase of racialization and stigmatization.

In Chile in Latin America, where social inequality has rapidly been exacerbated over the past few decades, K-pop appeared to attract young people of primarily underprivileged backgrounds. The Chilean fans whom we observed and interviewed were keenly interested in K-pop's choreography and thus easily transcended the linguistic difference inherent in K-pop. K-pop fandom was frequently expressed through bodily practices. While K-pop and other genres of Korean popular culture constituted a subcultural form, the Chilean fans gathered to dance and/or watch. In the anti-government protests that were held in the streets of Chile in 2019 and 2020, some protestors identified themselves as K-pop fans. This implies that in Chilean youth culture, Hallyu may evolve as a resource for imagining alternative society.

In comparison, the German fans in Europe, most of whom were university students, initially appeared relatively quiet and even indifferent to the universe of Hallyu. Even the K-pop cover dancers whom we met in clubs during our field studies seemed less expressive than those whom we observed in Chile and Spain. However, the German interviewees somewhat quietly revealed their passion for K-pop, Korean stars, and Korean popular culture. While seemingly inexpressive on the surface, the German fans often turned out to be dedicated to and engaged in their favorite Hallyu genres and stars. For the young German fans, K-pop seemed to play a symbolic role as a cultural antidote to American pop music.

Interestingly, while the majority of the Hallyu fans interviewed in North America, Latin America, and Europe were in their teens or twenties, the research participants in Spain included a group of relatively older fans who attempted to distinguish themselves from younger Hallyu fans and to define themselves as relatively "mature fans."[1] They acknowledged the quality and values involved in Hallyu content and showed some concern regarding newer teenage fans' fad for K-pop and K-pop idols. For the older fan group, Hallyu is not a sudden K-pop fad but a cultural trend that has evolved across different media forms.

The macro- and microlevel analyses provided in this book should not be separately understood, as it is important to analyze how different forces engage with the transnational flows of Korean popular culture. By examining both the structure and lived experiences of Hallyu in transnational contexts, we have explored the history, context, and user engagement of this emerging transnational cultural trend, and thus, we have made efforts to capture the multifaceted process of the transnational cultural flows of Korean popular culture. We have also illustrated how transnational cultural flows are configured and reconfigured in relation to digital media environments and participatory audience cultures. Through the articulation of the political, economic, and cultural analyses of Hallyu as a unique global phenomenon, this book helps to enrich ongoing media globalization debates. Its extensive empirical data and comprehensive framework, which are used to conduct macro- and microlevel analysis, present the dynamism, complexity, and diversity of transnational Hallyu.

REVISITING THE TRANSNATIONAL
AND DIGITAL WAVES OF HALLYU

Throughout this book, we have analyzed Hallyu as a cultural trend or flow in which two interwoven processes are articulated. We have considered that Hallyu may be best defined by transnational and digital waves, and through our audience studies in different locations, we have made an effort to examine how transnational Hallyu has evolved. As discussed in chapter 1, contemporary Korean media and culture are consumed by its overseas fans and audiences as a set of diverse forms of content and practices. Compared with several previous contraflows emerging in non-Western countries, most of which have depended on one or two signature genre(s) from a country—such as Japanese anime, Bollywood cinema, Latin American telenovelas, and Turkish television dramas—Hallyu is composed of a wide range of cultural genres, including K-pop, K-dramas, webtoons, animation, games, and children's music videos,[2] which evolve through transmedia storytelling. While K-pop is leading and facilitating the recent transnationalization of Korean popular culture, Hallyu is not limited to this one genre; rather, it relies on several cultural forms, which are increasingly interwoven and converged. Hallyu is a cultural trend that is recognized as "a total work of art" or "universe." In fact, even though K-pop is the most visible Hallyu genre, the fans consumed the "universe" of K-pop idols: not only K-pop music and videos but also variety shows, TV dramas, films, and online games starring these idols.[3] The fans navigated and explored the transmediated worlds of Hallyu by consuming different but associated content of Korean popular culture.

While many young interviewees were enthusiastic about K-pop, K-dramas, and/or Korean variety shows, they often reported that their parents and peers seemed indifferent to or ignorant of Hallyu. In Chile and Spain, Hallyu and its local fans were often stereotyped as *Chinos* or *Chinitos* in public. Similarly, among the German public, Hallyu seemed to be racialized as a set of exotic Asian cultural items or junk culture. The interview participants' accounts confirmed that Hallyu may not yet be truly global but may be a transnational niche cultural form.

While Hallyu may not yet be the dominant or mainstream cultural content in the global mediascape, it is undeniable that Korean popular culture and its industries have increasingly been disseminated to overseas audiences. Major Korean media and entertainment companies no longer target solely domestic audiences but consider a much larger audience outside of their own country. Thus, the production system involves multinational groups of producers, composers, choreographers, and idols. Moreover, the K-pop industry has been keen on the global release of new music videos through global media platforms, such as YouTube, Instagram, and Twitter, to enable the penetration of overseas markets as rapidly as possible. Likewise, several recent major Korean TV dramas aimed to attract international audiences from their preproduction stage. For example, the 2016 megahit drama *Descendants of the Sun* (KBS), which was partly funded by a Chinese content company, was released simultaneously in Korea and China (E.-j. Jung 2016). For Korean cultural industries, the increasing transnationalism in the Hallyu production system may operate as a double-edged sword, as it offers not only opportunities for global collaboration but also risk, such as heavy reliance on foreign players and capital.

As demonstrated in this book, extensive transnational flows of Hallyu are observed among overseas fans' responses and engagement. While Hallyu content was sometimes considered exotic by not only the public but also overseas fans, it was appropriated as a new and alternative cultural reference. Especially for the fans who were interviewed in Chile and Spain, K-pop music videos and idol worlds seemed to provide an image of an advanced, soft, and forward-looking society that is differentiated from their own. Some fans had been to Korea, driven, at least in part, by their interests in K-pop and other Korean popular culture forms, while others were interested in visiting Hallyu's country of origin. By engaging frequently in the universe of K-pop idols via social media, the fans incorporated transnational Hallyu texts and contexts into their everyday lives. K-pop idols were role models for young overseas fans during their transition to adulthood. As illustrated by K-pop and its overseas fandom, audience experiences are no longer national or local but involve transnational imaginaries, practices, and communication.

Hallyu has become highly transnational in its outbound and inbound flows. The outbound flows have been increased through the exportation of local cultural products to overseas markets to an extent that no other non-Western countries have ever achieved. The Korean cultural industries have successfully transnationalized their cultural products in the global markets. While Asia is still the largest market for Hallyu, other regions, including North America, Europe, and Latin America, have emerged as significant reception points. In addition to such outbound processes, Hallyu involves inbound processes of transnationalization, such as the increasing influence of overseas corporations and talent on domestic cultural production, as well as the opening up of the domestic market to the global free trade of cultural products. Inbound flows of Hallyu have increasingly reinforced the hybrid nature of

Korean popular culture, which might enhance the outbound spreadability of Hallyu beyond local markets. In so doing, inbound and outbound modes of transnationalization mutually accelerate the viral circulation of Hallyu on a global scale.

In this transnational circulation (the "transnational wave"), social media and digital platforms have become integral components of Hallyu. Without the "digital wave," Hallyu would not be globally and virally circulated. Digital technology is not only the vehicle via which local content is delivered globally but is also important content itself, as evidenced by the increasingly global use of Korea-based smartphones, apps, and platforms. Social media and digital platforms have become integral components in the recent phase of Hallyu, as observed in young fans' participatory consumption of K-pop music videos, which involves activities such as commenting, sharing, and reacting to the videos. Notably, this digital Korean Wave signals a new paradigm of transnational cultural circulation, in which production and consumption are easily merged through transmedia practices that draw on media convergence. Hallyu fans deploy social media platforms and technologies to access Korean popular culture materials that are not always available via the conventional mainstream media.

By circumventing the institutional gatekeepers to access the transnational cultural flows through digital and social media, the global fans reveal the emergence of a new form of cultural consumption from below, which is similar to what Lukács (2010) refers to as "private globalization." In many cases, Hallyu fan bases have grown through grassroots media convergence—that is, user engagement with and appropriation of different media platforms to explore cultural content that is unavailable on mainstream media channels.

Comprising transnational and digital waves, Hallyu is one of the latest and most vivid examples that illustrate how transnational cultural flows are intensified and widely extended via digital technologies; therefore, globalization is not only driven by structural forces, such as institutional gatekeepers, but is also facilitated by grassroots fans. Given the global cultural industry market shares, Hallyu has not yet overtaken Western popular culture, and the dominant position of the U.S. production flow continues. However, Hallyu illustrates the transnational momentum of contraflows, especially through young people's engagement with digital technologies.

THE HYBRID TRANSNATIONALISM OF HALLYU

Our convergence of empirical audience studies and political economic analysis provides resources for the discussion and theorization of the Hallyu phenomenon in relation to the globalization of Korean digital and popular culture. Hallyu appears to be a transnational trend that enhances and disseminates hybrid cultural content and practices (Jin 2016; Ryoo 2009). As confirmed by the narratives of Hallyu fans, the transnational circulation of Korean digital media and popular culture is a new breed of cultural globalization (Iwabuchi 2002). Hallyu evolves and appeals to overseas individuals, while offering room for audience engagement.

Our findings suggest that Hallyu is a transnational wave that connects different locales and regions through networked media practices. It originated in Korea and is considered, especially by policy makers, as a part of the national branding of Korea through the lens of soft power (see Nye and Kim 2013). However, the Korean Wave is not simply an example of reverse media imperialism, nor is it a counter-hegemonic media phenomenon (see Tomlinson 1999). In this book, we do not celebrate the rise of non-Western cultural forms in global or Western markets. Rather, we propose an understanding of Hallyu as a set of hybrid and transnational flows of popular culture and digital media that have emerged and evolved through various routes. The continuous transnational flows of Hallyu may increase its already hybrid nature. Given Western and Japanese cultural influences on Korean media production over the past several decades, it is not difficult to find hybridity embedded in Korea's contemporary media and culture. The overseas fans also acknowledged a high level of hybridity in Hallyu. For them, this hybridity appeared to offer versatile and flexible room to participate in the cultural texts of different linguistic and cultural contexts.

While this hybridity, which is especially evident in the K-pop genre, has enhanced the participatory aspects of Hallyu, this attribute is not necessarily favored by some overseas Hallyu fans. For example, the foreign language mixing in K-pop lyrics was considered irrelevant and "manufactured." However, increasing hybridity seems to provide overseas Hallyu fans with moments of cultural or emotional connection. Indeed, as illustrated by the fans, the overseas fans engage with Hallyu in relation to their own hybrid experiences with Western and/or local media. The hybridity of contemporary Korean media texts and their overseas fans together augment the complex and versatile nature of Hallyu; perhaps this occurs primarily when this cultural trend is introduced and integrated into locales who have already inherited complex histories in relation to the West.

The hybridity of Hallyu is not only observed at the textual level but is also noticeable at the contextual level. While the hybrid *text* of Hallyu and its *reception* in different overseas locales enrich cultural globalization theory, the *context* of Hallyu production and circulation offers an intriguing case for the critical political economy of media and communication. In particular, the K-pop production process illustrates how cultural industries, IT sectors, and successive governments have synergistically shaped the infrastructure of contemporary Hallyu. Hallyu's structural formation and reformation reveal tensions, contradictions, compliance, and the partial resolution of market forces and the state, thus offering insights into the global–local dynamics of cultural industries (Ma 2000). In addition, the growth of Hallyu is an outcome of the collusion of neoliberal economic restructuring and the sentiments of cultural nationalism (S.-Y. Kim 2018). This seemingly odd marriage of neoliberalism and nationalism is not necessarily surprising, as the neoliberal state often mobilizes nationalism by hailing its population as competitive individuals who contribute to the national profit and by exploiting the ideology of nationalism as an imagined antidote to the highly fragmented and competitive social worlds (Harvey 2005, quoted in S.-Y. Kim 2018, 194). The structural forces behind Hallyu have shaped and led the wave by obscuring the contradictions implicated in the rise of this new cultural trend. Neoliberalized cultural industries, in collaboration with business-friendly governments supporting the discourse of cultural or creative industries, have reproduced or been affected by a particular mode of subjectivity, such as market-oriented and self-developing individuals (G. Kim 2019; Y. Kim 2011). In his critique of the recent rise of K-pop, G. Kim (2019) described Hallyu as a cultural product of neoliberal developmentalism. From this point of view, the hybridity embedded in Hallyu echoes Korean cultural industries' strategy, rather than being a "third space" (Bhabha 1994) that entails subversive forces of different cultures.

However, our audience studies have shown that Hallyu fans do not necessarily engage in the cultural industries' strategies or admire the soft power of Korean media and popular culture. The fans in the United States, Canada, Chile, Germany, and Spain were fascinated with K-pop, Korean dramas, TV shows, films, webtoons, and/or online/mobile games; however, many of them consumed Hallyu as a cultural resource that they used to negotiate their everyday lives. Thus, we argue that despite the existing structural forces being driven by the neoliberal economy, the Hallyu phenomenon illustrates how audiences engage with and reorient top-down globalization while exercising bottom-up transnationalism.

FURTHER QUESTIONS AND PROSPECTS: THE GLOBAL TRANSLATION OF HALLYU

In this book, we have examined how transnational Hallyu has evolved and how overseas fan audiences have engaged with this emerging trend as a resource for negotiating their everyday contexts. Hallyu as transnational and digital waves is still evolving; therefore, academic and public discussion of Hallyu is also evolving in several ways. The evolution of Hallyu as transnational and digital waves encourages further discussion about the future prospects of transnational Hallyu.

Most of all, we are curious about how transnational and digital Hallyu will be. BTS's continuous record-breaking hits in the global music market, *Parasite*'s worldwide box-office record, and the global success of the TV show *The King of Mask Singer*, whose format has been sold to more than ten countries, demonstrate that Hallyu is increasingly incorporated into mainstream audiences' media experiences around the globe. We argue that various Korean cultural genres are already widely integrated into the global mediascape and that ordinary audiences in many parts of the world are thus exposed to Hallyu in one way or another. For example, whether they recognize it or not, not only its American viewers but also its Italian, British, Canadian, Irish, Dutch, Brazilian, or Japanese viewers of ABC's TV series *The Good Doctor*, a remake of a K-drama of the same title, are not entirely free of the influences of Hallyu. At least to some extent, these global viewers are exposed to Hallyu through its American translation or hybridization. Although the global influences of Hallyu may still be nascent in terms of conventional market measurements (such as general viewer ratings and the exportation of products in official markets), we argue that Hallyu is almost everywhere, exploring a new horizon of transnational cultural circulation through grassroots and corporate media convergence, as well as transnational border crossing.

The important question is how Hallyu may change the cultural logic of the global mediascape. This emerging flow questions how cultural practices are becoming transnational through digital media. BTS and other K-pop groups sing primarily in Korean but communicate with young people beyond national borders; some fans volunteer and collaborate to translate and share the BTS stories and universe. Hallyu is an ongoing process of articulation between digital innovation and cultural practices that extends beyond local and national boundaries. For example, K-pop's reaction videos reveal audiences' local contexts and cultural translations of the original texts. In the videos, the fans not only discuss the texts but also make use of the originals. By "reacting," fans become content creators and express their identities (D. Oh 2017b). Viral cultural phenomena, such as Psy's *Gangnam Style*, and their related cultural practices tend to be "socially resistant to control" and to move beyond institutional gatekeepers' regulation (Nahon and Hemsley 2013, 130).

In this regard, Hallyu seems to invite its overseas audiences to engage in constant cultural translation. Interestingly, some of the world's best-known Hallyu content/stars are not those who strategically prepared for global penetration but, rather, those who were locally produced and targeted. For example, Psy's *Gangnam Style*, BTS's music, *The King of the Mask Singer*, and Bong Joon-ho's 2020 Oscar-winning *Parasite* initially targeted local audiences. The unexpected global attention and success that began with locally unique concepts and themes suggest a new mode of transnational cultural flow. *Parasite*'s director, Bong Joon-ho, seemed surprised by the film's global acclaim; his intention had been to create a locally themed film after his two previous multinational projects, for which he had been obliged to generate English-language films in consideration of global audiences.[4] The storytelling of *Parasite* and BTS regarding social inequality and youth's struggles, respectively, may unintentionally reveal the way in which the local meets the global through transnational cultural flows. Such encounters suggest the importance of not only linguistic but, more importantly, intercultural translation. When translated meaningfully, overseas audiences may engage with Hallyu and find it relevant to their everyday lives. In fact, one of the most significant effects of transnational Hallyu is its flows beyond ethnoracial and linguistic borders. This cultural wave has indeed helped to encourage global audiences to "overcome the 1-inch-tall barrier of subtitles"[5] and engage with different popular cultural worlds through diverse digital technologies.

In conclusion, given the contradictions and potential of Hallyu, it may be too early to predict whether Hallyu industries and markets will be sustainably integrated into the global mediascape and global audiences' everyday contexts.[6] However, Hallyu reveals a transnational momentum that signals a new method of cultural circulation that extends beyond geocultural boundaries and the Western-centric framework of media industries and markets. While enjoying the good-looking Korean idols, unrealistic dramas, and acrobatic/comical variety shows, some fans whom we met were able to seeing through the structural forces behind the presented images of the kaleidoscopic Hallyu world. By navigating and exploring the relevance of cultural texts and practices that come from a distant part of the world, transnational Hallyu fans seem to learn how to utilize transnational cultural resources to make sense of their own everyday contexts and, in so doing, to imagine globalization differently. Transnational Hallyu may function as an experiment to explore how cultural globalization can make non-Western cultural resources more diverse and inclusive. Despite the limitations in the Hallyu industry, such as its rapid and systematic commodification, the Korean Wave offers a moment and the momentum to redefine the global and the local while reminding us that culture is always being translated. Although there might be losses in the translation process, there are also gains.

NOTES

1. This does not necessarily mean Hallyu fans in Spain are relatively older than other global Hallyu fans. Our qualitative, in-depth studies drew on snowball sampling

and thus did not seek generalizable data. One probable reason that Spanish fans were relatively older is that they were members of a major Spanish Hallyu fan club we contacted for interview. Even if the older fans did not represent Spanish fans, they may reveal how older and longtime fans consider younger and newer fans.

2. It is not only K-pop that facilitates the spread of Hallyu on social media. While several K-pop music videos have been sensational short- or long-term viewer record breakers on YouTube, the Korean-made music video of the children's song "Baby Shark" has been even farther ahead than the YouTube viewer record of the phenomenal *Gangnam Style* video. The "Baby Shark" music video, produced by the Korean-based educational video company SmartStudy, is the second most-viewed YouTube video as of March 2020. "Baby Shark" has been globally viewed and sung by not only children but also many adults. The song went viral and generated numerous user-created parody videos while being sung in numerous public locations around the globe (Ritschel 2018).

3. K-pop band BTS has been leading transmedia storytelling strategies. BTS uses a wide range of media platforms to tell its stories. In June 2019, it teamed up with the Korean gaming developers Takeone Company Corp and Netmarble to launch an online game titled *BTS World*. This storytelling mobile and interactive game enables its user to assume the role of a BTS manager and experience the group's journey from its debut to global stardom.

4. Even when the film was nominated for the Official Selection for Competition at the 2019 Cannes Film Festival, *Parasite* director, Bong Joon-ho, said the following to Korean reporters: "I think it is very unlikely that *Parasite* will win the award (at Cannes). *Parasite* is full of Korean-specific nuances. As this film is so Korean, it would not be understood (by non-Koreans). The film includes many details that only Korean audiences can fully appreciate" (Yim 2019). However, the film went on to win the Palme d'Or (the Best Picture Award) at the Cannes Film Festival, which was followed by numerous international award and box-office hits in many countries, including the United States.

5. In his Golden Globe award acceptance speech, Bong Joon-ho stated, "Once you overcome the 1-inch-tall barrier of subtitles, you will be introduced to so many more amazing films." This quote went viral, rectifying many American moviegoers' aversion to foreign-language films (J. Chang 2020).

6. The outbreak of COVID-19 in late 2019 and early 2020 has affected the cultural industries and people's cultural activities. People around the globe have been forced to restrict their outdoor activities, including cultural activities due to growing concerns. The Korean Wave has been hit harder than other cultural industries, as it has been establishing its significant momentum. Several K-pop groups, including BTS, had to cancel their global tours, and local films could not find moviegoers for a while because people stayed at home. COVID-19 has certainly barred the further growth of Hallyu in the global cultural markets, and it is significant to analyze the Korean Wave trend in the post-COVID-19 era later.

References

Acuna, Kristen. 2016. "Millions in Korea Are Obsessed with These Revolutionary Comics—Now They're Going Global." *Business Insider*, February 11, 2016. http://www.businessinsider.com/what-is-webtoons-2016-2.

Ainslie, Mary. 2016. "Korean Overseas Investment and Soft Power: Hallyu in Laos." *Korea Journal* 56 (3): 5–32.

Allison, Anne. 2003. "Portable Monsters and Commodity Cuteness: Pokémon as Japan's New Global Power." *Postcolonial Studies* 6 (3): 381–95.

Annett, Sandra. 2011. "Imagining Transcultural Fandom: Animation and Global Media Communities." *Transcultural Studies* 2: 164–88.

Appadurai, Arjun. 1990. "Disjuncture and Difference in the Global Cultural Economy." *Public Culture* 2 (1): 1–24.

Appadurai, Arjun. 1996. *Modernity at Large: Cultural Dimensions of Globalization.* Minneapolis: University of Minnesota Press.

Arana, Ismael. 2017. "Una banda surcoreana celebra el culto a la cirugía plástica con la operación de todas sus cantantes" ["A South Korean Band Celebrates the Cult of Plastic Surgery with the Operation of All Its Singers"]. *El Mundo*, March 21, 2017. www.elmundo.es/sociedad/2017/03/21/58d13ee4468aeb61478b45c4.html.

Arora, Payal. 2012. "Typology of Web 2.0 Spheres: Understanding the Cultural Dimensions of Social Media Spaces." *Current Sociology* 60 (5): 599–618.

Bai, Stephany. 2017. "'Universal Stories' Help Korean Dramas Find International Success." *NBC News*, January 26, 2017. https://www.nbcnews.com/news/asian-america/universal-stories-help-korean-dramas-find-international-success-n698511.

BBC. 2014. "J-Pop and the Global Success of 'Kawaii' Culture." *BBC*, October 21, 2014. http://www.bbc.com/culture/story/20130603-cute-culture-and-catchy-pop.

BBC. 2016. "An Unlikely Story: Why Do South Americans Love Turkish TV?" *BBC*, September 8, 2016. https://www.bbc.com/news/business-37284938.

Beck, Ulrich, and Elisabeth Beck-Gernsheim. 2002. *Individualization: Institutionalized Individualism and Its Social and Political Consequences.* London: Sage.

Benjamin, Jeff. 2016. "K-pop Concerts Continue to Grow Outside Asia." *Billboard*, May 3, 2016. https://www.billboard.com/articles/columns/k-town/7350481/international-k-pop-concerts-growth-infographic.

Benjamin, Jeff. 2017. "What Does It Take for a K-Pop Band to Blow Up in South America?" *New York Times Magazine*, May 4, 2017. https://www.nytimes.com/2017/05/04/magazine/what-does-it-take-for-a-k-pop-band-to-blow-up-in-south-america.html.

Bennett, Andy. 1999. "Hip Hop am Main: The Localization of Rap Music and Hip Hop Culture." *Media, Culture & Society* 21 (1): 77–91.

Bennett, Andy, and Keith Kahn-Harris, eds. 2004. *After Subculture: Critical Studies in Contemporary Youth Culture*. New York: Palgrave Macmillan.

beSUCCESS. 2016. "Five of Kakao's Daum Webtoon Titles to Appear on Chinese Screens through Partnership with Huace Group." *beSUCCESS*, March 14, 2016. http://besuccess.com/2016/03/five-of-kakaos-daum-webtoon-titles-to-appear-on-chinese-screens-through-partnership-with-huace-group/.

Bhabha, Homi K. 1994. *The Location of Culture*. New York: Routledge.

Billboard. 2011. "A Look Inside the 'K-Pop Cover Dance' Trend." *Billboard*, October 18, 2011. https://www.billboard.com/articles/news/465675/a-look-inside-the-k-pop-cover-dance-trend.

Billboard. 2012. "How the K-Pop Breakout Star Harnessed the Power of YouTube, SNL and More to Become Music's New Global Brand." *Billboard*, October 26, 2012. https://www.billboard.com/articles/columns/k-town/474456/psys-gangnam-style-the-billboard-cover-story.

BizFact. 2016. "A Mobile Game *Tower of God* Starts Its Official Service with Naver Webtoon." *BizFact*, February 18, 2016. http://news.tf.co.kr/read/economy/1626346.htm.

boyd, danah. 2014. *It's Complicated: The Social Lives of Networked Teens*. New Haven, CT: Yale University Press.

Boyd-Barrett, Oliver. 1977. "Media Imperialism: Towards an International Framework for the Analysis of Media Systems." In *Mass Communication and Society*, edited by James Curran, Michael Gurevitch, and Janet Woollacott, 116–35. London: Edward Arnold.

Buzzard, Karen. 2012. *Tracking the Audience: The Ratings Industry from Analog to Digital*. London: Routledge.

Capistrano, Erick Paolo S. 2019. "Understanding Filipino Korean Pop Music Fans: An Empirical Discourse." *Asian Journal of Social Science* 47 (1): 59–87.

Carranza Ko, Nusta, Song No, Jeong-Nam Kim, and Ronald Gobbi Simões. 2014. "Landing of the Wave: Hallyu in Peru and Brazil." *Development and Society* 43 (2): 297–350.

Castells, Manuel. 2011. "A Network Theory of Power." *International Journal of Communication* 5: 773–87.

CBS San Francisco. 2018. "K-Pop Fans Swarm Oracle Arena for Concert by Boy Band BTS." *CBS San Francisco*, September 12, 2018. https://sanfrancisco.cbslocal.com/2018/09/12/thousands-of-bts-k-pop-fans-ring-oakland-coliseum-complex.

Cha, Hyunhee, and Seongmook Kim. 2011. "A Case Study on Korean Wave: Focused on K-Pop Concert by Korean Idol Group in Paris, June 2011." In *Multimedia,*

Computer Graphics and Broadcasting: Conference Proceedings, edited by Dominik Slezak, William I. Grosky, Niki Pissinou, Timony K. Shih, Tai-hoon Kim, and Byeong-Ho Kang, 153–62. Berlin: Springer.

Chaney, David. 2004. "Fragmented Cultures and Subcultures." In *After Subculture: Critical Studies in Contemporary Youth Culture*, edited by Andy Bennett and Keith Kahn-Harris, 36–48. New York: Palgrave.

Chang, Justine. 2020. "Commentary: 'The 1-Inch-Tall Barrier of Subtitles': Bong Joon Ho Rightly Calls Out Hollywood Myopia." *Chicago Tribune*, January 7, 2020. https://www.chicagotribune.com/entertainment/movies/ct-ent-subtitles-par asite-0109-20200107-dchcnhgj7nhl5fp4qlcnqgv6uy-story.html.

Chang, WoongJo, and Shin-Eui Park. 2019. "The Fandom of Hallyu, a Tribe in the Digital Network Era: The Case of ARMY of BTS." *Kritika Kultura* 32: 260–87.

Chen, Lu. 2017. "The Emergence of the anti-Hallyu Movement in China." *Media, Culture & Society* 39 (3): 374–90.

Chin, Bertha, and Lori Hitchcock Morimoto. 2013. "Towards a Theory of Transcultural Fandom." *Participations* 10 (1): 92–108.

Cho, Heekyung. 2016. "The Webtoon: A New Form for Graphic Narrative." *The Comics Journal*, July 18, 2016. http://www.tcj.com/the-webtoon-a-new-form-for-graphic-narrative/.

Cho, Heeyoung, Taeyang You, and Chanjong Oh. 2017. "K-Webtoons on Mobile." *Maeil Business Newspaper*, November 12, 2017. https://www.mk.co.kr/news/business/view/2017/11/749674/.

Cho, Joanne Miyang, and Lee M. Roberts. 2018. *Transnational Encounters between Germany and Korea: Affinity in Culture and Politics since the 1880s*. New York: Palgrave.

Cho, Younghan. 2011. "Desperately Seeking East Asia Amidst the Popularity of South Korean Pop Culture in Asia." *Cultural Studies* 25 (3): 383–404.

Choi, Chungmoo. 1995. "Transnational Capitalism, National Imaginary, and the Protest Theater in South Korea." *boundary 2* 22 (1): 235–61.

Choi, Jaz Hee-jeong. 2006. "Living in Cyworld: Contextualizing Cy-Ties in South Korea." In *Uses of Blogs*, edited by Axel Bruns and Joanne Jacobs, 173–86. New York: Peter Lang.

Choi, JungBong. 2014. "Loyalty Transmission and Cultural Enlisting of K-Pop in Latin America." In *K-pop: The International Rise of the Korean Music Industry*, edited by JungBong Choi and Roald Maliangkay, 98–115. New York: Routledge.

Choi, JungBong. 2015. "Hallyu versus Hallyu-hwa: Cultural Phenomenon versus Institutional Campaign." In *Hallyu 2.0: Korean Wave in the Age of Social Media*, edited by Sangjoon Lee and Abé Mark Nornes, 31–52. Ann Arbor: University of Michigan Press.

Chon, Kilnam, Hyun Je Park, Jin Ho Hur, and Kyungran Kang. 2013. "A History of Computer Networking and the Internet in Korea." *IEEE Communications Magazine* 51: 10–15.

Chosun Ilbo. 2011. "Pop Idols Bringing the Korean Wave to Germany." *Chosun Ilbo*, July 29, 2011. http://english.chosun.com/site/data/html_dir/2011/07/29/2011072900515.html.

Chua, Beng Huat. 2012. *Structure, Audience and Soft Power in East Asian Pop Culture*. Hong Kong: Hong Kong University Press.

Chua, Beng Huat, and Koichi Iwabuchi, eds. 2008. *East Asian Pop Culture: Analyzing the Korean Wave.* Hong Kong: Hong Kong University Press.

Chua, Beng Huat, and Sun Jung. 2014. "Social Media and Cross-Border Cultural Transmissions in Asia: States, Industries, Audiences." *International Journal of Cultural Studies* 17 (5): 417–22.

Chun, Jin-Sung. 2018. "Specters of Schinkel in East Asia: Berlin, Tokyo, and Seoul from a Viewpoint of Modernity/Coloniality." In *Transnational Encounters between Germany and Korea: Affinity in Culture and Politics since the 1880s,* edited by Joanne Miyang Cho and Lee M. Roberts, 99–129. New York: Palgrave.

Chung, Peichi. 2013. "Co-Creating Korean Wave in Southeast Asia Digital Convergence and Asia's Media Regionalization." *Journal of Creative Communications* 8 (2, 3): 193–208.

Clarke, John. 1976. "Style." In *Resistance through Rituals: Youth Subcultures in Post-War Britain,* edited by Stuart Hall and Tony Jefferson. London: Hutchinson.

CNN Chile. 2019. " '¿Está el K-Pop detrás de la protesta chilena?': Medios coreanos reaccionaron al cuestionado informe de Big Data" [" 'Is K-Pop behind the Chilean Protest?']': Korean Media Reacted to the Questioned Big Data Report"]. *CNN Chile,* December 24, 2019. https://www.cnnchile.com/pais/medios-coreanos-reaccion-informe-big-data_20191224.

Coca, Laura. 2019. "¿Qué futuro le depara al K-pop?" ["What Future Will K-Pop Have?"]. *Los40,* June 22, 2019. https://los40.com/los40/2019/06/21/musica/1561 115701_486598.html.

Consalvo, Mia. 2017. *Atari to Zelda: Japan's Videogames in Global Contexts.* Cambridge, MA: MIT Press.

Cooper-Chen, Anne. 2012. "Cartoon Planet: The Cross-Cultural Acceptance of Japanese Animation." *Asian Journal of Communication* 22 (1): 44–57.

Cooperativa.cl. 2018. "Una estampida se produjo en Music Bank Chile y afectadas denunciarán ante el Sernac" ["A Stampede Occurred in Music Bank Chile and the Affected Girls Will Denounce before the Sernac (National Consumer Service)"]. *cooperative.cl.,* March 25, 2018. https://www.cooperativa.cl/noticias/entretencion/musica/shows-en-chile/una-estampida-se-produjo-en-music-bank-chile-y-afectadas-denunciaran/2018–03–25/013243.html.

Crane, Diana. 2014. "Cultural Globalization and the Dominance of the American Film Industry: Cultural Policies, National Film Industries, and Transnational Film." *International Journal of Cultural Policy* 20 (4): 365–82.

de Beukelaer, Christiaan, and Kim-Marie Spence. 2019. *Global Cultural Economy.* London: Routledge.

de Kosnik, Abigail. 2012. "Fandom as Free Labor." In *Digital Labor: The Internet as Playground and Factory,* edited by Trebor Scholz, 106–19. London: Routledge.

Denison, Rayna. 2011. "Anime Fandom and the Liminal Spaces between Fan Creativity and Piracy." *International Journal of Cultural Studies* 14 (5): 449–66.

DongA Ilbo. 2012. "UK Has Most Korean Wave Fans in Europe." *DongA Ilbo,* April 20, 2012. http://english.donga.com/List/3/all/26/403643/1.

Dorfman, Ariel, and Armand Mattelart. 1975. *How to Read Donald Duck.* New York: International General.

Duffett, Mark. 2013. *Understanding Fandom: An Introduction to the Study of Media Fan Culture*. New York: Bloomsbury.

Duffy, Brooke Erin. 2017. *(Not) Getting Paid to Do What You Love: Gender, Social Media, and Aspirational Work*. New Haven, CT: Yale University Press.

Dwyer, Tessa. 2012. "Fansub Dreaming on ViKi: 'Don't Just Watch but Help When You Are Free.'" *The Translator* 18 (2): 217–43.

Epstein, Stephen. 2017. "From South Korea to the Southern Hemisphere: K-Pop Below the Equator." *Journal of World Popular Music* 3 (2): 197–223.

Epstein, Stephen, and James Turnbull. 2014. "Girls' generation? Gender, (Dis)empowerment, and K-Pop." In *The Korean Popular Culture Reader*, edited by Kyung Hyun Kim and Youngmin Choe, 314–36. Durham, NC: Duke University Press.

Esposito, Anthony, and Natalia Ramos. 2019. "Chile Sees 2019 Economic Growth of 1.8% to 2.2% Due to Protests." *Reuters*, November 5, 2019. https://www.reuters.com/article/us-chile-economy-gdp/chile-sees-2019-economic-growth-of-18-to-22-due-to-protests-idUSKBN1XF2FC.

Expatica. 2013. "Why Is YouTube Blocking Gangnam Style and Justin Bieber in Germany?" *Expatica*, February 4, 2013. Accessed March 1, 2020. https://www.expatica.com/de/news/country-news/Why-is-YouTube-blocking-Gangnam-Style-and-Justin-Bieber-in-Germany_369200.html.

Featherstone, Mike, ed. 1990. *Global Culture: Nationalism, Globalization and Modernity*. London: Sage.

Fisher, Max. 2012. "Facebook's Amazing Growth in the Developing World." *The Atlantic*, May 18, 2012. https://www.theatlantic.com/international/archive/2012/05/facebooks-amazing-growth-in-the-developing-world/257392.

Fiske, John. 1989. *Reading the Popular*. London: Routledge.

Fiske, John. 1992. "The Cultural Economy of Fandom." In *Adoring Audience: Fan Culture and Popular Media*, edited by Lisa A. Lewis, 39–49. New York: Routledge.

Fluck, Winfried. 2004. "The Americanization of German Culture? The Strange, Paradoxical Ways of Modernity." In *German Pop Culture: How "American" Is It?*, edited by Agnes C. Mueller, 19–39. Ann Arbor: University of Michigan Press.

Fox, Susanna, and Lee Rainie. 2014. "The Web at 25 in the U.S." *Pax Research Center Internet & Technology*, February 27, 2014. Accessed February 20, 2019. https://www.pewresearch.org/internet/2014/02/27/the-web-at-25-in-the-u-s/.

Freeman, Matthew. 2015. "Up, Up and Across: Superman, the Second World War and the Historical Development of Transmedia Storytelling." *Historical Journal of Film, Radio and Television* 35 (2): 215–39.

Freire, Juan Manuel. 2019. "K-pop: la fábrica surcoreana de ídolos musicales que quiere dominar el mundo" ["K-Pop, the South Korean Idol Factory Which Wants to Dominate the World"]. *El Periódico*, May 27, 2019. https://www.elperiodico.com/es/ocio-y-cultura/20190527/blackpink-concierto-palau-sant-jordi-historia-fenomeno-k-pop-7476173.

Fuchs, Christian. 2014. *Social Media: A Critical Introduction*. London: Sage.

Fuhr, Michael. 2014. "K-Pop Consumption and Fandom in Germany." In *K-Pop on the Global Platform: European Audience Reception and Contexts*, edited by

KOFICE (Korea Foundation of International Culture Exchange), 141–200. Seoul: KOFICE. http://www.kofice.or.kr/z99_include/filedown1.asp?filename=K-pop_ on_the_Global_Platform(ENG).pdf.

Fuhr, Michael. 2016. *Globalization and Popular Music in South Korea: Sounding out K-Pop.* London: Routledge.

García Canclini, Néstor. 1995. *Hybrid Cultures: Strategies for Entering and Leaving Modernity.* Minneapolis: University of Minnesota Press.

Georgiou, Myria. 2006. "Diasporic Communities On Line: A Bottom Up Experience of Transnationalism." In *Ideologies of the Internet,* edited by Katharinem Sarikakis and Daya K. Thussu, 131–45. Cresskill, NJ: Hampton Press.

Ginsburg, Faye D., Lila Abu-Lughod, and Brian Larkin, eds. 2002. *Media Worlds.* Berkeley: University of California Press.

Giovagnoli, Max. 2011. *Transmedia Storytelling: Imagery, Shapes and Techniques.* Pittsburgh, PA: ETC Press.

Glynn, Basil, and Jeongmee Kim. 2013. "'Oppa'-tunity Knocks: PSY, 'Gangnam Style' and the Press Reception of K-Pop in Britain." *Situations* 7: 1–20.

Goebel, Michael. 2016. "Settler Colonialism in Postcolonial Latin America." In *The Routledge Handbook of the History of Settler Colonialism,* edited by Edward Cavanagh and Lorenzo Veracini, 139–52. New York: Routledge.

Goldsmith, Ben, Kwang-Suk Lee, and Brian Yecies. 2011. "In Search of the Korean Digital Wave." *Media International Australia* 141: 70–77.

Goodson, Scott. 2012. "Convergence Is the Future of Marketing." *Forbes*, March 1, 2012. https://www.forbes.com/sites/marketshare/2012/03/01/convergence-is-the-future-of-marketing/#47a2017f5401.

Grossberg, Lawrence. 1992. "Is There a Fan in the House? The Affective Sensibility of Fandom." In *Adoring Audience*: *Fan Culture and Popular Media,* edited by Lisa A. Lewis, 50–65. New York: Routledge.

Guback, Thomas H. 1984. "International Circulation of U.S. Theatrical Films and Television Programming." In *World Communications: A Handbook*, edited by George Gerbner and Marsha Siefert, 153–63. New York: Longman.

Gustines, George Gene. 2015. "Stan Lee and Michelle Phan Help LINE Webtoon, Digital Comics Site, Expand in U.S." *New York Times*, July 5, 2015. https://www.nytimes.com/2015/07/06/business/media/free-digital-comics-site-is-expanding-in-us-with-celebrity-help.html?_r=1.

Hall, Stuart. 1996. "The West and the Rest." In *Modernity: An Introduction to Modern Societies*, edited by Stuart Hall, David Held, Don Hubert, and Kenneth Thompson, 185–227. Malden, MA: Blackwell.

Han, Benjamin. 2017. "K-Pop in Latin America: Transcultural Fandom and Digital Mediation." *International Journal of Communication* 11: 2250–69.

Han, Jung Hoon. 2017. "'China Plagiarizes 29 Korean Entertainment Shows', Said MP Kim." *jtbc news*, October 4, 2017. http://news.jtbc.joins.com/article/article.aspx?news_id=NB11530591.

Hanaki, Toru, Arvind Singhal, Min Wha Han, Do Kyun Kim, and Ketan Chitnis. 2007. "Hanryu Sweeps East Asia—How *Winter Sonata* Is Gripping Japan." *International Communication Gazette* 69 (3): 281–94.

Harvey, David. 2005. *A Brief History of Neoliberalism*. Oxford: Oxford University Press.
Hassall, Isabella. 2016. "Smartphone Penetration by Country—Top 10." *smsglobal*, July 5, 2016. https://thehub.smsglobal.com/smartphone-penetration-by-country-top-10/.
Hills, Matt. 2013. "Fiske's 'Textual Productivity' and Digital Fandom: Web 2.0 Democratization versus Fan Distinction?" *Participations: Journal of Audience & Reception Studies* 10 (1): 130–53.
Hjorth, Larissa. 2011. "Locating the Online: Creativity and User-Created Content in Seoul." *Media International Australia* 141 (1): 118–27.
Holroyd, Carin. 2019. "Digital Content Promotion in Japan and South Korea: Government Strategies for an Emerging Economic Sector." *Asia and the Pacific Policy Study* 6 (3): 290–307.
Hong, Chansik. 2012. "Taiwan's Anti-Hallyu." *Dong A Ilbo*, January 1, 2012. http://news.donga.com/Column/3/04/20120101/43010775/1.
Hong, Seok Kyeong. 2013. *Hallyu in Globalization and Digital Culture Era: Full House, Gangnam Style, and After*. Paju: Hanul.
Hong, Seok-Kyeong, Daemin Park, and Sojeong Park. 2017. "Knowledge Network Analysis on Hallyu Research." *Korean Journal of Journalism & Communication Studies* 61 (3): 318–53.
Hong, Seok-Kyeong, Sojeong Park, Daemin Park, and Seungyun Oh. 2019. "Geography of Hallyu Studies: Analysis of Academic Discourse on Hallyu in International Research." *Korea Journal* 59 (2): 111–43.
Hong-Mercier, Seok-Kyeong. 2013. "Hallyu as a Digital Culture Phenomenon in the Process of Globalization: A Theoretical Investigation on the Global Consumption of Hallyu Seen in France." *Journal of Communication Research* 50 (1): 157–92.
Hoskins, Colin, and Rolf Mirus. 1988. "Reasons for the US Dominance of the International Trade in Television Programmes." *Media, Culture & Society* 10 (4): 499–515.
Howard, Keith. 2006. "Coming of Age: Korean Pop in the 1990s." In *Korean Pop Music*, edited by Keith Howard, 82–98. Kent: Global Oriental.
Hu, Kelly. 2005. "The Power of Circulation: Digital Technologies and the Online Chinese Fans of Japanese TV Drama." *Inter-Asia Cultural Studies* 6 (2): 171–86.
Hutchby, Ian. 2001. "Technologies, Texts and Affordances." *Sociology* 35 (2): 441–56.
IFPI (The International Federation of the Phonographic Industry). 2018. *IFPI Global Music Report 2018*. https://www.ifpi.org/downloads/GMR2018.pdf.
Iwabuchi, Koichi. 2002. *Recentering Globalization: Popular Culture and Japanese Transnationalism*. Durham, NC: Duke University Press.
Jang, Wonho, and Jung Eun Song. 2017. "Webtoon as a New Korean Wave in the Process of Glocalization." *Kritika Kultura* 29: 168–87.
Jenkins, Henry. 2004. "The Cultural Logic of Media Convergence." *International Journal of Cultural Studies* 7 (1): 33–43.
Jenkins, Henry. 2006a. *Convergence Culture: Where Old and New Media Collide*. New York: New York University Press.

Jenkins, Henry. 2006b. *Fans, Bloggers, and Gamers: Exploring Participatory Culture*. New York: NYU Press.

Jenkins, Henry. 2011. "Transmedia 202: Further Reflections." *Henry Jenkins Confessions of ACA-FAN*, July 31, 2011. http://henryjenkins.org/2011/08/defining_transmedia_further_re.html.

Jenkins, Henry, Sam Ford, and Joshua Green. 2013. *Spreadable Media: Creating Value and Meaning in a Networked Culture*. New York: New York University Press.

Jensen, Joli. 1992. "Fandom as Pathology: The Consequences of Characterization." In *Adoring Audience: Fan Culture and Popular Media*, edited by Lisa A. Lewis, 9–29. London: Routledge.

Jeong, Jaehyeon. 2020. "Webtoons Go Viral?: The Globalization Processes of Korean Digital Comics." *Korea Journal* 60 (1): 71–99.

Jeong, Jae-Seon, Seul-Hi Lee, and Sang-Gil Lee. 2017. "When Indonesians Routinely Consume Korean Pop Culture: Revisiting Jakartan Fans of the Korean Drama Dae Jang Geum." *International Journal of Communication* 11: 2288–2307.

Ji, Youngho. 2016. "Korean Dramas Conquering French Audiences." *KOFICE Overseas Correspondent Reports*, February 12, 2016. Accessed March 1, 2020. http://kofice.or.kr/c30correspondent/c30_correspondent_02_view.asp?seq=12067.

Jin, Dal Yong. 2009. "Where Is Japan in Media Studies in the Post-Cold War Era: Critical Discourse of the West and the East." *Social Science Research* 22 (1): 261–93.

Jin, Dal Yong. 2010. *Korea's Online Gaming Empire*. Cambridge, MA: MIT Press.

Jin, Dal Yong. 2011. *Hands On/Hands Off: The Korean State and the Market Liberalization of the Communication Industry*. New York: Hampton Press.

Jin, Dal Yong. 2013. "The Construction of Platform Imperialism in the Globalization Era." *tripleC: Communication, Capitalism and Critique* 11 (1): 145–72.

Jin, Dal Yong. 2015. "Digital Convergence of Korea's Webtoons: Transmedia Storytelling." *Communication Research and Practice* 1 (3): 193–209.

Jin, Dal Yong. 2016. *New Korean Wave: Transnational Cultural Power in the Age of Social Media*. Urbana: University of Illinois Press.

Jin, Dal Yong. 2017a. "Construction of Digital Korea: History, Use, and Implications of New Communication Technologies in the 21st Century." *Media, Culture & Society* 39 (5): 715–26.

Jin, Dal Yong. 2017b. *Smartland Korea: Mobile Communication, Culture, and Society*. Ann Arbor: University of Michigan Press.

Jin, Dal Yong. 2018. "An Analysis of the Korean Wave as Transnational Popular Culture: North American Youth Engage through Social Media as TV Becomes Obsolete." *International Journal of Communication* 12: 404–22.

Jin, Dal Yong. 2019. "Snack Culture's Dream of Big Screen Culture." *International Journal of Communication* 13: 2094–2115.

Jin, Dal Yong. 2020a. "Comparative Discourse on J-Pop and K-Pop: Hybridity in Contemporary Local Music." *Korea Journal* 60 (1): 40–70.

Jin, Dal Yong, ed. 2020b. *Transmedia Storytelling in East Asia: The Age of Digital Media*. London: Routledge.

Jin, Dal Yong, and Ju Oak Kim. 2018. "Korean Wave: Hallyu." In *Korean Communication, Media, and Culture: An Annotated Bibliography*, edited by Kyo Ho Youm and Nojin Kwak, 255–82. Lanham, MD: Lexington.

Jin, Dal Yong, and Kyong Yoon. 2016a. "The Social Mediascape of Transnational Korean Pop Culture: *Hallyu 2.0* as Spreadable Media Practice." *New Media & Society* 18 (7): 1277–92.

Jin, Dal Yong, and Kyong Yoon. 2016b. "Re-Imagining Smartphones in Local Mediascape: A Cultural Analysis of Young KaKaoTalk Users." *Convergence: The International Journal of Research into New Media Technologies* 22 (5): 510–23.

Jin, Dal Yong, and Nojin Kwak. 2018. "Introduction: Review and Future Prospects of Korean Communication Research." In *Communication, Digital Media and Popular Culture: Contemporary Research and Future Prospects*, edited by Dal Yong Jin and Nojin Kwak, xiii–xxiii. Lanham, MD: Lexington.

Jin, Dal Yong, and Tae-Jin Yoon. 2017. "The Korean Wave: Retrospect and Prospects." *International Journal of Communication* 11: 2241–2249.

Jin, Dal Yong, and Woongjae Ryoo. 2014. "Critical Interpretation of Hybrid K-Pop: The Global-Local Paradigm of English Mixing in Lyrics." *Popular Music and Society* 37 (2): 113–31.

J. K. 2020. "BTS's 'Map of the Soul: 7' Makes History as It Tops Album Charts in Germany, UK, France, and More." *Soompi*, February 28, 2020. Accessed March 5, 2020. https://www.soompi.com/article/1385624wpp/btss-map-of-the-soul-7-makes-history-as-it-tops-album-charts-in-germany-uk-france-and-more.

Ju, Young Jae. 2017. "Why Does People in 227 Countries Watch Korean Webtoons." *Kyunghyang Shinmun*, September 5, 2017. http://biz.khan.co.kr/khan_art_view.html?artid=201709051540001&code=920501.

Ju, Hyejung, and Soobum Lee. 2015. "The Korean Wave and Asian Americans: The Ethnic Meanings of Transnational Korean Pop Culture in the USA." *Continuum: Journal of Media & Cultural Studies* 29 (3): 323–38.

Jung, E. Alex. 2019. "Bong Joon-ho's Dystopia Is Already Here." *Vulture*, October 7, 2019. Accessed February 12, 2020. https://www.vulture.com/209/10/bong-joon-ho-parasite.html.

Jung, Eun-Jin. 2016. "'Descendants of the Sun' Hits 440m Views in China." *The Korea Herald*, 14 March. Accessed 26 March 2020. http://www.koreaherald.com/view.php?ud=20160314000815.

Jung, Eun-Young. 2009. "Transnational Korea: A Critical Assessment of the Korean Wave in Asia and the United States." *Southeast Review of Asian Studies* 31: 69–80.

Jung, Eun-Young. 2013. "K-Pop Female Idols in the West: Racial Imaginations and Erotic Fantasies." In *The Korean Wave*, edited by Youna Kim, 122–35. London: Routledge.

Jung, Eun-Young. 2014. "New Wave Formations: K-Pop Idols, Social Media, and the Remaking of the Korean Wave." In *Hallyu 2.0: Korean Wave in the Age of Social Media,* edited by Sangjoon Lee and Abé Markus Nornes, 73–89. Ann Arbor: University of Michigan Press.

Jung, Hyeri. 2017. "Transnational Media Culture and Soft Power of the Korean Wave in the United States." In *The Korean Wave: Evolution, Fandom, and Transnationality*, edited by Tae-Jin Yoon and Dal Yong Jin, 225–43. Lanham, MD: Lexington.

Jung, Sun. 2011. *Korean Masculinities and Transcultural Consumption: Yonsama, Rain, Oldboy, K-Pop Idols*. Hong Kong: Hong Kong University Press.

Kakao. 2017. "Korean Webtoon towards the Globe." *1boon*, November 16, 2017. https://1boon.kakao.com/appstory/171116_1.

Kang, Seung Tae. 2017. "Where Is Korea: Kakao, Line Standout." *Maeil Economic Daily*, September 29, 2017. http://news.mk.co.kr/newsRead.php?year=2017&no= 654005.

Kang, Tae-jun. 2014. "South Korea's Webtoons: Going Global." *Financial Times*, July 28, 2014. http://blogs.ft.com/beyond-brics/2014/07/28/south-koreas-webtoons-going-global.

KBS News. 2012. "The K-Pop Phenomenon in South America." KBS News, March 20, 2012. Accessed March 1, 2020. http://d.kbs.co.kr/news/view.do?ncd=2452580.

Kibria, Nazli. 2003. *Becoming Asian American: Second-Generation Chinese and Korean American Identities*. Baltimore, MD: Johns Hopkins University Press.

Kim, Bum Soo. 2017. "Rapidly Growing Webtoon Industries, and Their Vibrant Overseas Market Penetration." *Chosun Ilbo*, September, 12, 2017. http://biz.chosun.com/site/data/html_dir/2017/09/12/2017091201554.html.

Kim, Gooyong. 2017. "Between Hybridity and Hegemony in K-Pop's Global Popularity: A Case of *Girls' Generation*'s American Debut." *International Journal of Communication* 11: 2367–86.

Kim, Gooyong. 2019. *From Factory Girls to K-Pop Idols Girls: Cultural Politics of Developmentalism, Patriarchy, and Neoliberalism in South Korea's Popular Music Industry*. Lanham, MD: Lexington Books.

Kim, Hyelin, and Jihae Lee. 2019. "Korean Cultural Centers Offer K-Pop Academy Classes." *Korea.Net*, May 7, 2019. http://www.korea.net/NewsFocus/Culture/view?articleId=170771.

Kim, Jae Hong. 2004. "The Future of Korean Cinema: One Movie Is Comparable to a Mid-Sized Company." *Newsmaker*, no. 572, May 2004. http://weekly.khan.co.kr/khnm.html?mode=view&artid=7127&cod.

Kim, Jungmin. 2019. "Add K-Webtoon to K-Pop and K-Beauty. Popular Webtoonists Earn $100,000 Per Month Overseas." *Korea JoongAng Daily*, December 5, 2019. https://news.joins.com/article/23649795.

Kim, Jung-Yoon, and Hae-Yong Sohn. 2014. "Cyworld's Global Ambitions Are Over." *Korean JoongAng Daily*, January 14, 2014. http://koreajoongangdaily.joins.com/news/article/article.aspx?aid=2983356&cloc=joongangdaily.

Kim, Ki Chul. 2000. "Korean Music and Films Swept the Asian Market." *Monthly Chosun*, July 2000. http://monthly.chosun.com/client/news/viw_r.asp?ctcd=&nNews Numb=200007100071.

Kim, Sujeong, and Sooah Kim. 2015. "The Ethos of Collective Moralism: The Korean Cultural Identity of K-Pop." *Media & Society* 23 (3): 5–52.

Kim, Suk-Young. 2018. *K-Pop Live: Fans, Idols, and Multimedia Performance*. Stanford, CA: Stanford University Press.

Kim, Tae Gyun. 2017. "Naver Webtoon Global Users Reach 30 million." *Yonhap News*, October 26, 2017. https://www.yna.co.kr/view/AKR20171026054800033.

Kim, Yeran. 2011. "Idol Republic: The Global Emergence of Girl Industries and the Commercialization of Girl Bodies." *Journal of Gender Studies* 20 (4): 333–45.

Kim, Yongsoo, Tim Kelly, and Siddhartha Raja. 2010. *Building Broadband: Strategies and Policies for the Developing World*. Washington, DC: World Bank.

Kim, Youn-Jin. 2005. "America and Americanization: Images and Discourses as Revealed in Korean Journalism. *Journal of American Studies* 37 (3): 7–38.

Kim, Youna. 2013. "Korean Wave Pop Culture in the Global Internet Age: Why Popular? Why Now?" In *The Korean Wave: Korean Media Go Global*, edited by Youna Kim, 75–92. New York: Routledge.

King, Anthony D., ed. 1997. *Culture, Globalization and the World System: Contemporary Conditions for the Representation of Identity*. Minneapolis: University of Minnesota Press.

Korea Creative Content Agency. 2016. *2015 Whitepaper on Korean Games*. Naju: KOCCA.

Korea Creative Content Agency. 2017. *2016 Whitepaper on Korean Games*. Naju: KOCCA.

Korea Creative Content Agency. 2018a. *2017 Whitepaper on Korean Games*. Naju: KOCCA.

Korea Creative Content Agency. 2018b. *2017 Content Industries Prediction*. Naju: KOCCA.

Korea Creative Content Agency. 2019. *2018 Whitepaper on Korean Games*. Naju: KOCCA.

Korea Creative Content Agency. 2019. *2018 Content Industries Outcome and 2019 Prediction*. Naju: KOCCA.

Korean Film Council. 2009. *Korean Cinema Yearbook*. Seoul: Korean Film Council.

Korea Foundation. 2017a. *2017 Global Hallyu 2: Americas*. Seoul: Korea Foundation.

Korea Foundation. 2017b. *2017 Global Hallyu 3: Europe*. Seoul: Korea Foundation.

Korea Foundation. 2019. *2018 Global Hallyu 3: Europe*. Seoul: Korea Foundation.

The Korea Herald. 2016. "It's Time for Webtoons to Go Global in 2016." *asiaone*, January 6, 2016. http://www.asiaone.com/showbiz/its-time-webtoons-go-global-2016.

Korea Press Foundation. 2004. *Korean Media Yearbook 2004/2005*. Seoul: KPF.

Korea Press Foundation. 2014. *Korean Media Yearbook 2014*. Seoul: KPF.

Korean Statistical Information Service. 2018. "Overseas Koreans." Accessed March 1, 2020. http://kosis.kr/index/index.do.

KOTRA (Korea Trade-Investment Promotion Agency). 2016. *A Study of Hallyu's Economic Effects in 2015*. Seoul: KOTRA.

Kraemer, Jordan. 2014. "Friend or Freund: Social Media and Transnational Connections in Berlin." *Human–Computer Interaction* 29 (1): 53–77.

Kraidy, Marwan. 2005. *Hybridity or the Cultural Logic of Globalization*. Philadelphia, PA: Temple University Press.

K-Stat. 2018. "Korea's Top 10 Trade Partner Countries." Accessed December 27, 2019. http://stat.kita.net/stat/world/major/KoreaStats06.screen.

Kwon, Hyuk Ki. 2016. "THAAD after Storm: Warning of Chinese Anti-Hallyu." *Newszum*, July 15, 2016. http://news.zum.com/articles/31854323.

Kwon, Joshua Oshu. 2014. "Korean Webtoons Go Global with LINE." *Medium*, March 6, 2014. https://medium.com/the-headline/korean-webtoons-go-global-with-line-b82f3920580e.

Kwon, Seung-Ho, and Joseph Kim. 2014. "The Cultural Industry Policies of the Korean Government and the Korean Wave." *International Journal of Cultural Policy* 20 (4): 422–39.

Laing, Aislinn. 2019. "Chilean President Pinera Sparks Fury with Fake News Claims." *Reuters*, December 27, 2019. https://www.reuters.com/article/chile-protests-fakenews/update-1-chilean-president-pinera-sparks-fury-with-fake-news-claims-idUSL1N29200Z.

Larkin, Brian. 2008. *Signal and Noise: Media, Infrastructure, and Urban Culture in Nigeria*. Durham, NC: Duke University Press.

Lau, Tuenyu, Siwook Kim, and David Atkin. 2005. "An Examination of Factors Contributing to South Korea's Global Leadership in Broadband Adoption." *Telematics and Informatics* 22 (4): 349–59.

Laughey, Daniel. 2006. *Music and Youth Culture*. Edinburgh: Edinburgh University Press.

Lee, Claire S., and Yasue Kuwahara. 2014. "'Gangnam Style' as Format: When a Localized Korean Song Meets a Global Audience." In *Korean Popular Culture in Global Context*, edited by Yasue Kuwahara, 101–16. New York: Palgrave.

Lee, Dong-in, and Minu Kim. 2018. "Korea's Gaming Industry, Fourth Largest in the World, but Lacks Top 10 Players." *Maeil Business News Korea*, December 18, 2018. https://pulsenews.co.kr/view.php?year=2018&no=787789.

Lee, Hyangjin. 2017. "The Korean Wave and Anti-Korean Wave Sentiment in Japan." In *The Korean Wave: Evolution, Fandom, and Transnationality*, edited by Tae-Jin Yoon and Dal Yong Jin, 185–208. Lanham, MD: Lexington.

Lee, Hye-Kyung. 2013. "Cultural Policy and the Korean Wave: From National Culture to Transnational Consumerism." In *The Korean Wave: Korean Media Go Global*, edited by Youna Kim, 185–98. London: Routledge.

Lee, Hyo-won. 2017. "Netflix Sets Okja Theatrical Release Date." *The Hollywood Reporter*, May 14, 2017. https://www.hollywoodreporter.com/news/okja-hit-netflix-south-korean-cinemas-june-28-1003685.

Lee, Jung-yup. 2009. "Contesting Digital Economy and Culture: Digital Technologies and the Transformation of Popular Music in Korea." *Inter-Asia Cultural Studies* 10 (4): 489–506.

Lee, Kwang-Suk. 2015. *IT Development in Korea: A Broadband Nirvana?* London: Routledge.

Lee, Sangjoon. 2015. "From Diaspora TV to Social Media: Korean TV Dramas in America." In *Hallyu 2.0: The Korean Wave in the Age of Social Media*, edited by Sangjoon Lee and Abé Markus Nornes, 171–92. Ann Arbor: University of Michigan Press.

Lee, Sangjoon, and Abé Markus Nornes, eds. 2015. *Hallyu 2.0: Korean Wave in the Age of Social Media*. Ann Arbor: University of Michigan Press.

Lee, Soo Man. 2016. "SMTOWN: New Culture Technology." https://www.youtube.com/watch?v=Ky5NvWsXnn8.

Lee, Soobum, and Hyejung Ju. 2010. "Korean Television Dramas in Japan: Imagining 'East Asianness' and Consuming 'Nostalgia'." *Asian Women* 26 (2): 77–104.

Lee, Yujin. 2018a. "A BTS Germany Concert Sold-Out in 9 Min." *KOFICE Overseas Correspondent Reports*, June 7, 2018. Accessed March 2, 2020. http://kofice.or.kr/c30correspondent/c30_correspondent_02_view.asp?seq=15563&page=1&find=&search=&search2=%EB%8F%85%EC%9D%BC.

Lee, Yujin. 2018b. "Opening of the K-Pop Section in a Major German Media Retailer Shop." *KOFICE Overseas Correspondent Reports*, April 9, 2018. Accessed March 2,

2020. http://kofice.or.kr/c30correspondent/c30_correspondent_02_view.asp?seq=15329&page=1&find=&search=&search2=%EB%8F%85%EC%9D%BC.

Lessig, Lawrence. 2004. *Free Culture: How Big Media Uses Technology and the Law to Lock Down Culture and Control Creativity*. New York: Penguin Books.

Lie, John. 2012. "Where Is the K in K-Pop? South Korean Popular Music, the Culture Industry, and National Identity." *Korean Observer* 43 (3): 339–63.

Lie, John. 2015. *K-Pop: Popular Music, Cultural Amnesia, and Economic Innovation in South Korea*. Oakland: University of California Press.

Liebes, Tamar, and Elihu Katz. 1993. *The Export of Meaning: Cross-Cultural Readings of Dalls*. Oxford: Polity.

Lim, Susanna. 2018. "How Korean Boy Band BTS Toppled Asian Stereotypes—and Took America by Storm." *The Conversation*, June 7, 2018. http://theconversation.com/how-korean-boy-band-bts-toppled-asian-stereotypes-and-took-america-by-storm-97596.

Lim, Tania. 2008. "Renting East Asian Popular Culture for Local Television: Regional Networks of Cultural Production." In *East Asian Pop Culture: Analysing the Korean Wave*, edited by Beng Huat Chua and Koichi Iwabuchi, 33–52. Hong Kong: Hong Kong University Press.

Ling, Jinqi. 1997. "Identity Crisis and Gender Politics: Reappropriating Asian American Masculinity." In *An Interethnic Companion to Asian American Literature*, edited by King-Kok Cheung, 312–37. Cambridge: Cambridge University Press.

Llanos Martínez, Héctor. 2019. "Radiografía del ascenso del K-Pop en España" ["X-Ray of the Rise of K-Pop in Spain"]. *Verne*, April 17, 2019. Accessed July 25, 2019. https://verne.elpais.com/verne/2019/04/11/articulo/1554998633_602406.html.

Lukács, Gabriella. 2010. *Scripted Affects, Branded Selves: Television, Subjectivity, and Capitalism in 1990s Japan*. Durham, NC: Duke University Press.

Ma, Eric Kit-Wai. 2000. "Rethinking Media Studies: The Case of China." In *De-Westernizing Media Studies*, edited by James Curran and Myung-Jin Park, 21–34. New York: Routledge.

Maase, Kaspar. 1992. *Bravo Amerika*. Hamburg: Junius.

Madrid-Morales, Dani, and Bruno Lovric. 2015. "'Transatlantic Connection': K-Pop and K-Drama Fandom in Spain and Latin America." *Journal of Fandom Studies* 3 (1): 23–41.

Malone, Paul M. 2010. "The Manga Publishing Scene in Europe." In *Manga: An Anthology of Global and Cultural Perspectives*, edited by Toni Johnson-Woods, 315–31. New York: Bloomsbury.

Marinescu, Valentina, ed. 2014. *The Global Impact of South Korean Popular Culture: Hallyu Unbound*. Lanham, MD: Lexington Books.

Marinescu, Valentina, and Ecaterina Balica. 2013. "Korean Cultural Products in Eastern Europe: A Case Study of the K-Pop Impact in Romania." *Region: Regional Studies of Russia, Eastern Europe, and Central Asia* 2 (1): 113–35.

Mazaná, Vladislava. 2014. "Cultural Perception and Social Impact of the Korean Wave in the Czech Republic." In *The Global Impact of South Korean Popular Culture: Hallyu Unbound*, edited by Valentina Marinescu, 47–63. Lanham, MD: Lexington.

McClintock, Pamela. 2020. "Globally, the South Korean Film Celebrated Its Best Picture Victory by Crossing the $200 Million Mark." *The Hollywood Reporter*, February 18, 2020. https://www.hollywoodreporter.com/news/box-office-parasite-heads-huge-50m-us-oscar-win-1279671.

McSweeney, Anna, and Claudia Hopkins. 2017. "Editorial: Spain and Orientalism." *Art in Translation* 9 (1): 1–6.

Min, Wonjung. 2015. "Korean Wave." In *Estudios coreanos para hispanohablantes: un acercamiento crítico, comparativo e interdisciplinario* [*Korean Studies for Spanish-Speaking People: A Critical, Comparative and Interdisciplinary Approach*], edited by Wonjung Min, 63–79. Santiago: Ediciones UC.

Min, Wonjung. 2017. "Korean Wave Reception and the Participatory Fan Culture in Latin America: What Lies beyond the Media Reports." In *The Korean Wave: Evolution, Fandom, and Transnationality*, edited by Tae-Jin Yoon and Dal Yong Jin, 145–61. Lanham, MD: Lexington.

Min, Wonjung, Dal Yong Jin, and Benjamin Han. 2019. "Transcultural Fandom of the Korean Wave in Latin America: Through the Lens of Cultural Intimacy and Affinity Space." *Media, Culture & Society* 41 (5): 604–19.

Ministry of Culture, Sports, and Tourism. 2012. *2011 Contents Industry Statistics*. Seoul: MCST.

Ministry of Culture, Sports, and Tourism. 2014. *2013 Content Industry Final Statistics*. Seoul: MCST.

Ministry of Culture, Sports, and Tourism. 2016. *2015 Contents Industry Whitepaper*. Seoul: MCST.

Ministry of Culture, Sports, and Tourism. 2017. *2016 Contents Industry Whitepaper*. Seoul: MCST.

Ministry of Culture and Tourism. 2000. *Cultural Industries White Paper*. Seoul: MCT.

Ministry of Culture and Tourism. 2006. *Establishment of Film Development Fund*, 22 December. Seoul: MCT.

Ministry of Foreign Affairs. 2017. *Total Number of Overseas Koreans (2017)*. Seoul: Ministry of Foreign Affairs.

Ministry of Science and ICT. 2017a. *Mobile Telephone Statistics of 2017*. Seoul: MCICT.

Ministry of Science and ICT. 2017b. *Study on Globalization Strategy of Webtoon Platform*. Seoul: MCICT.

Morán, David. 2019. "Blackpink en Barcelona: artillería coreana para asaltar el pop (Blackpink in Barcelona: Korean Artillery to Storm Pop)." *ABC*, May 29, 2019. https://www.abc.es/espana/catalunya/disfruta/abci-blackpink-barcelona-artilleria-coreana-para-asaltar-201905291222_noticia.html.

Morelli, Sarah. 2001. "Who Is a Dancing Hero? Rap, Hip-Hop, and Dance in Korean Popular Culture." In *Global Noise: Rap and Hip-Hop Outside the USA*, edited by Tony Mitchell, 248–57. Middletown, CT: Wesleyan University Press.

Motion Picture Association of America. 2017. *Theatrical Market Statistics of 2017*. Los Angeles, CA: MPAA.

Murthy, Dharij. 2012. "Towards a Sociological Understanding of Social Media: Theorizing Twitter." *Sociology* 46 (6): 1059–73.

Nahon, Karin, and Jeff Hemskey. 2013. *Going Viral*. Oxford: Polity.

Nair, Roshini. 2017. "Is Vancouver the New Gangnam? Korean Pop Video Filmed in Vancouver Gets Millions of Views upon Debut." *CBC*, October 31, 2017. http://www.cbc.ca/news/canada/british-columbia/is-vancouver-the-new-gangnam-korean-pop-video-filmed-in-vancouver-gets-millions-of-views-upon-debut-1.4380373.

NationMaster. 2020. "Chile Media Stats." Accessed March 3, 2020. http://www.nationmaster.com/country-info/profiles/Chile/Media.

Newsis. 2017. "Why Chinese Broadcasters' Copy of Korean Entertainment Programs Continue." *Chosun Ilbo*, August 20, 2017. http://news.chosun.com/site/data/html_dir/2017/08/20/2017082000358.html.

Newsis. 2018. "BTS's ARMY, How Has It Become the World's Most Strong Fandom?" *Chosun Ilbo*, May 31, 2018. http://news.chosun.com/site/data/html_dir/2018/05/31/2018053100008.html.

Nixon, Brice. 2017. "Critical Communication Policy Research and the Attention Economy: From Digital Labor Theory to Digital Class Struggle." *International Journal of Communication* 11: 4718–30.

Noll, A. Michael. 2003. "The Myth of Convergence." *International Journal of Media Management* 5 (1): 12–13.

Nye, Joseph, and Youna Kim. 2013. "Soft Power and the Korean Wave." In *The Korean Wave: Korean Media Go Global*, edited by Youna Kim, 31–42. London: Routledge.

Obama, Barack. 2012. "Remarks by President Obama at Hankuk University of Foreign Studies." The White House: Office of Press Secretary, March 26, 2012. https://obamawhitehouse.archives.gov/the-press-office/2012/03/26/remarks-president-obama-hankuk-university.

Oh, David C. 2017a. "Black K-Pop Fan Videos and Polyculturalism." *Popular Communication* 15 (4): 269–82.

Oh, David C. 2017b. "K-Pop Fans React: Hybridity and the White Celebrity-Fan on YouTube." *International Journal of Communication* 11: 2270–87.

Oh, Ingyu. 2013. "The Globalization of K-Pop: Korea's Place in the Global Music Industry." *Korea Observer* 44 (3): 389–409.

Oh, Ingyu, and Hyo-Jung Lee. 2013. "Mass Media Technologies and Popular Music." *Korea Journal* 53 (4): 34–58.

Oh, Ingyu, and Gil-Sung Park. 2012. "From B2C to B2B: Selling Korean Pop Music in the Age of New Social Media." *Korea Observer* 43 (3): 365–97.

Oh, Kyu-wook. 2011a. "Berlin Becomes Hub of Korean Studies in Europe." *The Korea Herald*, June 21, 2011.

Oh, Kyu-wook. 2011b. "Learning Korean in London." *The Korea Herald*, June 21, 2011.

Olmedo Señor, Teresa. 2018. *Estereotipos raciales y de género en el K-pop: el caso español* [*Gender and Racial Stereotypes in K-Pop: A Spanish Case*]. Master's thesis. Universidad de Valladolid. http://uvadoc.uva.es/handle/10324/33344.

Ono, Kent A., and Jungmin Kwon. 2013. "Re-Worlding Culture." In *The Korean Wave: Korean Media Go Global*, edited by Youna Kim, 199–214. London: Routledge.

Otmazgin, Nissim K. 2008. "Contesting Soft Power: Japanese Popular Culture in East and Southeast Asia." *International Relations of the Asia-Pacific* 8 (1): 73–101.

Otmazgin, Nissim K. 2013. *Regionalizing Culture: The Political Economy of Japanese Popular Culture in Asia*. Honolulu: Hawaii University Press.

Otmazgin, Nissim, and Irina Lyan. 2014. "Hallyu across the Desert: K-Pop Fandom in Israel and Palestine." *Cross-Currents: East Asian History and Culture Review* 3 (1): 32–55.

Park, Changsun. 2014. *Introduction to Hallyuology*. Seoul: Sun.

Park, Changsun. 2015. "Why Did the Export of Korean Dramas Actualize in Harbin?" *Hankook Ilbo*, December 16, 2015. http://daily.hankooki.com/lpage/col umn/201512/dh20151216163900141170.htm.

Park, Jung-Sun. 2013. "Negotiating Identity and Power in Transnational Cultural Consumption: Korean American Youths and the Korean Wave." In *The Korean Wave: Korean Media Go Global*, edited by Youna Kim, 136–50. London: Routledge.

Park, Seokyung. 2013. "The Golden Days of Webtoon." *Postech Times*, March 20, 2013. http://times.postech.ac.kr/news/articleView.html?idxno=6814.

Park, Youngwoong. 2017. "Storytelling in the SNS Era: The Case of BTS's Global Success." *Chosun Ilbo*, February 26, 2017. news.chosun.com/site/data/html_ dir/2017/02/26/2017022600594.html.

Peterson, Richard A. 1992. "Understanding Audience Segmentation: From Elite and Mass to Omnivore and Univore." *Poetics* 21 (4): 243–58.

Pitcher, Ben. 2014. *Consuming Race*. London: Routledge.

Poole, Robert Michael. 2009. "No Constrictions on BoA's Ambitions." *The Japanese Times*, March 20, 2009. https://www.japantimes.co.jp/culture/2009/03/20/music/ no-constrictions-on-boas-ambitions/#.XmI3LRNKjs0.

Potts, Jason, and Stuart Cunningham. 2008. "Four Models of the Creative Industries." *International Journal of Cultural Policy* 14 (3): 233–47.

Poushter, Jacob. 2016. "Smartphone Ownership and Internet Usage Continues to Climb in Emerging Economies." *Pew Research Center Global Attitudes & Trends*, February 22, 2016. Accessed March 1, 2020. http://www.pewglobal.org/ 2016/02/22/smartphone-ownership-and-internet-usage-continues-to-climb-in- emerging-economies.

Poushter, Jacob, Caldwell Bishop, and Hanyu Chwe. 2018. "Social Network Adoption Varies Widely by Country." *Pew Research Center Global Attitudes & Trends*, June 19, 2018. Accessed March 1, 2020. http://www.pewglobal.org/2018/06/ 19/3-social-network-adoption-varies-widely-by-country.

Prado-Fonts, Carles. 2018. "Writing China from the Rest of the West: Travels and Transculturation in 1920s Spain." *Journal of Spanish Cultural Studies* 19 (2): 175–89.

PricewaterHouseCoopers. 2006. *Global Entertainment and Media Outlook, 2006*. New York: PriceWaterHouseCoopers.

PriceWaterhouseCoopers. 2018. *Global Entertainment and Media Outlook, 2018–2022*. New York: PriceWaterHouseCoopers.

Prieto, Mónica G. 2018. "K-pop: Un tsunami de colores inunda el mundo desde Corea del Sur" ["K-Pop: A Colorful Tsunami Floods the World from South Korea"]. *El Mundo*, February 26, 2018. www.elmundo.es/cultura/musica/2018/02/26/5a92faee 268e3ee93e8b4630.html.

Pulver, Andrew. 2019. "*Parasite*'s Box Office Figures Surge after Oscar Triumph." *The Guardian*, February 12, 2019. https://www.theguardian.com/film/2020/feb/12/parasite-box-office-figures-surge-after-oscar-triumph.

Rainie, Lee, and Barry Wellman. 2012. *Networked: The New Social Operating System.* Cambridge, MA: MIT Press.

Ramirez, Elaine. 2018. "Kakao Will Use Wildly Popular South Korean Webtoons to Build an Audience in Japan and China." *Forbes*, January 16, 2018. https://www.forbes.com/sites/elaineramirez/2018/01/16/kakao-will-use-wildly-popular-south-korean-webtoons-to-build-an-audience-in-japan-china/#2aebd23149c6.

Regatieri, Ricardo Pagliuso. 2017. "Development and Dream: On the Dynamics of K-Pop in Brazil." *Development and Society* 46 (3): 505–22.

Richard, Birgit, and Heinz Hermann Kruger. 1998. "Ravers' Paradise?: German Youth Cultures in the 1990s." In *Cool Places: Geographies of Youth Cultures*, edited by Tracey Skelton and Gill Valentine, 161–74. London: Routledge.

Ritschel, Chelsea. 2018. "What Is the 'Baby Shark Song', Where Did It Come From and Why Do Children Love It?" *The Independent*, February 7, 2018. https://www.independent.co.uk/life-style/baby-shark-song-baby-shark-challenge-pinkfong-youtube-instagram-a8507036.html.

Rockingham, Graham. 2018. "'BTS Army' Invades Hamilton for K-Pop Band's Three Sold-Out Shows." *Toronto Star*, September 20, 2018. https://www.thestar.com/entertainment/2018/09/20/bts-army-invades-hamilton-for-k-pop-bands-three-sold-out-shows.html.

Rolling Stone. 2017. "10 New Artists You Need to Know: July 2017." *Rolling Stone*, July 2017. https://www.rollingstone.com/music/lists/10-new-artists-you-need-to-know-july-2017-w491865/bts-w491866.

Rosati, Sara. 2018. "'Chiñol': The Dilemma of Being Second-Generation Chinese in Spain." *El País*, January 8, 2018. https://elpais.com/elpais/2018/01/08/inenglish/1515409434_109052.html.

Ryoo, Woongjae. 2009. "Globalization, or the Logic of Cultural Hybridization: The Case of the Korean Wave." *Asian Journal of Communication* 19 (2): 137–51.

Ryoo, Woongjae, and Dal Yong Jin. 2020. "Cultural Politics in the South Korean Cultural Industries: Confrontations between State-Developmentalism and Neoliberalism." *International Journal of Cultural Policy* 26 (1): 31–45.

Said, Edward. W. 1978. *Orientalism.* New York: Pantheon Books.

Sakai, Naoki. 1988. "Modernity and Its Critique: The Problem of Universalism and Particularism." *South Atlantic Quarterly* 87 (3): 475–504.

Sandvoss, Cornel. 2005. *Fans: The Mirror of Consumption.* Oxford: Polity.

Schiller, Herbert. 1976. *Communication and Cultural Dominance.* New York: International Arts and Sciences Press.

Scholz, Trebor, ed. 2013. *Digital Labor: The Internet as Playground and Factory.* New York: Routledge.

Seguel, Omar, and Patricia Galilea. 2016. "Social-Spatial Segregation and Urban Mobility in Santiago." *Journal de investigación de pregrado* 6: 76–93.

Shahzad, Ramna. 2017. "Here's the Unexpected Reason Why Korean Language Courses Are So Popular at U of T." *CBC*, March 13, 2017. https://www.cbc.ca/news/canada/toronto/programs/metromorning/korean-interst-1.4022395.

Shim, Doobo. 2006a. "Korean Women Television Viewers in Singapore." In *Cultural Space and Public Sphere in Asia Conference*, 163–81. Seoul: Korea Broadcasting Institute.

Shim, Doobo. 2006b. "Hybridity and the Rise of Korean Popular Culture in Asia." *Media, Culture and Society* 28 (1): 25–44.

Shim, Doobo. 2008. "The Growth of Korean Cultural Industries and the Korean Wave." In *East Asian Pop Culture: Analysing the Korean Wave*, edited by Beng Huat Chua and Koichi Iwabuchi, 15–32. Hong Kong: Hong Kong University Press.

Shin, Jeeyoung. 2005. "Globalization and New Korean Cinema." In *New Korean Cinema*, edited by Chi-Yun Shin and Julian Stringer, 51–62. Edinburgh: University of Edinburgh Press.

Silver, Laura. 2019. "Smartphone Ownership Is Growing Rapidly around the World, but Not Always Equally." *Pew Research Center Global Attitudes and Trends*, February 5, 2019. https://www.pewresearch.org/global/2019/02/05/smartphone-ownership-is-growing-rapidly-around-the-world-but-not-always-equally/.

SM Entertainment. 2018. *Overview*. http://www.smentertainment.com/Overview/History.

Sohn, JiAe. 2016. "K-Drama Masterpieces (6): Jealousy." *Korea.net*, December 15, 2016. http://www.korea.net/NewsFocus/Culture/view?articleId=142680.

Sohn, Seunghye. 2012. "Local Context and Global Fandom of Hallyu Consumption: The Case of Korean Connection in France." *Journal of Media Economics & Culture* 10 (1): 45–85.

Sohn, Seunghye. 2013. "Transnational Online Fandom in the Digital Network Era: An Analysis of the Interviews with the Members of 2PM Fan Forum Wild2Day." *Media, Gender, and Culture* 25: 73–111.

Sone, Yuji. 2014. "Canted Desire: Otaku Performance in Japanese Popular Culture." *Cultural Studies Review* 20 (2): 196–222.

Song, Jung-Eun, and Kee-Bom Nahm. 2016. "The Meaning of Hallyu and Its Sustainability in Bulgaria." *Journal of the Korea Contents Association* 16 (6): 19–39.

Song, Jung-Eun, Kee-Bom Nahm, and Wonho Jang. 2014. "The Impact of Spread of Webtoon on the Development of Hallyu: The Case Study of Indonesia." *Korea Entertainment Industry Association Journal* 8 (2): 357–67.

South China Morning Post. 2018. "Chilean Teenagers Are in Love with K-Pop, South Korean and Home-Grown Alike." *South China Morning Post*, May 1, 2018. https://www.scmp.com/news/world/americas/article/2144114/pictures-chilean-teenagers-are-love-k-pop-south-korean-and-home.

Spangler, Todd. 2016. "Korea's Line Webtoon Digital Comics Publisher Signs with CAA for TV and Film Projects." *Variety*, August 31, 2016. http://variety.com/2016/digital/news/line-webtoon-comics-caa-tv-film-1201847907/.

Spangler, Todd. 2018. "Warner Bros.' Drama Fever Korean-Drama Streaming Service Is Shutting Down." *Variety*, October 16, 2018. https://variety.com/2018/digital/news/dramafever-k-drama-shutting-down-warner-bros-1202982001/.

Stade, Philip. 2014. "'This Video Is Not Available in Germany': Online Discourses on the German Collecting Society GEMA and YouTube." *First Monday*, 19 (10). http://journals.uic.edu/ojs/index.php/fm/article/view/5548.

Statistisches Bundesamt. 2018. "Migration and Integration." Accessed March 3, 2020. https://www.destatis.de/EN/FactsFigures/SocietyState/Population/Migra tionIntegration/MigrationIntegration.html;jsessionid=6DED165D4F6BBD3DD40 96EF6E822E661.InternetLive2.

Stevens, Carolyn S. 2008. *Japanese Popular Music: Culture, Authenticity, and Power*. London: Routledge.

Straubhaar, Joseph D. 1991. "Beyond Media Imperialism: Asymmetrical Interdependence and Cultural Proximity." *Critical Studies in Mass Communication* 8 (1): 39–70.

Straubhaar, Joseph D. 2007. *World Television: From Global to Local*. London: Sage.

Sung, Sang-Yeon. 2013. "Digitization and Online Cultures of the Korean Wave." In *The Korean Wave: Korean Media Go Global*, edited by Youna Kim, 135–47. London: Routledge.

Sung, Sang-Yeon. 2014. "K-Pop Reception and Participatory Fan Culture in Austria." *Cross-Currents: East Asian History and Culture Review* 3 (1): 56–71.

Takacs, Stacy. 2014. *Interrogating Popular Culture: Key Questions*. London: Routledge.

Taylor, Paul A. 2012. "Participation and the Technological Imaginary: Interactivity or Interpassivity." In *The Participatory Cultures Handbook*, edited by Aaron Delwiche and Jennifer Jacobs Henderson, 247–56. London: Routledge.

Taylor, T. L. 2015. *Raising the Stakes: E-Sports and the Professionalization of Computer Gaming*. Cambridge, MA: MIT Press.

Telles, Edward, and René Flores. 2013. "Not Just Color: Whiteness, Nation, and Status in Latin America." *Hispanic American Historical Review* 93 (3): 411–49.

Templeton, Inez H. 2006. *What's So German about It? Cultural Identity in the Berlin Hip Hop Scene*. PhD thesis, University of Stirling.

Terranova, Tiziana. 2000. "Free Labor: Producing Culture for the Digital Economy." *Social Text* 18 (2): 33–58.

Terranova, Tiziana, and Joan Donovan. 2013. "Occupy Social Networks: The Paradoxes of Corporate Social Media for Networked Social Movements." In *Unlike Us Reader: Social Media Monopolies and Their Alternatives*, edited by Geert Lovink and Miriam Rasch, 296–311. Amsterdam: Institute of Network Cultures.

Thussu, Daya K. 2006. "Mapping Global Media Flow and Contra-Flow." In *Media on the Move: Global Flow and Contra-Flow*, edited by Daya K. Thussu, 10–29. London: Routledge.

Tomlinson, John. 1991. *Cultural Imperialism*. Baltimore, MD: Johns Hopkins University.

Tomlinson, John. 1999. *Globalization and Culture*. Oxford: Polity.

Um, Haekyung. 2014. "K-Pop Fandom and Scene in the UK." In *K-Pop on the Global Platform: European Audience Reception and Contexts*, edited by KOFICE (Korea Foundation of International Culture Exchange), 41–200. Seoul: KOIFICE. Retrieved from http://www.kofice.or.kr/z99_include/filedown1.asp?filename= K-pop_on_the_Global_Platform(ENG).pdf.

UNESCO. 1980. *Many Voices, One World: Communication and Society Today and Tomorrow*. Paris: UNESCO.

UNESCO. 2017. "Cinema Data Release." *UNESCO News*, June 4, 2017. http://uis. unesco.org/en/news/cinema-data-release.

United Nations Educational, Scientific, and Cultural Organization. 1999. *Statistical Yearbook*. Paris: UNESCO.

Van Elteren, Mel. 2014. "Reconceptualizing 'Cultural Imperialism' in the Current Era of Globalization." In *The Handbook of Media and Mass Communication Theory*, edited by Robert S. Fortner and P. Mark Fackler, 400–19. Malden, MA: Wiley-Blackwell.

Webb, Andrew, Andrea Canales, and Rukmini Becerra. 2018. "Denying Systemic Inequality in Segregated Chilean Schools: Race-Neutral Discourses among Administrative and Teaching Staff." *Race Ethnicity and Education* 21 (5): 701–19.

Wee, Willis. 2014. "Razmig Hovaghimian: From Failed Pizza Maker to Founder of Viki." *Techinasia*, April 20, 2014. https://www.techinasia.com/story-of-viki-and-razmig-hovaghimian.

Williams, J. Patrick. 2011. *Subcultural Theory: Traditions and Concepts*. Oxford: Polity.

The World Bank. 2019. "GDP Per Capita, PPP (Current International $): Chile." Accessed March 1, 2020. https://data.worldbank.org/indicator/NY.GDP.PCAP.PP.CD?locations=CL.

World Internet Project-Chile. 2011. "WIP Chile 2011: *Usos y prácticas en el mundo de Internet*" [Uses and Practices in the Internet World]. Santiago: World Internet Project Chile.

Yang, Eun-Kyung. 2003. "A Study on the Trade of Trendy Drama in East Asia." *Korean Journal of Broadcasting & Telecommunications Research* 56: 197–220.

Yano, Christine Reiko. 2013. *Pink Globalization: Hello Kitty's Trek across the Pacific*. Durham, NC: Duke University Press.

Yim, Haksoon. 2002. "Cultural Identity and Cultural Policy in South Korea." *International Journal of Cultural Policy* 8 (1): 37–48.

Yim, Hyunjoo. 2019. "Bong of Parasite Says, 'Unlikely to win at Cannes'." *Korea Economic Daily Hankyung*, April 22, 2019. https://www.hankyung.com/entertainment/article/201904229822k.

Yoon, Kyong. 2017. "Cultural Translation of K-Pop among Asian Canadian Fans." *International Journal of Communication* 11: 2350–66.

Yoon, Kyong. 2018. "Global Imagination of K-Pop: Pop Music Fans' Lived Experiences of Cultural Hybridity." *Popular Music and Society* 41 (4): 373–89.

Yoon, Kyong. 2019. "Transnational Fandom in the Making: K-Pop Fans in Vancouver." *International Communication Gazette* 81 (2): 176–92.

Yoon, Kyong. 2020. "Diasporic Korean Audiences of Hallyu in Vancouver, Canada." *Korea Journal* 60 (1): 152–78.

Yoon, Kyong, and Dal Yong Jin. 2016. "The Korean Wave Phenomenon in Asian Diasporas in Canada." *Journal of Intercultural Studies* 37 (1): 69–83.

Yoon, Sunny. 2013. "New Korean Wave and Deterritorialization of Social Network Communication in Europe." *Korean Journal of Journalism & Communication Studies* 57 (3): 135–61.

Yoon, Sunny. 2014. "Korean Wave in Eastern Europe and Cultural Identity." *Korean Journal of Broadcasting and Telecommunication Studies* 28 (3): 94–131.

Yoon, Tae-Jin, and Dal Yong Jin, eds. 2017. *The Korean Wave: Evolution, Fandom, and Transnationality*. Lanham, MD: Lexington.

Yoon, Tae-Jin, and Bora Kang. 2017. "Emergence, Evolution, and Extension of 'Hallyu Studies': What Have Scholars Found from Korean Pop Culture in the Last Twenty Years?" In *The Korean Wave: Evolution, Fandom, and Transnationality*, edited by Tae-Jin Yoon and Dal Yong Jin, 3–21. Lanham, MD: Lexington Books.

Yoon, Yung Sil. 2018. "Korean Gov't to Develop the Tech for Illegal Content Distribution Blacking." *Business Korea*, April 9, 2018. http://www.businesskorea.co.kr/news/articleView.html?idxno=21528.

You, Sangchul. 1998. "Drama *What Is Love All About* Made a Huge Hit in Chinese Households." *Korea Joongang Daily*, June 1, 1998. https://news.joins.com/article/3652656.

Zubernis, Lynn, and Katherine Larsen. 2011. *Fandom at the Crossroads: Celebration, Shame and Fan/producer Relationships*. Newcastle upon Tyne: Cambridge Scholars.

Index

About the Authors

Dal Yong Jin is Distinguished SFU Professor. He completed his PhD at the Institute of Communications Research at the University of Illinois in 2005. Jin's major research and teaching interests are on digital platforms and digital games, globalization and media, transnational cultural studies, and the political economy of media and culture. Jin has published numerous books and journal articles, book chapters, and book reviews. Jin's books include *Korea's Online Gaming Empire* (MIT Press, 2010), *New Korean Wave: Transnational Cultural Power in the Age of Social Media* (University of Illinois Press, 2016), S*martland Korea: Mobile Communication, Culture and Society* (University of Michigan Press, 2017), and *Globalization and Media in the Digital Platform Ag*e (Routledge, 2019). He is the founding book series editor of Routledge Research in Digital Media and Culture in Asia, while directing Center for Policy Research on Science and Technology (CPROST) at SFU.

Kyong Yoon is an Associate Professor of Cultural Studies at the University of British Columbia Okanagan, where he teaches cultural industries, Asian pop culture, and Internet culture. He completed a PhD in Cultural Studies at the University of Birmingham and held postdoctoral fellowships at the University of Sheffield and Korea University. His research focuses on digital culture, migration, Korean popular culture, and transnational youth. His recent studies of transnational Korean popular culture have been published in several journals, including *International Communication Gazette*, *Popular Music and Society*, and *Journal of Youth Studies*. His monograph *Digital Mediascapes of Transnational Korean Youth Culture* (Routledge, 2020) examines transnational flows of Korean youth and their digital media practices.

Wonjung Min is an Adjunct Assistant Professor of History Department and Executive Committee Member of the Asian Studies Center at the Pontificia Universidad Católica de Chile. She holds a PhD in Latin American Literature. Her research focuses on the fandom of Asian pop culture in Spanish-speaking world, identity formation of Latin American societies, and comparative culture between Asia and Latin America. She is the editor of the book, *Estudios Coreanos para hispanohablantes: un acercamiento crítico, comparativo e interdisciplinario* (*Korean Studies for the Spanish-Speakers: A Critical, Comparative and Interdisciplinary Approach*) (Ediciones UC, 2015). She has published numerous articles and book chapters on the reception of Asian pop culture in Latin America.

www.ingramcontent.com/pod-product-compliance
Lightning Source LLC
Chambersburg PA
CBHW022316280326
41932CB00010B/1122